Misadventure
Stabbed Act(

FELLOW DUELLIST EXONE

A verdict of misadventure was recorded by the Oldham Borough Coroner (Mr. J. L. Watson) on Harold Norman (Mr. Harold Edward Thompson), who died in Oldham Royal Infirmary on Wednesday in last week as a result of a stabbing accident while playing in "Macbeth" at Oldham Repertory Theatre on January 30.

Among the exhibits were four daggers and the tunic which Harold Norman was wearing when the accident happened. The Coroner held that no blame could be attached in any shape or form to Antony Oakley, Harold Norman's antagonist in the fatal duel.

The Coroner's verdict was that death was due to general peritonitis following the perforation of the bowels due to a stab wound in the abdomen accidentally received while in the course of his employment.

The Coroner added that Mr. C. Buckley (Messrs. Taylor and Buckley), who appeared for the widow, had raised questions about what had happened at Oldham Royal Infirmary, but he (the Coroner) was concerned only with criminal negligence, and there had been no evidence of that.

Sympathy Expressed

Mr. J. W. Stansfield (instructed by Mr. Fred Hollis, of Manchester), who represented the Oldham Repertory Theatre Club, expressed sympathy with the relatives of the deceased, who, he said was one of the stars at the Repertory Theatre and whose death was a great loss.

Mr. J E. Driver (Messrs. Ponsonby's), who appeared for the Oldham Royal Infirmary, also paid a tribute of sympathy, in which the Coroner joined.

Mr. C. Buckley said it must be a source of gratification to the widow to realise the high esteem in which her husband was held.

Mrs. Audrey M. Thompson, the widow, who witnessed the duel scene from the wings of the stage, said it seemed to be rather muddled and did not run strictly to routine as it had done on other nights. The moods were rather different from what they had been. She did not actually see her husband stabbed.

Her husband had said to her at the Infirmary that such dangerous weapons should not be used again.

James S. Dickinson, employed by Messrs. S. B. Watts, Ltd., theatrical costumiers, of Manchester, said his firm had supplied the costumes and the properties for the performance of "Macbeth." The weapons required were eleven swords, two daggers and eleven shields. Two more daggers were afterwards called for.

Cut in Tunic

On February 5 the costumes and property were returned, and he saw a small cut in the tunic that had been worn by Macbeth. Certain of the daggers had been picked up at antique shops. One of them had a blunt end. They were the usual type supplied.

In reply to Mr. Buckley witness agreed that originally they were not made for theatrical purposes.

Answering Mr. Stansfield, witness said they knew that the daggers were to be used in the show. They were of the type that had been supplied for years for the production of "Macbeth."

In reply to the Coroner, witness said they would not supply daggers so made that the blade would go into the handle unless they were asked for. Such a dagger was used in "The Vagabond King."

Douglas Emery, the producer at the theatre, said he had occupied that position for the last six and a half years Harold Norman joined the company in September, 1945, and stayed until February, 1946, returning about Christmas, 1946. Mr. Oakley joined the company in April, 1946, and they had played together for many weeks. So far as he knew they got on quite well together and were quite good friends.

While the play was being rehearsed he allowed them to make their own arrangements about how the duel scene should be fought. Afterwards they rehearsed for him, and it seemed to be quite satisfactory. On the night of January 30 he was standing in the wings and there was nothing unusual about the scene until he saw Norman crawling off the stage towards him. Instead of dying on the stage, according to the script, he crawled off, holding his stomach.

"He said: 'Douglas, I have been stabbed.'

"I thought he had been winded," witness added, "and I said: 'Harold, go back and take your call.' He said: 'I am sorry I cannot,' and looking at his tunic I thought I saw blood. I rang down the curtain and went on the stage, making a short announcement.

"I asked him if I should get a doctor and he replied: 'Yes, I wish you would. I rang for Dr. Booth, but he was out. I dialled 999, and he was taken to the Infirmary."

When the accident occurred the two combatants were facing one another, and Harold had his back to the audience He did not think that anyone other than the two combatants could tell what happened. Witness was sure that no blows were struck in anger. They were both very happy about the fight, being like a couple of kids

..., had such dagger, and had used it a few weeks ago. Witness did not anticipate any danger in using the particular dagger. If any actor had objected to a particular dagger, he would have given him another, and a spring-handled one if he wanted.

The Coroner then intimated that he was not going to call Mr. Oakley, but that his statement to the Police would be read later.

Dr. J. F. Cogan, casualty officer at the Oldham Royal Infirmary, said he examined Norman when he was admitted. There was then no evidence of perforation of the bowels. Dr. Stephens, the senior resident surgical officer, came to the same conclusion. The wound was explored but no evidence of a perforation could be found, and the patient was admitted to a ward.

Witness told the night staff to inform him if the patient's condition became worse. On seeing him again at ten o'clock the following morning witness was rather doubtful about his condition. At 2 p.m. the same day it was obvious that there was a perforation, and he was at once operated upon by one of the honorary surgeons. His condition improved after the operation, which disclosed a small perforation.

Later it deteriorated again and the patient died.

Doctor Explains

In reply to Mr. Buckley, witness said the deceased had told him how the accident had happened. It would have been possible to open up the wound to the bowel when the case was first admitted. There was a chance if that had been done that they would have seen the perforation. Sometimes, however, the perforation sealed itself up. If the perforation had been seen at the time, he would have operated upon then.

Mr. Buckley commented that the operation was performed twelve to eighteen hours afterwards, and that the chance of recovery would have been better had he been operated upon at once.

In answer to further questions witness said he qualified as a doctor in June of last year. Since January of this year he had been the casualty officer, having been previously orthopaedic officer and assistant casualty officer. The cause of death was general peritonitis.

In reply to Mr. Driver witness said the patient had stated that he did not think that the dagger had gone in more than four inches. He did not see any physical signs of perforation because the perforation had probably sealed itself off. That was probably why, when he explored the wound, he thought that he had got to the end of it.

General Peritonitis

Dr. G. Stewart Smith, the director of the pathological services at Manchester who performed a post-mortem examination, said the cause of death was general peritonitis following the perforation of the bowels due to the stab wound.

In answer to Mr. Buckley witness said deceased would get weaker with each operation.

Detective-Sergeant Marr read the statement that had been made by Mr. Antony S. Oakley, which was to the effect that he was 34 years of age and was lodging with his wife in Churchill Street.

He was a native of London, and did not know the deceased before the latter rejoined the company. Their acquaintance had been purely of a business nature, and they had played together in various productions. They had been very good friends, and had had no differences.

Explaining how the accident happened when he was playing the part of Macduff with Norman as Macbeth, Mr. Oakley suggested that Norman, on twisting his wrist in the duel scene, went too far forward and got on to the dagger before it could be turned outwards.

THE CURSE OF MACBETH

Richard Huggett as Macbeth. 'The worst performance I ever gave and I am lucky to be alive to write about it.'

THE CURSE OF
MACBETH
AND OTHER THEATRICAL
SUPERSTITIONS

an investigation by

RICHARD HUGGETT

PICTON PUBLISHING

1981

©Copyright 1981 Picton Publishing & Richard Huggett
First published in Great Britain by Picton Publishing 1981
ISBN 0 902633 72 4

Photoset in 11/13½ Times Roman
by Chippenham Typesetting, Bath Road, Chippenham, Wiltshire.
Text paper supplied by Howard Smith Papers, Bristol.
Bound by Western Book Company, Maesteg.
Printed in Great Britain by Picton Print
Citadel Works, Bath Road, Chippenham, Wiltshire.

Chapter Opening Illustrations by Alan Cameron, Bath
Jacket Design by Adrian Hillier, Pictons

DEDICATION

I humbly dedicate
this book, *The Curse of Macbeth*
to the spirit of wisdom and goodness
as enshrined in the White Goddess,
the Virgin Mary. May she, on its passage
to publication and from there
and thence to homes and libraries,
protect it and all who read it.

October 25th 1979

On a more earthly plane,
I would like to dedicate this book to two men.
To John Dunn, whose interview programme
made the existence of this book known and also
to David Picton-Phillips who, in deciding to
publish this book, has shown an initiative and
enterprise which is noticeably lacking
in the publishing world.

March 13th 1981

Contents

†

1 · Superstitions in the Theatre

We actors are undoubtedly the most superstitious of all profession-als a fact which is freely, indeed cheerfully, admitted. It is interest-ing to speculate why this should be so and the answer must surely lie in the character of the actor and the rather peculiar nature of our work. Actors have a strong imagination and a sense of fantasy: this is essential, otherwise we could never be actors. We tend to be highly-strung, nervous, optimistic, apprehensive, credulous and sensitive. Underneath whatever façade of smiling confidence we choose to show to the world there is frequently a bottomless pit of hopes and fears, of insecurity and tensions. We live on such talents which a mainly benevolent Deity has seen fit to give us, and if our work does sometimes offer artistic satisfaction, it never guarantees security, a serious handicap to those encumbered with wives, chil-dren and domestic responsibilities. Poverty, neglect and frustration alternate in an actor's life with affluence, fame and fulfillment. If actors live to please, then we must please to live and we must please not only the public and the critics but also – and this is probably more important – our employers, past, present and future.

If actors are different from other people then it is because our work is like nothing else. Nobody who has never acted can have the least idea just what it means to step onto a stage before an audience. Our lives consist of a series of painful and nerve-wracking experi-

1

ences whether it is the first take in a film, the recording of a TV play, a live radio broadcast or – and this is by far the worst – a big first night in a West End or Broadway theatre. An actor is under a continual strain. He lives on his nerves, and in contradiction of the popular glamorous image, his life is a very difficult one, whether he is humble novice, esteemed supporting actor, popular leading man or international superstar. Everybody wants good luck and dreads the bad, but in few people is the desire so urgent or the fear so passionate as in an actor facing his nightly ordeal. Is it any wonder that we should be superstitious?

It is a gross and insulting over-simplification of the facts to describe actors as children playing at make-believe, but there is, surely, a childlike simplicity and emotional naïvety – irrespective of education, intelligence and background – which transforms the whole of our glittering world into a highly sophisticated and enchanting game of 'Let's Pretend'. The theatre is an enclosed, isolated world with its own rules and laws, its own traditions and disciplines; and however accurately it may appear to mirror real life it is, in fact obstinately and justly cut off from it. The sailor, soldier, airman, coalminer, steeplejack, fisherman, all these people lead dangerous lives and are naturally superstitious, but it is not our bodies which we actors endanger, but our hearts and souls; it is not bullets, storms, bombs nor coal-gas we fear, but the most deadly and unpredictable and relentless of all natural forces – public opinion and fashion. It is precisely in this sort of artistic and emotional hothouse that superstitions take root and flourish.

Most actors have a talisman, a lucky mascot which they keep in their dressing-rooms and will take religiously from theatre to theatre, from TV to film studio. A random survey of the mascots belonging to a number of stars and lesser luminaries has produced some intriguing items. Wilfrid Hyde White has a collection of china ornaments; there is a pigeon with a broken beak, a recumbent cow, a pig, an American silver dollar and – most highly prized of all – a beautiful framed coloured photograph of his Rolls-Royce. Every evening, before each entrance, and it doesn't matter how many there are, he will kiss each of these mascots, 'all presents from present friends and past mistresses', he smilingly states; each is

Amanda Reiss and her aged, tatty dressing-gown. Taken during the run of *Crown Matrimonial* by Royce Ryton.

gently touched in loving valediction before he leaves the theatre at night. Alec MacOwan clings to a navy-blue blazer which he first wore fifteen years ago in *The Elder Statesman.* 'You look like a second-hand car salesman' was Henry Sherek's (the producer) acid comment when he appeared with it at the dress rehearsal. Amanda Reiss also possesses a sartorial mascot, a blue and black check dressing-gown. This was a present from her mother in 1961 when she made her West End début in *The Irregular Verb to Love.* She wears it to make-up in and to receive her visitors after the performance. It is now showing its age and looking rather tatty but she will never part with it. Cardew Robinson treasures a magnificent colour portrait of Bransby Williams in the character of Chief Sitting Bull donated by a group of friends who know of his fanatical interest in Red Indians. Thora Hird always wears under her stage costume three large nappy pins which she once pinned to her daughter, Janette Scott, and her two grand-daughters. Jill Bennett's dressing-table is covered with lucky mascots – a silver ashtray with a 1936 penny welded to the base, donated and signed by the late Sir Godfrey Tearle; a green china boot given by Royal Ballet dancer, Donald Macleary; a little oriental knife with an unidentified goddess on the handle, and a row of six teddy-bears. These are religiously

3

Jill Bennett surrounded by a very small selection of her lucky mascots.
(*Daily Telegraph* Colour Library)

taken to every rehearsal and sat down in the prompt corner, the smallest lying snugly in her hand-bag. 'Disgusting, isn't it?' she comments happily. This is only a small section of the whole collection, the rest of it filling a whole room in her house.

Leslie Phillips has a beautiful frog given to him by Ciaren Madden in gratitude for his having obtained her first starring West End part for her. After thirty years, Derek Sydney still keeps a beautiful make-up box with a rabbit's foot in it given to him for his first job by his wife. Ken Dodd has a lucky shilling which he always carries in his pocket. Richard Dennis has a collection of postcards which must be arranged in a special order in front of his mirror – they include Dylan Thomas, Constable, David Garrick, and a Clown. He also has a woolly penguin given by a fan when he made his first appearance in the West End in *An Ideal Husband*. Peter Bull has a tie which is not only lucky for him but also for his friends. This is a very rare thing for good luck is seldom transferable, but whenever he lends it for auditions, his friends always get the job. However, he will not allow it to be photographed or it will lose its

4

Alec MacOwan and Richard Huggett comparing lucky cuff-links.

luck. He also takes worry beads to the theatre and carries them in his pocket throughout the performance.

I have a bizarre pair of odd cuff links which for many years I have either worn or carried on first nights. They are very colourful and in grotesquely bad taste – one is made of rubies, the other of emeralds, both surrounded by elaborate clusters of gold. At a casual glance you might think they cost thousands, but in fact they were bought in a bargain store in Times Square on my first euphoric visit to New York many years ago, and they cost one dollar. I once got into severe trouble with the management of Vienna's English Theatre on the first night of *Dear Liar* in 1972 but I firmly overruled their objections to them. I am happy to report that the production was a huge success and a three-week season was extended to twelve.

Tallulah Bankhead was a walking encyclopaedia of superstitions 'You name it, honey, I believe in it,' she used to say. Champagne was lucky and must be consumed in quantity before and during a performance. Visitors to her dressing-room must always enter with the right foot first; the left foot was unlucky and any offender must be sent out and told to re-enter correctly. But her favourite mascot was a hare's foot given to her by her father in 1936. She took it everywhere and it can be seen in the final photo of Brendan Gill's picturebook biography. After her death it was put into the coffin and buried with her. Ann Rogers once consulted the famous astrologer, Maurice Woodruff, before accepting an offer to play in *No No Nanette* in Chicago, because she also wanted to play it in London later in the year and did not know if she would be available. Woodruff predicted that the Chicago run would be off in time for her to take up the London offer and so it was. After that she invariably consulted him before making any serious decision in her career. Maurice Woodruff's death left a painful gap in the lives of many stars.

Gerry Jedd once found a four-leaved clover in Central Park on her way to an audition. It was a good audition and she was invited to give another. On her way to the second she found a six-leaved clover in the park. The second audition was very successful and two months later she found herself co-starring with Peter Finch at the Haymarket Theatre in *Two for the See-saw*. She thus enjoyed every unknown's dream of success and overnight stardom. Throughout the six-month run in London she kept the two clovers but she died at a tragically early age before she could repeat her success in America.

The three Barrymores, John, Ethel and Lionel, were very generous to each other but seldom to outsiders, charity most definitely began at home and stayed there. They invariably gave red apples to each other on their opening nights which must on no account be eaten. This was a very old, very personal family superstition and inherited from their theatrical parents, the famous Drews. It was John who took this one inevitable stage further; on opening nights he drank a jug of apple-cider, before and during the performance. A caretaker who once drank it by mistake was instantly dismissed.

Some of the old American vaudeville performers on the touring circuit had some very strange personal superstitions. Jack Pearl used to touch his ear for good luck, but if anybody else did it he would have to touch the other person's ear before he could go onto the stage. One practical joker who knew about this did touch Jack's ear on a very important Broadway opening and then ran away. Jack went berserk and followed him out of the theatre and all round the block before he finally managed to catch up with him. Jimmy Durante was once asked if he was superstitious. 'If I get a cold in da nose and I hear a raven croaking at da same time, then dat means trouble,' was his characteristic reply; but there was another he didn't talk about. He was very superstitious about hats which had not on any account to be placed on beds. The only antidote to the bad luck was to take the hat off the bed and hang it up and then it had not to be touched until the owner was wearing another. One day, when on tour, his friends in the company played a wicked joke. They bought twenty-five hats from a dime store and placed them all on the bed in his hotel bedroom and then retired to the bathroom to observe his reaction. This, when he arrived on the scene, caused boundless hilarity and thus added one more item to the Durante legend. If bad luck can attach itself to beds and other items of clothing, then gloves are no exception. Pennsylvania University Library claims that it possesses Shakespeare's own gloves (authority unstated), and tells all visitors that anybody who wears them will die within the year. Maurice Evans was shown them whilst on tour and asked if he would like to try them on for size. He refused because he said that if the gloves were not genuine then it was a waste of time and if they were then it was sacrilege. He firmly stated that he was *not* superstitious but the fact that the play he was currently touring was *Macbeth* may possibly have influenced his decision. There is, when all's said and done, no point in tempting fate.

Sometimes there are ad-hoc mascots for special occasions. Denis Shaw remembers that he was once rehearsing a melodrama called *Barren Soil*, playing an Irish boy called Mad Matt. During the rehearsals he was very bad, couldn't get the feel of the part or come to grips with it and worked himself up to a state of trembling apprehension about the first performance. A sympathetic old actor, seeing his distress, lent a special pair of cuff-links in the shape of a shamrock. The psychological effect was immediate. 'I cheered up rightaway,' said Shaw, 'and I was *superb!*' June Grey, a variety artiste, once picked up a rusty nail in the wings while waiting to make her first appearance in a provincial pantomime. The evening was a great success and ever since she has always picked up rusty nails. She keeps them in a trunk which travels everywhere with her and is now imbued with good luck. Jack Pearl always picks up pins, good-luck pins, ordinary pins, safety pins, nappy pins, and if the point is towards him as he stoops to pick it up, then this is particularly good luck.

Many actors like to carry their lucky mascots onto the stage whenever possible. Sometimes it is a coin, ring, tiny framed photo of their loved one, hare's foot, strip of yellow ribbon, playing card – the Queen of Spades, in spite of Pushkin, carries good luck associations for many people – fragment of costume from a previously lucky play or a tiny teddy-bear (very popular as lucky mascots). There is just one rather unfortunate thing about lucky mascots and that is that they can backfire in the most unpleasant and unpredictable way as with a certain young actor whom I shall call Peter Plinge. Peter's lucky mascot was a 1930s dinky-car, a souvenir of a happy boyhood. It measured four inches by two and fitted comfortably into his pocket. Throughout his professional career he wore it in the pocket of whatever costume he wore and if there was none then the wardrobe mistress would have to improvise one. One day he found himself playing Ariel in a touring production of *The Tempest* and the costume, as he found to his alarm on the day of the dress rehearsal, was that irreducible, pre-*Oh Calcutta* minimum, the skintight jockstrap. The director knew about his dinky-car. 'Well, dear boy,' he enquired sardonically, 'just *where* are you going to put it tonight?' Peter smiled sheepishly. 'There's only one place,' he said firmly, and he put it there. The result provoked from the first night audience not only crude laughter but also some rather bawdy anatomical speculation. But there was worse to come. The director was very balletically-minded and had at one time been a choreographer. He had devised some very spectacular *grands jetés, arabesques* and *cabrioles* for Peter who, whilst executing one of these, stumbled against a rock and fell flat on his face thus doing himself what is tactfully described as a 'mischief'. Doubled up, groaning and clutching himself in agony, Peter was carried offstage by Prospero and Caliban and spent the rest of the evening in the local hospital. Not surprisingly, the car fell from favour and was banished to his little boy's nursery where it could do no further harm.

Religious medals are popular, particularly those of St. Genesius: he is the patron saint of actors, though surprisingly few actors know this. St. Christopher inspires considerable devotion amongst actors and there are many who would no more walk onto a stage than they would embark on a jet-liner to Israel without their St. Christopher medal. This must be carried on the person (easier than a dinky-car) and must be blessed. St. Christopher's absence on a critical first night can fill the unhappy performer with real agonising fear. Kathie Warren, who used to do a William Tell act on ice in which her partner, Scott, would leap over her and slice the apple in two with his razor-blade-sharp ice-skates, invariably carried a St. Christopher medal. One evening she forgot it and went through her dangerous ordeal in a state of trembling terror. Happily, the act passed without incident but she privately swore she would never forget it again and she never did.

Broadway actors talking about their own special superstitions will always come to the famous Gipsy Robe. 'Gipsy' in American theatre slang refers to the singing and dancing chorus of the big musicals. The gipsies are the toughest, most hard-working, most fiercely dedicated bunch of professionals on Broadway and the American theatre's debt to them is vast and incalculable. The Gipsy Robe is a dressing-gown covered with souvenirs of previous musicals and it is passed from one company to another. On the first night of a new musical, the current owner brings it to the theatre and presents it to the senior gipsy of the new show. There is no sexual or racial apartheid in this, it can be given to anybody, black or white, man or woman. The lucky recipient will put on the Robe and parade round the stage so that everybody can see it. Sometimes the company will assemble on the stage to witness the ritual, sometimes the Gipsy will visit all the dressing-rooms so that everybody can see it and touch it for luck. Once this has been completed to everybody's satisfaction the show can go on in an atmosphere of hilarity and confidence. The Gipsy keeps the Robe in his dressing-room until the next Broadway musical opens. He will then attach

Don Bonnell, wearing the Gypsy Robe, accepting a copy of *The Truth about Pygmalion* (a lucky book) from the author. Renée Rose, a former owner of the Gypsy Robe, is in attendance. (Sam Reiss Photography)

by pins or thread some small souvenir of his own show: it might be a programme, or a photo of the star, a piece of costume or a small prop, appropriately marked with the name of the show and the date. He will then take it round to the new theatre and pass it on to the Gipsy of his choice, and to receive the Gipsy Robe is a colossal honour, though nobody knows who will get it until it arrives.

I was given a privileged glimpse of this unusual ritual on the first night of *Molly* at the Alvin Theatre in October 1973. This was arranged by the Assistant Director, Jay Fox and his wife Bonnie Walker. An attractive young coloured dancer from *Raisin*, named Renée Rose, was the previous owner and she duly brought it round to the stage door of the Alvin. Surrounded by the electricians, stage-hands, the press and the producer's party of friends, she solemnly presented it to a young dancer called Don Bonnell. Speechless with delight he wore it, posed for photographs and then toured the dressing-rooms where he was kissed, hugged, touched and generally made much of by a laughing, crying, highly emotional company. The Robe was a very handsome garment and very heavy ... To it were attached a sword and coffin (*Cry For Us All*), a balloon (*Gantry*), gold tapes (*No No Nanette*), a tambourine (*Coca*), gold handprints (*Applause*), a coat-of-arms with money (*The Rothschilds*) Danny Kaye's photo (*Two by Two*) and a fragment of birthday cake (*Company*).

Molly was the season's Jewish musical (there is always at least one on Broadway), based on a popular TV series, *The Goldbergs* and starring the popular and immensely vital Kay Ballard. On the opening night, it was performed with enormous gusto, received with hysterical delight by a mainly Jewish audience, was later described by the *New York Post* as a warmed-up corpse and was withdrawn within a month. All of which goes to show that even the Angels of Luck take the occasional night off.

The history of the Robe is interesting, and unlike most superstitions its origin can be pinpointed to a place and a date. It started in October 1950 with a chorus singer called Florence Baum who was appearing in *Gentlemen Prefer Blondes*. She had in her dressing-room a white satin gown trimmed with maribou. One of the dancers, Bill Bradley, admired it and as a rather camp little joke asked permission to wear it backstage to cheer up the other gipsies. The show was a huge success and a week later he sent it round to his friend, Arthur Parrington, who was due to open in *Call me Madam*. Attached to it was a note saying that this was the famous Gipsy Robe and to wear it backstage and thus show it to everybody would bring good luck to the show. Arthur Parrington obediently followed the instructions and was delighted that *Call Me Madam* was a huge success also. From then it went to Forrest Bonshire in *Guys and Dolls* and so the new superstition was kicked off to a flying start. During the years that followed the original Robe became so encrusted with souvenirs that it began to fall to pieces and though the wardrobe mistress of *Can-Can* in 1953 did her best to sew and darn it together, it finally disintegrated in 1954 and was presented to the Drama Collection in the Lincoln Centre where it is occasionally put on show. In twenty-four years there have been no less than five Gipsy Robes; some fall to pieces, some have been lost, one has even been stolen.

Claire Bloom never walks on pavement cracks, a childhood superstition which has mysteriously survived into adult life. She touches wood in moments of crisis, as many of us do and – rather curiously – if she accidentally walks under a ladder then she goes straight to bed. Frankie Vaughan cherishes a silver-topped cane for luck and Ted Lewis, a famous American vaudeville comedian once cancelled a $5,000 engagement because his lucky top-hat was lost *en route* to Chicago. Ed Wynne, another American comic, who can occasionally be seen in Hollywood musicals, always wore the same pair of shoes in his act and managed to make one unusually well-made pair last for twenty years. According to the *New York Times*, good luck could be bought like any other commodity. An advertisement for a Chinese lucky ring selling at the modest price of $1.50 ('Buy now to avoid disappointment!') found one curious customer in Fanny Brice. Within a week of buying and wearing it she won $2,000 in a lottery. The news spread like wildfire round Broadway, and amongst those who queued up at the sale counter to buy them were W. C. Fields, Francine Larrimore, Robert Mantell and Raymond Hitchcock. History has not recorded the extent of the luck they were thus able to buy.

Certain actors and actresses are regarded by their colleagues and employers as lucky mascots: Mrs Patrick Campbell, Gladys Cooper and Vivien Leigh all carried with them an aura of imperishable luck and success far in excess of mere stardom, partly owing to their extraordinary beauty and partly their unique talents. All had the ability to drag unlikely and unpromising plays out of the rut and transform them into hugely popular successes. Richard

Goolden and Robertson Hare were both regarded as lucky and producers over the decades queued up to employ them. Also in this category is the mysterious figure of Walter Plinge, whose identity requires a word of explanation for the public. 'Who is Walter Plinge?' is a popular quiz question which recurs with some frequency in the intellectual press. If an actor is playing two parts in the same play, the second heavily disguised, he will use a fictitious name in the programme to conceal his identity; by a long tradition the name used is Walter Plinge. His appearance on any programme was once regarded by his colleagues as a sign of good luck: actors used to love displaying their versatility at a time when this was encouraged (not so much now, alas), and audiences loved watching it. Mr Plinge's presence in a play was an indication that the evening was going to be full of old-fashioned theatrical delights. From time to time, the more esoteric magazines will start a correspondence in which Walter Plinge's origins are the subject of learned speculation. Nobody has ever been able to state with certainty when he made his first appearance in the West End but he is believed to have started his career sometime in the 1870s. Though he never became a star he acted with the greatest companies and his career in the profession can be truthfully described as distinguished. At the turn of the century he was very busy and even contrived the major miracle of appearing in three plays simultaneously. (Did a taxi wait at the stage door to take him from one theatre to the next, one wonders?) During the 20s and 30s he virtually left the West End and acted mainly in the provinces, and after the war his retirement was complete. It is believed that his farewell appearance was in a musical called *Chrysanthemum* at the Apollo in which he played a Dickensian old washerwoman. Few playgoers will forget that supreme *coup de theâtre* when he lifted off his grey wig to reveal the smiling features of Richard Curnock, a popular comedy actor of the post-war years. According to Wilfrid Granville, author of the definitive *Theatrical Dictionary*, the original Walter Plinge was a theatre-crazy landlord who managed a pub opposite the Theatre Royal, Drury Lane and who extended unlimited credit to the company. Not unnaturally he was greatly liked by them, and one historic Sunday evening they permitted him to satisfy a lifelong ambition by appearing on the stage in a benefit performance given in his honour and under his own name.

In America his equivalent is George Spelvin. As with Walter Plinge his ancestry is obscure, but he is thought to have originally been a member of the Lambs Club. His career didn't last as long as that of his English counterpart, a fact which can only be due to overwork. At one time (1900–03) he played no less than 210 parts in three years, a fact which, if Equity had existed at that time, would certainly have aroused its sympathetic concern. The Spelvin family, unlike the Plinge family, includes a sister, Georgina Spelvin. In 1973 she appeared in a very controversial sex film which nearly became the subject of legal action.

Between the wars, the Music Box Theatre boasted a lucky backstage worker. Sam Roseman, Master Property Man, was the object of this belief and to guarantee success every leading lady had to be photographed sitting on his lap. Margaret Sullivan in *Dinner at Eight* in 1933, started it just as a joke, and it worked. Helen Broderick in *Thousand Cheer*, Tallulah Bankhead in *Rain*, Claire Luce in *Of Mice and Men*, Martha Scott in *The Male Animal*, are only a few of the lucky leading ladies. Nobody knows who started this idea, but it is believed to have been Sam Roseman. In *Ceiling Zero*, there was no leading lady, so Osgood Perkins the leading man sat on his lap, but strangely enough this didn't work and the play was not a success.

So much for the lucky people. Contrariwise, there are unlucky actors who, although dedicated and talented, contrive to bring misfortune to a play and unhappiness to a company. Peter Bull relates how he once accepted a West End engagement and enquired after his colleagues. A list of names was rattled off. 'That's not a cast-list,' he exclaimed in horror, 'that's a suicide pact.' Kate Claxton, a popular American musical comedy star of the 90s was thought to be highly unlucky. Her career was dogged by an amazing number of burned down theatres, train accidents, and other disasters. In spite of this she was always in work for she had special qualities which the public flocked to see, a superb singing voice, a rare beauty and, if that wasn't enough, a fair measure of acting ability.

Then there are those first-night rituals which give strength and reassurance and calm the nerves and which are faithfully performed on first nights in the theatre and the recordings of TV plays. Not every actor has one, but most of us do, and some of these are exceedingly bizarre. The public misunderstands, for the public doesn't realise what an actor goes through on these distressing occasions. Some of us take it much worse than others. Some actors feel sick, quite literally sick, like Bob Hoskins who has been sick on first nights so many times that he gets worried if he isn't sick, and then somehow has to contrive to make himself sick before he can act. Alec Guinness develops a crippling pain in his knees and back. George Arliss would walk round the theatre several times before he dared enter, not only on first nights, but every night. José Ferrer, by a monumental effort of mind, convinces himself that everybody in the audience is a personal friend. Al Jolson did likewise which was a little easier in his case as many of them were, and those who weren't felt that they were. It was a thousand pities that he could never nerve himself to cross the Atlantic and perform in England. Money beyond the dreams of Solomon was laid at his feet for a brief London season and after his films were released his fan-mail from England could have left him in no doubt as to the warmth of his reception here, but he regarded foreign appearances as very bad luck and the thought of appearing in front of a strange audience filled him with superstitious terror. 'If there's just one guy who ain't enjoyin' the show,' he once said in explanation, 'I'll know it and that'll kill me.'

Sir Henry Irving on first nights would always walk to the theatre instead of taking a cab as was his custom. From his rooms in Grafton Street to the Lyceum Theatre was a thirty minute walk, but the exercise calmed his nerves, and the open, unashamed adoration of all he met on this Royal Progress – paper-sellers, flowergirls, shop-keepers, ordinary pedestrians – went far to banish the nightmare of insecurity and inadequacy which had haunted him throughout his life. He was very popular with the Dickensian substrata of London life: he tipped them generously, chatted unselfconsciously to them, and generally felt far more at home in their company than with the much grander people who filled his theatre.

They in turn would cheer and salute him as he walked past, smooth his path and in many small ways, look after him. Passing through Covent Garden he would invariably buy a small posy of violets from one of the flower-girls there and place it on his dressing table. The sad thing about this routine is that it didn't really help him. Irving was always at his worst on first nights and one of the reasons was the presence of his wife in the stage-box. Although they had parted in 1871 on rather less than amicable terms (full details of this sad story in Laurence Irving's biography), and although they never again spoke to each other, Irving continued to discharge what he felt to be his marital duty (or was it a secret masochism rising from God only knows what sense of guilt?) by giving her seats for all his premières. She would sit there gazing at him with cold, implacable hatred, willing him to fail and, although he was very short-sighted, he must have been able to see her.

There are some interesting first-night rituals. Derek Fowldes has a carefully worked-out routine which is not untypical of many actors. He always comes to the theatre a full hour before the performance, reads the evening paper with his feet up and then has a shower when the half-hour is called. He then prepares a drink of honey, lemon and warm water and luxuriously sips this whilst making up and dressing. When the five minutes is called, he performs a complicated series of vocal exercises and then takes a tablet of Vitamin C. He does all this in the same sequence religiously every night, and although it could be described by cynics as a simple commonsensical way of relaxing, it has, over the years, acquired a definite aura of good luck, and he admits that he would be seriously alarmed if circumstances compelled him to omit any part of it.

Peter Barkworth has a ritual by which he always travels to the theatre by the same route. (Sir John Gielgud, perversely, never does; that's his ritual). It started when he was playing at the Savoy in 1955 in *A Woman of No Importance.* He would always travel from St. John's Wood to Trafalgar Square by a 159 bus and then walk down the Strand. But instead of taking the obvious short cut down by, or through, the Coal Hole Pub, he would go further along and turn into Savoy Place before going down to the stage door. On

Peter Barkworth holding a lucky stick of Leichner's No.5. He always travels to the theatre the same way.

one memorable occasion he met some of the company on the Embankment whither he had gone to see a film during the afternoon. They were returning to the theatre and rather than embarrass or aggravate them, he walked with them to the stage door and then excused himself and dashed up to the Strand and returned to the stage door by his usual route. On the one occasion when he did come by a different route, he gave a bad performance and he has no desire to run the risk of repeating it. He always tries to avoid going past the front of the theatre and if this is not possible, he takes very good care not to look at the pictures of himself outside. During rehearsals he will never on any account watch the scenes he is not in, nor will he watch other people's scenes on the monitor set whilst acting in a TV play.

Sir Laurence Olivier states firmly that he is not in any genuine sense of the word superstitious but he does admit that when driving to the theatre he will look hard at any water of the Thames whenever he drives over it (the water of a river is the bringer of life and thus represents good luck), and if he is passing under a bridge on which a train is passing over he will not alter speed. Jim Dale is superstitious about clean fingernails and will hold up the curtain if he has not cleaned them. Leslie Phillips jumps up and down in his dressing-room and burps, a simple routine which is also used by boxers (exponents of another theatrical art). Jack Lemmon always whispers the words 'magic time' just before the cameras begin to turn, a hangover from his early days in TV. Magic is, after all, what every actor wants to produce and all audiences want to experience. Jenny Laird hypnotises herself into thinking that it's not her in the part but somebody else, and that she is standing in the wings watching this *alter ego*; once she has done this, the first night has no further terrors for her. Tilly Losch, Austrian musical star of the 20s and 30s, will never open on October 23rd, or even go out of her home on that day if she is working. Apparently two near-fatal accidents occurred on the October 23rd of two consecutive years. The first was a car accident and the second was a fire in her hotel. She escaped from both, but only just, and that particular day clearly has the jinx on it. John Bryans has a very peculiar ritual before he records a TV play, which most actors agree is ten times more nerve-wracking than a theatrical first night; he goes to the lavatory, sits on the seat and silently recites the names of actors he admires ... Wilfrid Walter, Conrad Veidt, Wilfrid Lawson, Donald Wolfit, Henry Ainley ... Ken Waller always eats a sweet called Cherry-Ripe, originally supplied by his mother in his early days in the North. He believes that it is good for the voice and, like aspirin, cures headache and calms the nerves.

Some young actors tend to scoff at superstitions but not Michael Ridgeway who spent three years as the youngest son of the Barrett family in the musical, *Robert and Elizabeth*. He admits to being riddled with irrelevant and illogical superstitions. He is always first out of the dressing-room and he likes, when possible, to dress on the empty stage. He considers it very good luck to iron his trousers on the stage. If he touches something with his left hand while he is dressing then he must immediately touch the same thing with his right hand: this balances things up and a good balance between extremes is traditional part of good augery. When the call, 'Beginners Please' is announced three minutes before the opening of the play, he embarks on a curious little ritual: he puts the tips of his fingers together which will store the energy in the tips, holds his cupped hands together and then follows upwards the line of his fingers. He then gazes fixedly at whatever object lies immediately ahead, which might be a picture, light-fitting or curtain rail. He then looks hard at it and swallows: this gives him that feeling of assurance and confidence without which nobody can act.

Gerry Small, the Jamaican actor, thinks that dressing-rooms are unlucky and will avoid them; instead he will prowl round the empty wings where he can be alone. Richard Dennis, following the example of his father, a variety star of the 20s, walks round the empty theatre to get the feel of it. Many actors do this and there is a sound, practical reason for it; only by this reconnaissance can you discover the size and test the acoustics. Cardew Robinson has a curious superstition about forgotten errands; if he has to return to his dressing-room to get something he has forgotten, he will always count ten before going in, though he cannot give a logical explanation for it. Marlene Dietrich is superstitious about the stars as are many theatre people; she lives under the sign of Capricorn which she says is not a good Zodiac sign but it helps her to organise things – she cannot endure an untidy dressing-room which is bad luck to her, or an untidy stage, which is why her dressing-rooms and theatres are always religiously clean. Joe Melia goes one stage further in this; his dressing-room is not merely tidy, he likes to keep it in a state of monastic simplicity – functional and unlived in: not for him the cosy domestic touches whereby most actors like to transform their dressing-room into a second home. This bleakness helps him to concentrate and give a good performance.

John Graham regards it as very bad luck to consult his script before the performance and banishes it from his dressing-room, whereas most actors would die a thousand deaths if it wasn't on their table and wide-open for endless consultations. Likewise, having a script on the stage for discreet consultation in a moment of crisis is regarded as very bad luck by some old actors, but actors faced with the nightmare ordeal of a one-man show will usually find a way of getting something on the stage to help them out in an emergency. When I started doing my *First Night of Pygmalion* in which I was on the stage continuously for two and a quarter hours, I always had two scripts lying round the stage disguised as props and would never think of embarking on the performance without them. For this reason, I am convinced, the moment of crisis never occurred. Beerbohm Tree took this one stage further: his first-night memory was so treacherous that he had all the difficult parts written out on separate pieces of paper and pinned in likely places all round the stage so that wherever he found himself in trouble, help was near at hand.

Carol Channing stays up all night before an opening going over every word. Sir Laurence Olivier did this on the night before his first *Richard III* at the New Theatre in 1944, a very nerve-wracking and traumatic night, as he was later to remember. *Richard* was the third play to be launched in the historic Old Vic season; the other two were *Peer Gynt* and *Arms and the Man* and they had been hugely successful. During the dress rehearsals of *Richard* he had suffered some alarming lapses of memory which, for one who enjoys almost photographic recall of the text, was a very sinister omen. He was filled with a superstitious fear that the play would be the ugly duckling of the repertoire and that he would experience a really crucifying failure. The night before the opening he and Vivien Leigh and Garson Kanin went over the whole part in a suite at Claridges, again and again and again. The rest is history.

The Lunts had two superstitions as I remember well from the six months I spent with them during the London production of *The Visit* in 1960. They would never cross anybody on a staircase and I remember a couple of occasions when they insisted, politely but firmly, on standing on the top stair until I had climbed up and passed them to the point of safety. My bewilderment clearly showed and Lynn Fontanne gently explained to me. 'It's terribly bad luck to cross whilst inside in a theatre,' she said. 'Ellen Terry told me this and I've never forgotten it.' It was strange to be reminded so directly that she had been a friend of Ellen Terry's fifty years earlier (and mentioned in the lady's diary) and it was remarks like this which triggered curious speculation amongst the company as to her age. The theatrical reference books were discreetly silent on the subject and Lynn Fontanne will doubtless take the secret to her grave. Their other superstition was a very strong belief that it was good luck to come to theatre at least four hours in advance and sometimes more. For a 7.30 performance they were comfortably installed in their two dressing-rooms by 3.00 in the afternoon; they would have a light lunch, Alfred would read the papers and do the crossword and she would slowly get into the rather complicated wig and costume in which she made her first entrance. For two hours they would enjoy a monastic silence and seclusion – and there is nothing more tomb-like than an empty theatre. This was their way of soaking up the atmosphere of the play and relaxing.

Contrariwise, Charles Hawtrey, the consecrated darling of the Edwardian comedy theatre, believed it to be very bad luck to come early to the theatre as this gave him plenty of time to get curtain nerves and since he was already a very highly-strung man, this would effectively stop him from acting well. He liked to appear in the theatre not the usual thirty-five minutes of theatre tradition and law, but just before his entrance. The stage door keepers of the different theatres in which he appeared would well remember his nightly arrival. He would rush out of the taxi, through the stage door, down the corridors and onto the stage arriving just in time for his first line. This was, of course, a distinctly worrying situation for the stage manager who never knew if Hawtrey would appear or not until he did, so the understudy was kept in a state of permanent readiness. This lateness was against all the accepted rules of the theatre, but since Hawtrey was an actor-manager and his own employer he was entitled to make and break them to his own satisfaction.

Sir Henry Irving, like most men of destiny, would have firmly regarded himself as master of his own fate and entirely independent of augery, but a Cornish ancestry and upbringing cannot be lightly cast-off; although his grandson and biographer was unable to find much evidence of a superstitious nature, it seems that he did attach good luck to a little fox-terrier called Fussy who was his insepar-able companion. Irving lavished on him all the pent-up, frustrated affection which a lonely and loveless man is liable to extend to an

21

Mrs Patrick Campbell holding her lucky Pekinese, the obnoxious Moonbeam. This picture of beauty and quality in its final sad decline is one of the saddest the author knows. (London Express News & Feature Services)

animal, and Fussy's death in 1897 was one of the greatest emotional blows he suffered. After that his fortunes declined rapidly; a South London warehouse was burned down and with it the accumulated scenery and costumes and furniture for twenty-five productions, the mainstay of his repertory; a series of unsuccessful productions brought him almost to the point of bankruptcy and he was finally forced to sell out to a syndicate and was thus no longer master of his own theatre.

Mrs Patrick Campbell was superstitious about a loathsome little pekinese called Moonbeam. Her refusal ever to be separated from him even for a moment resulted in her rejecting a number of very lucrative film offers (Mrs Higgins in *Pygmalion*, Lady Britomart in *Major Barbara*) at a time in her final years when she was suffering great financial hardship. In view of the quality of these two films both directed by Anthony Asquith, the loss to posterity is beyond calculation.

Barbra Streisand has been reticent on the subject but she did admit with characteristic humour that she considered it very bad luck to step in front of an express train going at 80 miles per hour. Noël Coward once informed the press that the only superstition he had ever had was that it was bad luck to sleep thirteen in a bed. The laughter which followed encouraged him to repeat the joke in his next play which was the very successful *Nude With Violin*. Robert Morley has shown a distinct impatience with the existing superstitions and has brought his splendidly creative imagination to bear on the subject. He now invents his own and has firmly announced to the world that it is very bad luck while travelling to the theatre to listen to *The Archers* in the car. It is difficult to avoid the conclusion that other people have brought similar powers of invention when answering my appeal for information.

What is one to make of 'bad luck to eat peanuts in the dressing-room ... to play chess in the Wardrobe ... to read Thackeray in the wings ... to talk to your agent on the stage door telephone ... to act on a Sunday ... to wear striped underwear ... ?'

Praying is important, particularly if it is directed to a particular saint. St. Genesius is the most popular for he is the patron saint of actors; he was an actor in the ancient theatres of Rome and was

23

martyred by the Emperor Diocletian. St. Christopher is another and so is St. Cecilia, the patron saint of music. Derek Ayleward prays to St. Anthony, an unusual choice. 'I'm not a Catholic and I'm not even particularly religious, but I always say a prayer to St. Anthony on first nights. He's the patron saint of lost property and supposing I lost my lines … ?' The prayers are usually muttered quickly and quietly in the wings just before the moment of entrance but there are some very religious actors who will go down on their knees in the privacy of their dressing-rooms and pray at length; Catholics will say a complete Rosary, Protestants will read from the Bible and Jews will recite the Talmud. But it must be remembered that good luck rituals can be overdone and to be too crawlingly servile when asking favours from the lucky angels is bad luck, for it is liable to trigger off a very unwelcome streak of sadism. Before the opening of Noël Coward's play *Waiting in the Wings* in 1960, Marie Lohr went to St. Mark's Church and prayed long and hard for a good first night. On the way to the theatre she slipped and broke her arm. 'No good deed ever goes unpunished' was Coward's acid comment. Sir Alec Guinness remembers with a painful smile the night he played Hamlet for the Festival of Britain in 1951 at the New Theatre. An hour before he arrived at the theatre he went round the Garrick Club anxiously touching all the busts and portraits of Shakespeare for luck. One would have been enough, but to touch all three was definitely overdoing it. A detailed description of the famous theatrical disaster which followed is not within the scope of this book and will doubtless be told elsewhere in all its colourful detail. The play was in the hands of a well-known radio producer who had never directed Shakespeare in his life. The production opened ice-cold without the benefit of a pre-London tour, for this was the Dark Ages before the preview had been invented. A new switchboard had been installed whose workings caused great confusion and which played havoc with the complex lighting cues and effects. The company included some of the most talented and distinguished actors then available, including the fledgling critic, Kenneth Tynan, making his first and last appearance on the professional stage as the Player King: but the Kiss of Death was on the production and all managed to give the worst performances of their lives. The public took a great hate to the beard which Guinness wore for the part and for the first and only time in his career there were boos from the gallery at the end.

I myself once called in on a church on my way to the audition for a part which I very much wanted and appeased my excessive nerves by putting a pound note into the poor box and paying another pound for a candle. I arrived at the theatre glowing with high moral satisfaction and complacency, saying to myself, 'Well, after all that, I've just *got* to get it.' The audition was a terrible failure and not only did I not get the part but I didn't work again for three months, so the only possible conclusion is that God, like the Metropolitan Police, doesn't take kindly to attempted bribery.

Continuity is important. Many actors, like John Moore, will always keep a prop from the previous play, an ash-tray, a pencil, a pair of spectacles, a scarf. Some actors will always use an old set of make-up sticks on a first night and will never break into a new stick, bottle or tube until the play has been running at least a week. Peter Barkworth takes this idea one stage further: he won't start a new tin of pancake at the beginning of a performance any night, he must wait until half-way through the evening, perhaps until after the interval. This distrust of newness extends to clothes: Richard Dennis will never wear an entirely new, freshly laundered shirt on a first night, it must have been worn once before at the dress rehearsal. Al Jolson always wore old clothes on his opening nights and Jim Dale will never change a costume during a long run. If it wears out and has to be replaced then a fragment of the original costume must somehow be incorporated in the new one. On the other hand, newness can bring good luck. Some actors, like Robert Selbie, regard it as lucky to wear something new on the first day of rehearsal and there was once a certain eminent actress, luckily with a wealthy husband, who invariably bought a new piece of jewellery and wore it throughout the rehearsals of a new play. Before the War actors were expected to look like gentlemen and to dress smartly, but Laurence Olivier's habit of appearing on every day of the *Mary Queen of Scots* rehearsals in a different suit, aroused a certain jealous hostility from his colleagues. 'Each suit is a relic of a different flop,' was Olivier's prompt explanation, a remark which

Robert Selbie (left) wearing his 'good luck' new suit on the first day of rehearsals for the 1974 season of the Chichester Festival. Also in the picture Anthony Chardet and Timothy West. (Peggy Leder)

greatly endeared him to the company and started lifelong friendships which survive to this day.

† † †

All these superstitions are personal, but there are dozens of general ones which, in total defiance of logic or common sense, are regarded by the theatrical fraternity as Holy Writ. Their origins are lost in the mists of antiquity and theatrical history and between them they cast a very intriguing light on human gullibility. It's good luck if your shoes squeak on your first entrance for this means the audience will love you; nobody has ever been able to explain why this is, but one old actress I knew in my early days in the theatre assured me that it was so and had frequently happened to her. For this reason she always bought rather cheap shoes as these were the only variety which could be relied on to squeak loudly enough.

If you get a first-night telegram then you must immediately destroy the envelope, and if you are writing a letter in connection with your work you must get the stamp from a friend *and not pay for it.* This means you will get the job. It's very good luck to fall flat on your face when you make your entrance; the play will then be a huge success and there is one interesting example of this in the first production of *Dracula* at the Little Theatre, London, when an actor called Stuart Lomath tripped over the Gothic doorway and fell heavily onto the stage. Apparently the effect was more sinister than amusing for the audience uttered a collective gasp of alarm instead of laughing, seeing in the incident yet another manifestation of Count Dracula's evil influence. Nobody had any faith in the play and all were greatly surprised when it ran two years in London and a year in New York with a lucrative film deal to follow.

Finding a piece of cotton is good luck as long as it is either backstage or on the stage itself (dressing-rooms don't count). This indicates a forthcoming contract with a producer whose initial corresponds with the number of times you can wind it round your finger. Once round means 'A' suggesting that Mr Tom Arnold will be requiring your services; three times round means 'C' indicating that it is Michael Codron, Ray Cooney or the Festival Theatre at Chichester who will be fighting for you. Seven times would be 'G' for Gale and if you were lucky enough to find a piece of cotton long enough to wind round your finger thirteen times, as once did happen to a certain aged American actor, then Mr David Merrick of the Mermaid Theatre would be smiling in your direction. There is an alternative version of this which I heard from a music hall lady ventriloquiste (old enough to remember the days when such people were called *artiste* and no nonsense about it). You must take the thread from somebody's jacket or dress and drop it onto the ground, and if it falls into the shape of a letter that will be the initial of your next employer. Leslie Banks was always intensely irritated by a certain actress who spent her time picking threads from his jacket and dropping them onto the floor whenever she played a scene with him. 'The dandruff-scraper and fluff-twirler' he would peevishly describe her. He always wondered why she did it and this would now appear to be the explanation.

It is very bad luck to whistle in the dressing-room or indeed anywhere inside the theatre for that means that the play will be finishing soon. Those who really do believe in the darker side of the supernatural will explain that by whistling you are summoning the Devil. 'Whistle and I'll come to you,' runs the old Cornish saying. It is further believed that the one sitting nearest the door will get the sack. There would seem to be some truth in this for in my first year in the theatre (1950) I was sacked from my first three jobs, the repertory companies at Watford, Bromley and Darlington.

I can remember that on all three occasions some actor in the dressing-room had whistled only the day before and that my place at the long trestle table was nearest the door; this being the coldest and draughtiest place is where the newcomer to the company traditionally sits. The first occasion had definitely been malice aforethought from an older actor I had unwittingly offended; the second and third were, I like to think, both accidents from actors as young and inexperienced as myself who presumably did not know any better. There is a simple, traditional way of cancelling the bad luck: you must leave the dressing-room, turn round three times, knock on the door and then beg humbly to be re-admitted. Profanity has a healthy neutralising effect and a stream of obscene words will quickly banish any evil spirit in hearing. In the stage area whistling is exceedingly dangerous for a good commonsensical reason; in the eighteenth and nineteenth centuries the stage-staff, who were responsible for the raising and lowering of the scenery, (known in professional jargon as 'flying'), were recruited from the navy, for it was ex-seamen who understood how to handle the hemp lines on which the scenery was strung. They were traditionally directed by the stage-manager who whistled at them, one for raise and two for lower. Any foolish actor or visitor whistling backstage could cause total confusion in the performance and could even get the scenery on his head.

Views on the supposedly bad luck of the number thirteen differ considerably within theatrical circles. For most people it is bad luck as with Dudley Moore who, in a typically witty letter, said, 'I'm not *really* superstitious, but if my play opened on Friday 13th and I found myself in No.13 dressing-room on the 13th floor and the theatre was No.13 in the street, then I might think that things were beginning to stack up on me.' Jean Kent remembers how very distressed she and the company she was leading were when they were flown out to South Africa on Friday 13th. Old actor-laddies used to say that if there are thirteen in the company then three will get the sack. Eddie Cantor would rewrite his entire script if the original was thirteen pages long and there are producers who will never open a play on the thirteenth of the month. One famous Edwardian theatrical lodging house in Brighton had a room No.13, but nobody would use it. The landlady tried to take off the jinx by redecorating it, putting in running water and room service (early-morning tea, an exotic luxury) but it was all useless. Nobody would touch it and it was eventually turned into a bathroom. A TV series called *Diana* and starring Diana Rigg, started in America to a fanfare of trumpets, failed to find the audience it had expected and it was on Episode 13 that the producers finally abandoned it. Pat Phoenix, much-loved star of *Coronation Street* which is coming near to breaking all world records for longevity, decided to leave the series after a financial dispute. She wanted an extra £100 a week and Granada TV would only offer her £20. Her departure and that of her husband, Alan Browning, who was also in the series, was loudly mourned by the fans but her decision was made and she stuck to it. She had been with the series for thirteen years.

On the other hand, the number carries a reassuring amount of good luck for some people. It was Eric Portman's favourite lucky number and it has been noticed that play titles with thirteen letters are usually very lucky; a random selection of these would include *The Magistrate, The Profligate, The Shaughrawn, A Scrap of Paper, The Wizard of Oz, The Silver King, Under Two Flags, The Wages of Sin, In Old Kentucky.* In America there is an interesting super-stition connected with the number. On Broadway and in many other cities (commercial theatres only) it is considered good luck to start the performance thirteen minutes late. This means a happy and responsive audience and a fine performance to match, for it is a sad and inescapable truth of theatrical life that if the audience is bad then the actors are unlikely to be good. There is a practical reason for this as with many superstitions and it stems from the notorious unpunctuality of American theatregoers. No power in heaven, earth, Broadway or the White House can persuade New Yorkers to get to the theatre on time, a phenomenon which is difficult to explain; in view of the insane prices they pay for their tickets, they might be expected to fall over backwards rather than miss a single minute of the entertainment. Rather than torment the unhappy company with the nuisance of chattering, rattling late-comers, the curtain is held for thirteen minutes. It seems to work.

Thirteen is a very lucky number for me. The first play I ever sold to a commercial West End producer, (Michael White who pro-duced *Sleuth* after everybody else had turned it down) was de-livered by hand on Friday 13th July. The address was 13 Duke Street, St. James and his enthusiastic card of acceptance arrived 13 days later. The contract was in my hands for signature on the 13th of the following month, the address of the agent who negotiated the very favourable and far-seeing contract was 113 Wardour Street, his name Laurence Fitch, had thirteen letters, and the first meeting I had with my new producer was on the 31st of the following month – the reverse of a lucky number is also lucky. It was and still is a matter of the keenest regret that the title *Weekend with Willie*, (it is about Somerset Maugham) did not contain thirteen letters nor did the cast number thirteen. In spite of all this the play could still be a terrible failure and time alone will reveal what the Fates have in store, but it cannot be denied that it has kicked off to a flying start.

† † †

It is bad luck to speak the last line of the play (called the tag-line) at rehearsal though there are some subtle variations on this. Some say it applies only to a new play; others say that, old or new, it applies only to the dress rehearsal, though I have known old actors who refuse to say it at any time and could only with reluctance be persuaded to say it on the first night. Nobody has ever been quite sure why this is unlucky but many a novice actor like myself who has innocently done so has been shot down in flames by the old actor-laddies in the company. One theory which has been tenta-tively advanced is this: if you don't say the tag-line then this is one little thing which hasn't been rehearsed; this knowledge will be a tiny pinprick of worry and this will produce an element of tension in your first night performance which is commonly regarded as an essential ingredient of good acting. This is only a theory and not a very convincing one because first nights are quite tense enough without going out of one's way to make them any worse. The other and much more plausible idea is that anything which is complete is tempting providence, for the impish humour of the Fates will bring them to destroy anything which is perfect, since perfection is the privilege only of the Gods; this is why builders won't put in the last brick or shipbuilders the last rivet and why Michaelangelo left unpainted a tiny section of the ceiling in the Sistine chapel. Some producers, particularly in the pantomime world, take this superstition very seriously and Emile Littler would never allow his principals even to know what the tag-line was until they came to the last scene at which point a uniformed attendant would enter the stage and give it to them in a sealed envelope. Patrick Ludlow who stage-managed a number of the postwar Littler pantomimes has preserved a couple of these state secrets, for posterity:

CINDERELLA: And now our evening work is done
                  We hope you've all had lots of fun.

ROBIN HOOD: And that's the story of Robin Hood
                  We know you'll come back to this wood.

Some producers go to what must surely be considered an unreasonable length to avoid trouble and will not allow the principal in question to speak the tag-line even on the first night. The principal concerned must speak some gibberish is rhythm. June Grey remembers reciting,

ALADDIN: di-dum, di-dum, di-dum, di-dum,
             Dumdiddi, dumdiddi, dumdiddi, DUM!

greatly to the bewilderment of the audience, though the orchestra was also playing and thus partially covered the gap.

Of all superstitions this is probably the most dangerous, for to leave anything unrehearsed, particularly the final line and curtain is to invite disaster. Ellen Terry remembers a significant incident in her youth when she was playing Julia in *The Rivals*. During the rehearsals she faithfully observed the then centuries-old tradition by never speaking the tag-line,

JULIA: But in judging passion will force the gaudier into the
           wreath whose thorn offends them when its leaves
           are dropped.
                                                    Exeunt omnes.

When the first performance came the prompter heard this for the first time and was greatly confused to hear her say it with an upward inflection, which she later claimed made good sense, rather than the traditional downward inflection. An upward inflection implies that there is more to come so the wretched man stood there with his hands on the curtain rope waiting for it. She recalled in her memoires that there was a terrible embarrassment while the company waited for the curtain to come down and it wasn't until Mr Buckstone as Bob Acres had shouted for all the audience to hear (he was very deaf), 'What the devil does all this mean, why don't you bring the damned curtain down?' that the prompter did so. A similar incident dogged a rep production of *The Importance of Being Earnest* in the early fifties. The final two lines, just in case there is any reader who does not know them, are as follows:

LADY BRACKNELL: My nephew, you appear to be displaying signs of
                triviality.

WORTHING: On the contrary, Aunt Augusta, I have just
             discovered for the first time in my life the vital
             importance of being Earnest.
                                                All embrace. Curtain.

The actor playing Ernest not only refused to speak his final line in the rehearsals but rashly assumed that all the back-stage staff knew about the superstition. On the first night the young and inexperienced stage manager who did not, and rather more surprisingly did not know the final line of the play, brought down the curtain on Lady Bracknell's line, thereby robbing the leading man of his privilege of ending the play. When the combined wrath of the company fell on his head, he defended himself, not unreasonably, by explaining that he had thought Lady Bracknell's line to be the final one because at no time during rehearsals had he heard any other.

Matheson Lang always liked to end his productions himself and, irrespective of the play or the part, would rewrite the final scene to give himself the tag-line, but in rehearsal he would always substitute the words 'Colleen Bawn' greatly to the bewilderment of the company's newcomers.

These are only three examples of an accident which can be duplicated endlessly in theatrical history and which confirm one basic fact of life – that to leave anything unrehearsed however trivial or apparently unimportant, is very dangerous.

Opening umbrellas on the stage doesn't seem to bother anybody in England but in America there is a lot of bad luck associated with it. It started in 1868 when an orchestral leader named Bob Williams, saying goodbye to the company before going away for the weekend, opened his umbrella whilst standing on the stage, and walked out into a very rainy day. An hour later he was standing on the boat waving goodbye to a party of friends. As it sailed away from the jetty one of the engines exploded and Williams was killed instantly. In the resulting publicity it seemed that the accident and the open umbrella were connected and thus a new theatrical superstition was born. This then produced a rather bizarre little problem for producers for although in the legitimate theatre the opening of an umbrella might well be avoided with a little judicious rearrangement of text and production, the twirling parasol, either singly or collectively, was always an essential ingredient of the late nineteenth century musical stage. Rose Coghlan, a big musical star of the nineties, twirled her red parasol in *Fashion* at Wallacks Theatre with unmatched zest and skill but was severely criticised in a very ungentlemanly manner by the press for thus endangering the future success of the entertainment. It was Marie Tempest in her big Broadway success *The Marriage of Kitty* who, with her usual cool, forthright, commensensical way of organising her life, decided that opening an umbrella or parasol on the stage was not unlucky provided you pointed it towards the floor and opened it down-

33

wards, thus indicating that you had all your troubles under your feet. From then on, umbrellas were always opened downwards and Jeanne Eagels on the first night of *Rain* was reminded of this in a first night telegram. She went on to score the greatest success of her career.

It was just as well there were no peacocks involved in *Rain* for peacocks are very unlucky. If the play involves peacocks' feathers or peacock fans or peacock designs on the stage, there will be trouble, not the least from mutinous principals. Oscar Asche had all the peacock fans destroyed at the dress rehearsal of *Chu Chin Chow* which then proceeded to break all existing records with a run of five years. Tom Walls would go berserk if any importunate designer tried to sneak peacock patterns into the setting of the Aldwych farces, and there is an intriguing story about Sir Henry Irving playing Othello with Edwin Booth's Iago at the Lyceum Theatre in 1880s.

Booth, who had sharp eyes, reported to Irving (who was very short-sighted) in the interval that there was a woman in the front row of the stalls who had a large peacock fan. Irving became greatly agitated and sent a letter to her by one of the attendants. It said: 'For God's sake, take your peacock's fan out of the theatre to avoid disaster!' The woman, anxious to obey, handed it to the attendant for disposal who, terrified, refused to take it. Eventually the woman left the theatre herself and threw it away into a nearby dustbin. Unfortunately it was too late to save the evening from disaster for his Othello was one of the few complete failures in Irving's long and glorious career and after the brief engagement he never played it again. Booth had good reason to dread the bird for when he built his huge and splendid theatre in 6th Avenue in the 1870s, a close friend gave him a magnificent stuffed peacock. Booth was very reluctant to hurt his friend's feelings; he accepted it with a convincing show of gratitude and placed it in the front lobby. The theatre and his management was a failure: one disastrous production followed another and within a couple of years he was bankrupt. In later years he not only quarrelled violently with his so-called friend when doubting his benevolence, but also attributed the downfall of his managerial ambitions to 'that miserable bird of malignant fate!' His unhappy experience would seem to have gone unheeded by other managers for when the Bijou Theatre was built in 1892, a dado of peacock feathers was painted round the auditorium. Once again bad luck hit the theatre with one failure after another. Soon the word circulated that it was an unlucky theatre and it wasn't until some years later that the dado was repainted a cheerful blue and the theatre enjoyed its first success with a light comedy *Midnight Belle*. From then it became one of New York's luckiest theatres.

An expensive and highly prestigious TV series, *The Pallisers* included some very decorative peacocks on the title designs. My heart sank as I watched the first episode. I telephoned the production office, warned them of the danger, and suggested that a new and peacock-free design be substituted for all future episodes. 'Nobody has ever heard of *that*,' said a voice very petulantly, 'and it's going to be very expensive. And nobody here takes that sort of thing seriously. After all, this is a TV studio not a theatre and I don't think these outmoded superstitions apply.' But they did. The BBC technicians went on strike just before the last episode was due to be recorded and it had to be cancelled. When the strike finished some months later the actors and sets were re-assembled but it was a hideously expensive and time-wasting business. Peacocks, I'm happy to learn, are no longer welcome in the TV Centre.

Then there are some unlucky colours. Yellow is bad luck because this is the colour worn by the Devil in the mediæval mystery plays. Yellow roses in a bouquet mean the death of an old friend, and a yellow dog in a play means a death in the company. Yellow clarinets are considered unlucky in America and though they have vanished completely from the theatre world they were once in common use in orchestra pits. Nat Goodwin, the vaudeville comedian, would go berserk if he saw one and would threaten to walk out if the offending musician did not take his instrument away. Black is unlucky because of its old association with death and people will refuse to wear it on the stage. There used to be a time when actors would get their dinner jackets, tails and dress-trousers made of midnight blue instead of black; it looked like black under the lights and was considered exceedingly smart.

But the unluckiest colour of all is undoubtedly green. You must not wear it, nor must you have it on the stage or anything connected with the play. There are a number of ingenious explanations for this: one is that it dates back to the days when stages had green cloths on the floor or when actors invariably performed out-of-doors on green lawns (hence the old actors expression, 'see you on the green'). So if an actor was wearing green while standing on something green, he would not be properly visible. The other theory puts it down to the traditional green spotlight which illuminated the eighteenth and nineteenth centuries' leading actors. It was known as the 'lime' (hence the *limelight*) and was particularly popular for illuminating the villains in olde-tyme melodramas. So it you were foolish enough to wear green whilst bathed in a green spotlight, the two colours would cancel each other out with a subsequent loss of visual interest. Green was once the symbol of sexual perversion as was shown by the specially dyed green carnation of the nineties which was the unofficial badge of the top-level homosexual society of that period; sexual perversion as a subject for drama was not, until recently, considered acceptable to either the public or the authorities. Witches and those involved in the occult profession will explain it very simply: green is the fairies' own special colour and they are jealous and hostile if mere mortals wear it, even if the mortal in question is impersonating a fairy. But there is a very practical explanation for green's unpopularity and that is the problem it gives to theatre electricians and designers; Michael Sinclair, an English actor and stage manager now resident in New York, sums it up tersely: 'Green is a real bitch to light, it always looks like muddy brown.' But whatever the reason, people will go out of their way to avoid green. One West End producer will not allow it on stage or in any company he employs. Even the two male volumes of *Spotlight*, inescapable to any theatrical organisation, are banished to the outer office where they can't be seen because of the two strips of green on the cover. Michael Codron admits quite cheerfully that he believes in this superstition and to further being a mass of 'unformulated and illogical belief'. He states that one evening during the run of *There's a Girl in my Soup* he discovered that the set was predominantly green, there were green books in the shelves and that the poster advertising it was green. He is now cautiously reconciled to the colour because the play had at that point been running for two years which by any standards can be called successful. But I remember an actress of considerable antiquity in my early days at Watford who found herself rehearsing on a green carpet, was given a script with a green cover and a green shawl to wear and her first line was 'my dear how beautiful you are, I'm positively green with jealousy.' She lost her voice, had to be replaced, and left the theatre cursing the colour and convinced that this had been the source of her troubles.

On the other hand, the theatrical fraternity has always been happily reconciled to the communal sitting-room backstage being called the Green Room, and there is in London a well-known and very prosperous actors club of that name. Green writing-paper appears to be lucky and it's interesting to note that Shaw invariably wrote his famous letters on paper of this colour, claiming that it was restful to his eyes. These letters found their way to many dressing-room tables, particularly those of Ellen Terry and Mrs Patrick Campbell and few playwrights enjoyed such an unbroken string of successes as Shaw did between 1900 and 1932. I invariably used green notepaper embossed with Shaw's address in Whitehall Court when impersonating him in *Dear Liar* and *The First Night of Pygmalion* and both of these plays have been very lucky for me. Play titles with the word 'Green' are also blessed with luck, *Green Julia*, *Green for Danger*, *The Corn is Green*, *How Green is my Valley*, *The Green Bay Tree* and *Green Pastures*, to name only six which spring instantly to mind.

Green Pastures provides an interesting footnote to this enquiry. Its success in the 30s on Broadway and round the American continent was legendary but the aura was slightly tarnished by a series of unaccountable and sinister deaths. Wesley Hill, the actor playing the Archangel Gabriel, was killed by a passing taxi. Sam Davies, his successor in the part died of a heart attack. The third actor in the part committed suicide. By now the company was getting extremely worried for there was a serious casting problem facing them; clearly there was a jinx somewhere, but why? Was it the part and if not, then what was it? It was finally suggested by one of the

37

company who had a knowledge of witchcraft that the curse was not on the part but on the horn which Gabriel has to play in De Lawd's office, the horn having a rather sinister significance in certain forms of voodoo. Thus reassured, the fourth actor, Orlando Jeffs, consented to play the part but not the horn and thus a superstition was born which has survived into the present day. In the film version, (MGM 1935) Oscar Polk insisted on following the tradition and the scene was tactfully re-written. Gabriel picks up the horn looks sadly at it, puts it to his mouth silently, and then replaces it on De Lawd's desk, saying rather guiltily as De Lawd enters, 'Ahm jest itchin' to blow one good toot on dat horn, Lawd.' De Lawd smiles gently, and Gabriel puts away the horn which is never seen or referred to again.

Old actors consider it very bad luck to have a tin trunk whilst on tour; it must be leather or one of those spacious wicker baskets known in the profession as skips. Tin trunks are unlucky because they resemble coffins and anything which even remotely resembles or reminds you of death is to be avoided. For this reason you must never have a real coffin on the stage and if the play – as with *Loot* or *Richard III* – requires one you must never hire it from a local undertaker; it must be specially constructed in the theatre workshop. In America, a camelback trunk, which is one with a rounded top, is considered unlucky; they are difficult to pack inside the lorry or coach when touring and in the old touring days many managers simply refused to allow them. Any young hopeful thus encumbered would be given the choice of either dismissal or being forced to replace it very expensively with one of the conventional shape. Likewise, a corded trunk is bad luck because the cord represents the hangman's rope and thus the company will be hanged with bad notices. Ethel Barrymore once in her very early days travelled with a corded trunk and was sternly ordered by the company manager to uncord it immediately and substitute leather straps. But it's good luck to have dozens of travelling labels pasted all over the trunk, for this is evidence of prosperity and experience and will thus get more respectful treatment from the porters and carriers.

Anything associated with death must naturally be avoided and there was an interesting example of this in 1950 during the run of

His Excellency. Owen Fellowes, playing a Middle Eastern prime minister, was involved in a very unpleasant accident in the underground. He fell onto the rails, his legs were amputated by a passing train and he died shortly afterwards in hospital. His replacement, Richard Littledale, moved into the empty dressing-room and wore his suit; shortly afterwards, he died from gas poisoning. With two fatalities so close to each other of two actors playing the same part, the company was getting worried. The part, the dressing-room, the suit and the props were all clearly unlucky, and so the third actor, Walter Horseborough, was strongly advised to keep away from the fatal dressing-room and not to use the suit or the props. He took their advice, and played it successfully and without incident for the remainder of its two-year run.

The Spanish theatre takes quite a different view of death – in Spain they love it, they are obsessed with it and their art, in all its forms, is coloured by the death wish. What the Spanish theatre public likes about plays and acting is the presence of death and this is how they judge it: *con fuende* meaning *with death* is the highest praise they can bestow on a play or a performance. The plays of Lope de Vega and all the other Spanish playwrights can only be understood properly in the light of this.

† † †

It is very ironic that when the whole point and purpose of an actors art is to produce an illusion of reality that the actual reality should be so carefully avoided. It's bad luck to have real money and real jewels on the stage. Apart from the obvious danger that they might be stolen there is the strange paradox that real jewels never look real; from a distance they look small and colourless and a competent property master with a supply of coloured glass and tin is able to outshine a whole shop window of Cartier and Fabergé. Gertrude Lawrence took this superstition so seriously that when Douglas Fairbanks Snr in a gesture of well-meaning generosity substituted real diamonds for the paste ones she wore during the run of *Private Lives* in 1930, she threw them back again into his face and refused ever to speak to him again.

Real antiques are bad for the same reason, for they never look entirely authentic no matter how splendid is their reality. A good illustration of this is a legendary story of Sir Herbert Beerbohm Tree being asked to give a special Royal Gala performance of his Hamlet as part of the 1911 Coronation festivities and deciding that to suit the occasion he would use in the play, not the usual painted cardboard goblets, but a set of antique mediæval chalices made of real gold and liberally studded with rubies, diamonds and sapphires. They were borrowed from the British Museum at enormous cost and trouble. The insurance against loss, the deposit, the police escort to, during and from the play added enormously to the costs of the operation but the resultant publicity provided some compensation – Sir Herbert in fur-lined astrakhan coat and top-hat formally receiving the goblets (which did, it must be admitted, look marvellous) flanked by uniformed police constables, Sir Herbert supervising their unwrapping in his dressing-room, Sir Herbert stating to the press that 'nothing is too good for His Majesty and His Majesty's Theatre', and finally Sir Herbert (aged 58 but who cared?) in his Hamlet costume holding up one of the goblets and soliloquising soulfully over it. The sad result of all this extravagance was a complaint from *The Times* critic, who had clearly not heard of all the fuss, that it was a great pity that the otherwise excellent production should have been spoiled by the use of goblets which were so obviously faked.

Real food is unlucky on the stage and there are some very hidebound old actor-laddies who will bluntly refuse to eat it. The tradition is that it must be fabricated to resemble real food but must not be what it is supposed to be; on the other hand it must be edible since it does have to be eaten. Actors are very long-suffering and in the interests of our Art we will eat and drink some unusually revolting things. As an unpaid student Assistant Stage Manager at the Palace Theatre, Watford in 1950 my duties during my first week included preparing a full breakfast for the first act of a trouserless army farce of unusual ineptitude entitled *The Maiden's Prayer*. The meal, which the unhappy actors were forced to eat with every appearance of enthusiasm, consisted of strips of bread coated with gravy-browning to represent bacon, circles of bread coloured red to represent a tomato, and further circles of bread with a dab of mustard in the middle to look like a fried egg. The coffee was more diluted gravy-browning (a very useful and ubiquitous commodity backstage) and the whisky was cold tea. You could always rely on there being somebody in the stage box with a pair of binoculars so the food had to look convincing under scrutiny. Preparing all this for six was a long and cumbersome task and one day I asked innocently why we couldn't use the real thing which, I pointed out, would be much easier to prepare and would have the added advantage of being pleasanter to eat. 'Quite impossible,' said my immediate superior, a young acting Stage Manager named Michael Wynne, 'you'd have to cook it just before it's needed and you're busy elsewhere. Those bastard electricians would nick the lot if they could and anyway, Wilkie wouldn't stand for it!' Wilkie was our resident old actor-laddie; his full name was Harold Wilkinson, a vintage example of his breed and it was from him that I learned much of the mystique and tradition of the Theatre. So bread and gravy-browning it continued to be and, I fear, still is.

Real flowers on the stage are unlucky and although this superstition goes back a very long time there are a number of eminently practical reasons for it. Real flowers require water in the vase and if it is accidentally upset during the play there is a nasty mess for the stage management to clear up at the end as well as providing a terrible distraction for the unlucky actors involved. Real flowers are expensive and in the winter insanely so and if the stage had to be filled with flowers for a wedding or funeral scene their daily renewal would be a prohibitive addition to the running costs; admittedly artificial flowers are not exactly cheap but at least they do last for a long time and require only occasional washing and dusting. Real flowers can give hayfever and did so once to the star of a West End play who sneezed so violently that he was unable to finish his performance. Real flowers shed their petals on the ground and this can be very dangerous as with one eminent West End actress who slipped on a real rose petal, broke a vital bone in her ankle, sued the producer and won her case with substantial damages. A famous nineteenth century courtesan, said to be Lola Montez, went several stages further; when dancing before the Emperor Franz Josef with a real rose in her corsage, she made an unusually convulsive movement, the rose fell to the floor, she trod on the thorn, slipped, and broke her neck, dying instantly. White flowers and those with five petals are sacred to the White Goddess and so are unlucky to mortals. Whoever started this superstition was probably thinking of hawthorn which is both white and five-petalled and associated chiefly with funerals.

It's unlucky to have real mirrors on the stage; you must use a piece of polished tin, and if you must have a real mirror then the surface must be smeared with soap to dull the reflection. This probably dates back to the mediæval mistrust of mirrors and the belief that if you looked into one you would see the Devil standing behind you. There is a curious legend that a performance of Marlow's *Doctor Faustus* was enlivened by the appearance on the stage of the six devils as specified by the author but when the actor playing Faustus turned to count them there were seven. He thought the seventh was a reflection in a mirror but it wasn't; it was the Devil himself who had chosen that moment to enter the stage. The audience ran out screaming and the actor playing Faustus died of a heart attack.

It's bad luck to have a real Bible on the stage for this is disrespectful to God; it must be an ordinary book painted to look like a Bible. It is unlucky to make the sign of the cross the correct way from left to right – it must be from right to left in the Greek Orthodox manner. The correct way is regarded as a mild form of blasphemy and will surely bring down Holy Wrath from somewhere up above as many hundreds of actresses impersonating nuns in the various productions of *The Sound of Music* were taught. On this point a number of interesting regional differences are to be found. In Ireland the superstition about the sign of the cross also applies to a number of pious objects as I found to my cost. In 1962 I played a singing bishop in a musical called *Fursey* which starred Dublin's darling, the irrepressible and inimitable Milo O'Shea. Amongst the holy relics I wore was a pectoral cross. It was authentic, purchased in Rome, blessed by the Pope and correct in every detail. A howl of anger rose from the Catholic pressure groups; there were many of them, they kept a watchful eye on the Dublin Theatre, they wielded a terrifying power and influence and they combined to denounce

Richard Huggett as the singing Archbishop in *Fursey*, Dublin Festival 1962. The saintly medallion which was acceptable to an Archbishop, the producer and Catholic pressure groups, is in fact a horse-brass.
(Pat Sweeney)

the use of a real pectoral cross as a terrible and dangerous blasphemy. A moan of anguish likewise rose from the company who swore it would bring bad luck not only to me but to them, to the show and to the whole of the Dublin Theatre Festival of which *Fursey* was a proud and glittering centrepiece. With a stubborness and determination worthy of a better cause I refused to accept this nonsense and accordingly paid a visit to the head of the Catholic Church in Ireland, Archbishop Macquoid known, none too affectionately, as John Charles and not to be confused with a very popular footballer of the same name. I received an assurance that the pectoral cross was *not* offensive and triumphantly passed this on to the producer, John Ryan, who received it very coldly.

'I don't give a damn for the Archbishop,' he said angrily. 'It's the fock'n Legion of Mary you've got to watch out for because they don't give a damn for him either.' If I went ahead and wore the pectoral cross in defiance then the Legion of Mary would picket the theatre; there would be riots, a lot of adverse publicity and the show, whose décor he had himself designed and in which he had invested so much money, would be ruined. This threat was a very real one so I then produced a substitute which had been mocked up in the Gaiety Theatre property room; it was a piece of cross-shaped tin studded with little beads of glass and suspended from a length of lavatory chain. But this was not acceptable either. 'Sure, it may not *be* real but it *looks* real and that's just as bad!' I was told by the director, Alan Simpson. A compromise was eventually reached; I was allowed to wear a highly polished horse-brass on a chain which might, at a distance, pass for a saintly medallion. This rather peculiar solution satisfied everybody, including the dreaded Legion of Mary.

† † †

There are a great number of curious superstitions relating to the dressing-room and the use of make-up. Whereas some always use old make-up sticks on first nights, there are others who will always arrange to have a completely new set in times of crisis and will go to considerable expense to get it. This is probably due to the ancient tradition of revenging yourself on your enemy; you placed a needle down the centre of the stick and he, all unsuspecting, would rip his face to pieces. Some consider it good luck to arrange the accessories on the dressing-room table in a special pattern – wigblock on the left, hand-mirror on the right and the Leichner sticks arranged in a fan shape in the centre. But most actors after a few years in the profession regard it as good luck to use an old cigar box and to keep everything in it in rather an untidy, haphazard manner. It is quietly believed that only amateurs and enthusiastic beginners are religiously clean and tidy in the dressing-room and no actor wants to be thought a beginner; only beginners sport those expensive Leichner metal make-up boxes with separate sections for each stick and

44

sliding trays inside for the accessories, usually the present from a proud parent at the beginning of a a career. A touch of elegant untidiness and artistic sleaziness inspires confidence in your age, expertise and experience; in fact, I know one old actor who proudly boasts that he hasn't cleaned or tidied his make-up box for twenty-two years. Some actors consider it bad luck to unpack the make-up box until after the first night and the notices, for better or worse, are out. Sascha von Scherler, the American actress, never unpacks her box until the end of the first week; to unpack any earlier indicates a smug assumption that you will be in residence for a long time and the Angels of Luck are quick to punish complacency. This practice is commonly observed in the American theatre and is thought to have originated with Booth. There are, in addition, some old actors who consider it rather good luck to piss into the dressing-room basin and don't consider that a young actor can truly call himself a professional until he has performed this rather distasteful ceremony of initiation. Chorus girls believe that it's bad luck to spill powder on the floor but if you stamp and dance on it then you will very quickly become a star. It is not known whether or not this ever actually happened but the belief survives strongly. If you drop a pair of scissors on the ground you must always get somebody else to pick them up. It's bad luck to look over another actor's shoulder into his section of the dressing-room mirror for this has associations with the evil eye, and the reason why so many actors carry hand-mirrors for making up is due to the shortage of full-size mirrors in some of the more primitive theatres on tour. To break a mirror in a dressing-room is dreadfully unlucky and will result in seven years bad luck; I have known a very nervous actress of some distinction refuse to dress in a room where a mirror had been broken.

Sometimes superstitions cancel each other out since there exists irreconcilable views as to their significance. Suppose you stumble as you enter the stage; some say this is good luck, some say it is bad: the reader must take his choice. Supposing you go to a strange producer's office for an interview and by mistake you go into the wrong door, an easy thing to do especially in America where a single corridor in an office block will house a dozen producers whose offices are not always easily identified. Some say that this is good and you will get the part, some say it is bad and that you'll never work for him; once again the reader must take his choice.

Then there is the peculiar superstition about soap in the dressing-room. Everybody agrees that it represents good luck but should you take it with you on tour or should you leave it behind? Some old actors say you must leave it behind if you wish to return to the same theatre in the future; others say with equal firmness that you must take it with you if you wish to enjoy good notices and a return engagement with the same management. The obvious solution would appear to be to have two cakes of soap, one to leave behind and one to take with you; and it is surprising that nobody has thought of this simple answer before. But perhaps the Angels of Luck don't take kindly to those clever people who hedge their bets. Telegrams are another source of dissent: some actors keep their first night telegrams and cards and hopefully watch them grow dustier and yellower as the months and years flick by. Others say that this is bad luck and that they must be destroyed after the opening. Some actors keep one telegram for their next play, another example of how important continuity is in people's lives, whereas some believe continuity to be a bad thing and will always destroy something in their dressing-room on the last night – it might be a light bulb, a plate or an ashtray – as a gesture of absolute finality which is thought to prevent any evil impulse or spirit from following them into their next play.

You mustn't look through the gap in the front curtains to watch the audience coming in as this means 'curtains' for the play. It is also regarded as unspeakably amateurish, the only insult you can throw at an actor which really hurts. For the same reason it's unlucky to lower the front curtain at the end of the dress rehearsal. This would be regarded as a symbolic gesture of finality which would result in a bad opening and a short run. But some actors always touch the curtain when it has finally come down: the curtain in some mysterious way represents good luck and if you touch it then you will get good notices. The 1940 film, *Yankee Doodle Dandy*, starring James Cagney as George M. Cohan, was correct on this small point and did, in fact, give a very authentic picture of

46

the sleazier side of vaudeville in the 90s.

If a star replaces another during a long run, it's very bad luck as well as bad manners for the incoming star to see the outgoing star's final performance, or to see it at all once the take-over has been decided. And it is equally bad luck and bad manners for the outgoing star to see the incoming star's first performance, nor must a good luck telegram be sent. Instead a message must be scrawled on the dressing-table mirror with a stick of Leichner No.5, this being a light creamy colour and most visible on the polished surface.

Many superstitions go in threes. If one actor gets the sack then two more will follow. If you get one engagement at the Theatre Royal, Drury Lane (the luckiest of all theatres), then you will get three. If you get a job offered, two more will be offered within the week. If you have one successful play then you'll have three in a row. In America it is believed that the best people go in threes: the three Barrymores, the three Frohmanns (David, Charles and Guy, all producers), the three Sirens, three Slocums, three Whitstucks, all comedy trios from Vaudeville. But old actors have traditionally been cautious of joining a company with three women, for it is believed that when two women get together they always talk and gossip about the third; this makes trouble and is very bad for the company's morale and inevitably their performances. Failure can also go in threes. Noël Coward always denied that he was in any way superstitious, but even he had to admit that there were definitely sinister elements at work when he had three flops in quick succession – *This was a Man, Home Chat* and *Sirocco*, all within four months. The young Laurence Olivier had no less than six failures in one year, 1929 and it was only his appearance in the uniquely successful *Private Lives* immediately afterwards that reassured him that there was no jinx on his career.

The ritual of good luck wishes on first nights is fraught with superstitious distaste and it is getting worse within our lifetime. To wish good luck on another person, so they say, is to part with it yourself: it also means that you are inviting the hostile and rather contemptuous intervention of the Gods if you draw attention to your desperate need for fortune. I knew one neurotic actor who would go quietly berserk if anybody wished him good luck, or sent a telegram or tried to give him a first night present; he would creep on stage by a back staircase and skulk in the darkness of the wings until his entrance, avoiding, like the plague, meeting or even seeing anybody on the way. In recent years a curious and rather repulsive tradition borrowed from the continent has grown up of offering gruesome first night wishes like 'break a leg' or 'fall down backwards' or 'give them hell' or 'go and perform an impossible action', or just a stream of good-natured obscenities. But usually actors say pleasant, encouraging things like 'be brilliant' or 'enjoy yourself' or 'have a marvellous time'. A popular greeting much quoted by wits is Dorothy Parker's famous telegram to Uta Hagen, 'a hand on your opening and may your parts grow bigger' and in America, according to Tenniel Evans, 'knock them for a loop' has gained a wide currency. Amongst the old actor-laddies a popular greeting was 'skin off your nose' and this, according to Tenniel Evans, has a special significance. It apparently referred to the bad old days before Mr Leichner came to our rescue when make-up was crude, coarse, untested and when applied it invariably had a disastrous effect on the skin which started to peel off in patches. This is why the actors in the early part of the nineteenth century could always be identified by their blotchy complexions. So if you said 'skin off your nose' you were in effect hoping that he would be in a position where he must continue to apply his make-up; in other words, to be in work and that is the best wish you can extend to any actor. Nowadays, good wishes are extended at dress rehearsals and this leads to another curious superstition, that it is good luck to have a bad dress rehearsal as this means that the first performance will be good. Contrariwise, it is bad luck if the dress rehearsal is good as this means a bad opening. I doubt if there is an actor in the theatre who hasn't experienced the forbidding truth of this. Good dress rehearsals are liable to make the company complacent and lazy and leads them to underrate the strain and difficulties of the actual first performance. If they have been acting up at a high dynamic level they won't have enough energy left for the first night and the performance will suffer accordingly. It must be stated very firmly that the dress rehearsal mustn't be too bad, for total disaster merely makes everybody very angry and despair fills actors with a careless death-wish. A dress rehearsal which is tense, nervy, strained with a few technical hitches and lapses of memory is acceptable. Of course in recent years the excellent custom of previews which started in New York and has happily spread to London has gone a long way to taking the edge off a first performance. Of course a first night is a first night no matter how many weeks of previews you have, but at least they are now marginally less miserable.

Cats are traditionally the object of superstitious awe, both good and bad. Inside a theatre they usually represent good luck and are spoiled and cherished by the actors and stage staff, led firmly by the wardrobe mistress whose room provides a warm and comfortable home. If it takes an interest in the rehearsals and watches from the wings then this is lucky, but if it strays onto the stage or, worse still, actually crosses it then this is very bad and one hysterical actress to my certain knowledge refused to work all day when it happened. But if it makes a mess in the dressing-room then this is the luckiest event of all. This very thing happened to Noël Coward on the first night of *The Vortex* in London. It was just before the curtain and everybody assured him that it was a lucky omen. He was paralysed with nerves and refused to cheer up, firmly stating that it was a very sensible comment on the whole play. *The Vortex* was a triumphant success and set its youthful author on the way to true stardom, so perhaps there's something in it. If this little accident happens in a performance then the result is obviously going to be disastrous, for animals and children are traditional show-stealers. Rachel was a victim; her death scene in *Judith* was one of the greatest experiences the Comedie Française offered its patrons. One night a black cat walked on the stage and left its candid comment on the floor. It stopped the play and reduced the audience to hysterical laughter, but what Rachel did not know was that it had been lured onto the stage by a rival tragedienne in the company.

† † †

Superstitions are not confined to the stage and the dressing-room: they are to be found in the managerial offices and even in that little temple of hard-headed materialism, the box office. Box office managers believe that if a queue is outside the window after a successful first night and the first person pays with a torn banknote, this is unlucky and the play will be off within a week. But if the first person is an old man then the play will run for a year. 'What happens if the old man at the head of the queue pays with a torn banknote?' I asked my informant. 'It did happen,' he smiled, 'and the Fates neatly split the difference. We ran exactly six months.' Producers have good reason to be nervous since the financial risks they habitually run are considerable. Some will never open their plays on a Tuesday or an even-numbered day. Some will never open on a Friday or an odd-numbered day. Some producers regard it as good luck to open after a flop because the critics, having vented their spleen will probably be more kindly disposed. Some producers will never give free tickets to a cross-eyed man or to a woman.

Seat attendants and usherettes have their own pet superstitions particularly relating to the number 13. If the first person in the audience sits in row 'M' which is the thirteenth row then it will be a bad evening with a loss of tips and plenty of worry and aggravation. If a woman tries to tip them this is frequently regarded as bad luck and many usherettes won't accept it. If anybody actually sits in the thirteenth seat in a row, this is regarded as potential trouble and a watchful eye is kept on the occupant. It's bad luck if a woman faints in the theatre and if a woman buys a programme instead of her male escort, two superstitions which will not bring joy to the supporters of Women's Lib. It's bad luck if the usherette doesn't hear the first line of the play and this accounts for the fact, noted by many patrons, that when the curtain rises the usherette will momentarily stop whatever she is doing and listen intently. These worthy ladies believe that if they make a mistake about seating somebody, then they will make two more before the evening is finished; they further believe that the first tip of the play's run on the first night is lucky and must be rubbed against the leg; after that it must be kept permanently in the pocket for the rest of the play's run as a coaxer, a spur to fate. It's bad luck if the first customer in the theatre has a complimentary ticket; the first ticket must be bought and paid for or there will be more 'comps' than money in the house thereafter. Some producers believe that it is bad luck for the show if the first customer is a woman and there is record of a rather misogynistic producer trying to prevent a lady from entering until a man arrived to save the situation. William Wheatley, manager of America's Niblo Garden Theatre used to employ a man to stand and wait in the lobby especially to avoid this disaster.

Some producers are superstitious about titles. *Three Blind Mice* is known to be an unlucky title though nobody knows why; Christopher Fry was going to use it for one of his early plays but was persuaded to change it. Agatha Christie used this title for one of her crime plays in the early fifties and sent it to Peter Saunders who promptly changed it – not, he firmly maintains, because it was unlucky, but because there was already a play with that title. Whatever the reason, it turned out to be a very lucky decision because the new title was *The Mousetrap* which is currently in its twenty-ninth record-breaking year and has made an immense fortune for all concerned. 'Miracle' in the title is unlucky and few plays with it have ever succeeded since this suggests a rather tedious preoccupation with religion and this, in most Englishmen's eyes, has no place in a popular entertainment. 'Peacock' is unlucky for the reasons already stated and its presence in a title prophesies real trouble. Peter Bull lost a lot of money over Noel Langley's *Cage Me A Peacock*, Anouilh's *Cry of a Peacock* was a failure both in London and Paris, and *Juno and the Paycock*, though rightly regarded as a classic masterpiece, has never enjoyed a long run nor has it made money; it remains obstinately a great play which everybody admires but only a few actually want to see. Two popular words whose presence in the title is a fair guarantee of success are 'Sex' and 'Murder'. It is thought that T. S. Eliot had a shrewd awareness of the latter when his play about St. Thomas à Becket was named, not after the hero as might be expected, but *Murder in the Cathedral*. Admittedly many of the people who flock to see it do so in the happy expectation of seeing yet another crime drama by the indefatigable Agatha Christie (confusing it, doubtless, with her immensely popular *Murder in the Vicarage*) but flock they do, not once but many times. As Shaw perceptively commented, there is a strong vein of the purest masochism in the English public and anybody who can bore them stiff in the interests of culture can reap huge profits. A singularly death-wishing title in England was a musical originally called *Give Me The Bird* (1957), the brainchild of two Americans who hopefully launched it in London with Gladys Cooper making a late appearance in the treacherous field of musical comedy. She pointed out to the authors what they clearly did not know, that in English theatre slang, getting the bird means being booed off the stage, and to title a play thus was literally to ask for trouble. Reluctantly, they consented to change it to *The Crystal Heart* but it didn't make any difference. Gladys Cooper had a solitary number in the show from which the title had been taken. The words, and I quote from memory, were:

> Give me that bird, Where is that bird?
> Oh *give* me that bird that maddening –
> – saddening –
> – gladdening –
> BIRD!

It was too much. The gallery which had been very patient while ineptitude and triteness burst like an avalanche of yesterday's porridge over the stalls, finally screamed out their contempt and anger. And that was the end of *The Crystal Heart*, though it struggled on to empty houses for a full month.

In France the unlucky word is *ficelle* meaning *string*. It must never be mentioned in the dialogue, nor in the title and if the sense makes it necessary, then the word *corde* must be used instead. Nor must the actors speak the word backstage or in the dressing-rooms. In America the unlucky words are 'bomb' and 'turkey'. How curious that 'bomb' should mean opposite things on the two sides of the Atlantic, for in England 'bomb' means success, as in the phrase 'it went like a bomb, old boy,' which one actor could well use to another in the dressing-room while the cheers of the first night audience are still echoing round the theatre. By general agreement with the theatrical fraternity, the one place where this gruesome expression was never used was in Belfast during the years of civil strife. During this explosive period the expression came painfully near to the truth. This is yet another example of the truth of Bernard Shaw's oft-quoted saying that England and America are two countries separated by a common language. As for 'turkey', the all-time record for the shortest Broadway run is unarguably held by a drama called *Cage Me A Turkey*. The play was about, and performed by, a group of dwarfs whose talent and experience of the theatre was – to put it very diplomatically – somewhat limited; amongst the decorations prominently displayed in the drawing-room set were a stuffed turkey and a stuffed peacock. Many plays finish after the first performance, there is no longer any novelty in that; but *Cage Me A Turkey* has made a tiny footnote in history by failing even to finish the first. It seemed that a violent argument broke out amongst the company in the interval; some of them ended up in hospital, and the audience had to leave the theatre without seeing the final act. But the most self-destroying title in American theatre history was a wartime play produced in 1967 called *We Bombed in New Haven,* a verbose slice of sub-Pirandello, set in a timeless world on an empty stage. New Haven is one of those indispensable places on a pre-Broadway tour whose audiences are notoriously difficult to please and which is known as a theatrical graveyard where the bones of countless Broadway shows lie rotting in the autumn sun. *We Bombed in New Haven* didn't do what the title said. It did, however, struggle into Broadway and lasted a month.

Closing in New Haven was one of the occupational hazards of the American touring theatre to which all actors were resigned but there were many others. For fifty years, between roughly 1880 and 1930, America was covered with a vast network of touring theatres of formidable complexity; it kept thousands of actors in perpetual employment and kept its multi-million audience happily entertained before the talking cinema killed it. The scruffier side of touring life is shown with praiseworthy accuracy in the silent film *Exit Smiling* which gave Beatrice Lillie her first and greatest starring part and which, in addition, contrives to be as excruciatingly funny as the best of Chaplin and Keaton. This rather specialised theatrical life stimulated and accumulated a series of rather unusual superstitions which are lovingly preserved in the bottomless archives of the Lincoln Centre Theatre Collection. A brief look at the relevant files reveals that Sunday rehearsals were bad luck and meant that a death would occur in the company and that the salaries would not be paid. This last was possibly the more intimidating threat for being stranded and penniless in some remote outpost of the country was every touring actor's favourite nightmare. Unhappily it still is, for even in this day and age of easy communications and Equity it can happen, as with the unhappy group of English and American actors recently given eighteen-month contracts at a generous salary with a company in New Zealand. They discovered, when they arrived there, that the company had gone bankrupt and their salaries, contrary to managerial assurances, had not been deposited. Sunday rehearsals in America did take their toll and a number of victims are on record; Millie Cavendish, famous soubrette of the musical theatre in the nineties, was compelled to rehearse for three successive Sundays in a play called *The Crook* and died of a heart attack on the fourth. The play did open, and closed immediately. Jim Fisk, manager of the Grand Opera House in Chicago, had a rather more melodramatic ending as befitted the melodrama he was rehearsing. Not only did he rehearse on a Sunday but he even enforced performances on a Sunday which actors have always hated: in New York they are now an accepted part of the theatre scene but we in England have so far been mercifully spared them. Jim Fisk was shot dead by gangsters and the play was swiftly withdrawn having lost a fortune for all concerned. Fisk's death was generally regarded by the religious pressure groups as a highly fitting punishment for his blasphemy. But with a total lack of logic, it was said to be good luck to sign a contract on a Sunday.

If a train carrying the company arrives at a station with a graveyard on the right that was good luck; if it was on the left that was bad luck and the performance that evening would be a bad one. An old actors' poem neatly sums up the situation:

> Graveyard on right
> Goodhouse tonight.
> Graveyard to the left
> House will be bereft!

It was shockingly bad luck to have a corpse on the train and there are records of companies bluntly refusing to travel with such a neighbour and their touring schedule being drastically revised. One hunchback in the company is good luck but two is bad; it is not known, though, what sort of luck is produced by three hunchbacks. Certain tunes were unlucky: *Home Sweet Home* and *Marriage Bells* are bad and indicate the early closing of the play. Anybody heard singing them either in the theatre or in their lodgings or even in the train would be dismissed instantly. After 1912 and the Titanic disaster (whose victims included Charles Frohman) *Nearer My God To Thee* was added to the list. Once again it can be seen that anything remotely connected with death acquires bad luck and must be carefully avoided. This accounts for the striking absence from the American scene of a hugely popular comedy, *Our American Cousin*, which every American schoolboy knows is the play Lincoln was watching on the night of his death.

When a touring company arrives in a town the custom was, and happily still is sometimes, to parade through the streets on a cart or coach, in costume, dancing, singing and distributing leaflets and thus publicising that evening's performance. If a haycart passed on this royal progress, this was good luck. But if you saw a funeral procession coming towards you then it was essential to go down a sidestreet and wait till it went by, for never under any circumstances must you allow a corpse to pass you. If there was no sidestreet then the parade must disband temporarily, the cart drawn into the side and the company must turn their backs to the street since even to look on death was bad luck. It was bad luck to see the full moon through glass but good luck to sign a contract under moonlight. But would it be very cynical to wonder which parsimonious, pleasure-killing landlady managed to convince her lodgers that prunes for dinner represented good luck provided they were all eaten, and that failure to do so meant a bad house and loss of receipts?

Poverty and hardship, cheerfully and unresentfully accepted, was the lot of most of the profession, and particularly the blacks. *Green Pastures* and *Porgy and Bess* gave them a new lease of life and self-respect, but until then their professional careers were exceedingly hard and artistically frustrating. Comic and servile stereo-types were the order of the day and not many of those. Hardship breeds determination and determination breeds hope and thus a whole series of minor but intriguing superstitions grew up amongst the theatrical negroes. It was bad luck to applaud any number at rehearsal for it meant that it would be cut at a later stage or fail dismally on the first night and thus be cut later. It was bad luck to count the audience if it was scattered sparsely over the house unless it could be done so discreetly that nobody could see it. It was bad luck if the actors came to the theatre to ask them if they felt well or were in good voice. The Lafayette Theatre in 7th Avenue was a black theatre and there was an elm tree standing in front of it. Nobody knows why, when or how it started, but a distinct aura of good luck gathered round this tree and actors on their way to the theatre for an audition or opening would kiss it for good luck. Over the years the tree became a meeting place for actors and when a little café was built next to it the Elm Tree was put on the Broadway map. Producers and directors and agents looking for talent would go down to the Elm Tree and pick their fancy. It gradually became necessary to kiss it in moments of crisis; leaves and twigs from the tree became a favourite lucky mascot. Then in 1934 it was cut down for redevelopment but at the request of all the black actors the stump was left whose magic properties were considered to be no less potent than those of the whole tree. But it did not survive long for shortly afterwards a car ran into the stump and uprooted it and that was the sad end of the Elm Tree. A few months later the demolition squads moved in and that was also the end of the Lafayette Theatre.

† † †

Certain pantomimes are unlucky, *Robin Hood*, *Babes in the Wood* and *Aladdin*, particularly *Aladdin* because the excessive use of trap-doors, smoke and magical production effects represent a real haz-ard to life and limb. But *Cinderella* is a lucky pantomime and this happily overflows into any play which has a Cinderella theme: any play in which the heroine or hero appears in rags in Act One and in beautiful clothes in Act Three, and in addition goes to a ball or

Maxine Audley as Mrs Patrick Campbell in *The First Night of Pygmalion*
on its South African Tour, with Richard Huggett as Bernard Shaw. He
says, 'She was unquestionably the greatest Mrs Patrick Campbell I ever
acted with. I cannot imagine it being played better by anybody else.'

party or whatever, can be truthfully described as a modern-style
Cinderella. The obvious example of this is *Pygmalion* which is
nothing more than Cinderella brought up to date and this is one
reason (there are others) why *Pygmalion* is the luckiest play of this
century. It is always a huge success; it always makes money, there
hasn't been a day since its première in 1914 when it hasn't been
performed somewhere in the world and in its gold-filled history it
has always made reputations. The sensational first production
placed it firmly on the theatre map, the film version in 1938 bought
the film industry into the International market and made a star out
of Wendy Hiller and a much acclaimed director out of Anthony
Asquith and the unique epoch-making success of *My Fair Lady*
needs no further comment or explanation. It has always been a
lucky play for me. My two-handed comedy of bad manners *The*

First Night of Pygmalion was the big success of the 1968 Edinburgh Festival, and gave me my first real breakthrough as an actor, and is the only play which has earned me any real money. I have toured the American Universities and made my first off-Broadway appearance. I have toured all Europe and South Africa; it has brought me money and acclaim all over the world.

Actors who appear regularly in pantomine and variety have their own special superstitions which are not observed or even known in what is still called the *legitimate* theatre. There are two popular songs which have bad luck associations and should never be sung or hummed or whistled anywhere backstage or on stage even if the play requires it. The first is Tosti's *Goodbye* which has strong associations with death and which no singer will tolerate: Ellen Terry, though, had no such qualms for when Tosti himself met her he inscribed the fatal words on the back of a photograph of himself and gave it to her ... 'Goodbye, summer, goodbye.' ... She was enchanted. The second forbidden song is from Balfe's opera *The Bohemian Girl* which contains the ever-green and ever-popular aria 'I dreamt I dwelt in marble halls'. Harold Wilkinson once told me that in the twenties he had nearly been dismissed from the company when the producer heard him singing it in his lodgings. He was told by one of the old actor-laddies that if you start singing it accidentally, you must change it quickly to the words, 'I dreamt I was scratching my father's balls!' The origin of this superstition is interesting and it apparently dates back to the time at the turn of the century when the Adelphi Theatre owned by the Gatti Brothers, had a bar and a restaurant adjoining. The décor was ugly and pretentious and never enjoyed the success of the other Gatti establishments. Because of its decoration, the bar became known as 'The Marble Halls' and in addition to that became the haunt of unemployed actors, tramps and ill-kempt loafers from the Strand. So the Marble Halls came to be associated with the rougher and sadder elements of the theatrical profession and to be a regular patron was to be on the way down. There was even a song about it:

Oh! The Marble Halls, the Marble Halls!
A place in the Strand where everybody calls.

Where the actor out of collar
Often raises half a dollar
Oh! God bless Gatti and the Marble Halls!

There is at every time in theatre history a place where out-of-work actors can congregate to read the trade papers, buy inexpensive cups of coffee and snacks, pass on and receive useful information or just sit around and chat happily with similarly-situated colleagues and thus pass those long and frustrating hours of unemployment. In New York it is a dimly lit bar in 8th Avenue called the Haymarket: it is also the offices of Equity which has plenty of spare chairs and sofas, an informative noticeboard, telephones and all the accessories of a well-equipped club room; in Hollywood it was Schwab's drugstore where the young hopefuls could earn a little extra money serving milk-shakes behind the bar, in Dublin it was Neary's Pub whose back door faced the stage door of the Gaiety Theatre. In London there really isn't anywhere which fills this function but in my early days in the profession in the fifties the acknowledged meeting place was the snack-bar in the basement of the Arts Theatre Club. In those golden days the theatre itself was in the devoted and inspired hands of Alec Clunes whose policy was to produce a different play every month with the best possible people. He was a fanatical admirer of Bernard Shaw and some of the finest Shavian revivals of the post-war years were at the Arts. The standard was very high even if the salaries were low; transfers were not uncommon and many careers started and blossomed there. It was a period of great theatrical vitality and the unemployed actors nursing their sixpenny coffees, worrying about their *Spotlight* advertisements, and glancing irritably through *The Stage*, noticed that Alec Clunes himself, his directors, administrative staff and the resident company would use the snack-bar during their tea-breaks and lunch-hours. It was naturally hoped and assumed that he would use them and a certain amount of discreet jostling, lobbying and eye-catching did take place. Useless. It seemed that Clunes, whose apprenticeship in the theatre had not been difficult, had little sympathy for unemployed actors and was, furthermore, greatly irritated by the amount of space we took up in the snackbar and the noise we made in the course of the day (we were, admittedly, rather loud and convivial). He couldn't get rid of us as we did represent a source of valuable income to the Club, but he could refuse to employ us. He decided that nobody who was seen at all frequently in the snack-bar should ever be employed in the theatre and communicated this decision privately to his staff. Nothing was ever said to us and the matter was supposed to be a dark secret but inevitably the word did get round that the black mark was on us; it gradually became unlucky to be seen there and thus another superstition was born. But most of us – and this group included Barry Foster, Kenneth Haigh, Robin May, Walter Hall and Harold Pinter – continued to use it, partly because there was nowhere else to go except the Lyons Tea Shop next door which none of us liked, and partly because we just couldn't believe that the charming and glamorous Alec Clunes, whom we all greatly admired as a superb actor, could be so unreasonable and so unkind. But it seemed that he could and was, and throughout the years of his management none of us ever worked there.

It's bad luck to have worked in the first productions of somebody now famous and successful. Once they have achieved this enviable state they have a tiresome habit of consigning to outer darkness all memories of their early years and everybody associated with them. To have appeared in Mr H's production of *Worm's Eye View* at Manchester or Mr G's production of *Life With Father* at Cape Cod twenty years ago is a fair guarantee that you will never work with them again, even if you got on well with them and were good in the part. There are, naturally, some honourable exceptions, well-balanced, secure people who don't hold it against an actor that he knew them in their dog-days, but by and large this superstition appears to be justified. In fact the anticipation of a cold reception will serve as an active discouragement to an actor who will not even make a preliminary approach to a director or producer if he has worked with him years ago. This law applied to producers, casting-directors, managers who had once been actors, to anybody who has crossed to the other side of the desk. It doesn't apply to star actors who are touchingly loyal to their colleagues of their salad days. Sir Henry Irving was well known in the profession for giving preferential treatment to the old actors he had once known in his purgatorial early years and who formed the nucleus of his Lyceum Company; and many of the names in the programmes of Laurence Olivier's early appearances in the 20s appear with reassuring frequency in those of the 40s, 50s and 60s.

The rehearsal period is when an actor is at his most superstitious for then he is nervous and vulnerable. In America, nobody will blame him, for the truly appalling practice still survives whereby an actor is strictly on probation for the first five days and can be dismissed any time if the producer decides he is either miscast or just not good enough. The wretched actor may need the job desperately, because he hasn't worked for a year or because he needs the money to pay for his wife's pregnancy or his children's education. He has five days to make an impression and instead of allowing the performance to develop slowly and carefully over the four weeks, he is forced to get easy, striking effects overnight, to produced a tiresome form of instant acting which can seriously damage the final performance, just as Mr Crummles stunted his infant daughter's growth by feeding her on gin. After five days, if the producer is satisfied, he will receive the protection of a contract and he can breathe again, but by then the damage may have been done. These actors sometimes try to make an impression by learning the part in advance and arriving at the first rehearsal word perfect. This is invariably a waste of time and energy because there are always cuts in the text and an actor who has learned a section of the text which is later cut, finds it very difficult to forget it. This is one reason why older actors, particularly in England, regard it as bad luck to learn the part before rehearsals start, and it is probably this which explains the strange hostility to the youthful Noël Coward from the older actors in the companies he first appeared with. Coward always knew every word of his part at the first rehearsal and his efficiency in this matter was a source of great irritation to the others. This continued all his life and in later years when he directed plays, particularly his own, he insisted on the company being word perfect from the start, on the grounds that you couldn't act or develop with a script in your hands.

Some of the older actresses in these companies just could not cope; rehearsals were particularly frustrating for them and their performances did finally suffer from those terrifying lapses of memory which we all fear. Every actor has his own method and his own pace for working and to interfere arbitrarily with this by forcing them to develop at an unnatural speed is to ask for trouble.

† † †

It's bad luck to want something too much. If an actor is bursting to play a particular classic part and has been hoping and dreaming about it all his life, and then gets his big chance, this, as the old actor-laddies keep saying, is very unlucky. Some of the saddest theatrical disasters have stemmed from this and Charles Laughton's Lear – tragic in a sense the author didn't intend – is a case in point. He was a frustrated classical actor; Shakespeare was his greatest love and joy and the volume of the Complete Works, a school prize when he was a boy, was thumbed and tattered with a lifetime of study. He dreamt of playing all the great heroic parts, but it was only after his stupendous success in the film *Henry VIII* in 1933 that Lilian Baylis invited him to the Old Vic for a season. In quick succession he played a disastrous Macbeth (full details later in the book), a competent Henry VIII, a dullish Prospero and an interesting Angelo, but he had not been a success and it was quite evident that he just couldn't do Shakespeare. It was, and still is, difficult to explain why this should have been so. He was one of the most gifted and exciting actors of his day, with a strong star personality, an actor whom it was always tremendously stimulating to watch, but he had made a late entry into the profession at the age of twenty-six and his meteoric rise to fame came after only six years and ten plays, all but two in the West End. It is tempting to think that if he had enjoyed a longer apprenticeship involving a lot more stage experience (he never acted in a repertory company; he started in London and never went out of it during those early years), he would have acquired a stronger technique and a better voice without which classical acting is impossible. He was painfully aware of this and would sometimes describe himself as a gifted amateur, one of those sad half-truths which are the hallmark of the insecure actor.

62

Charles Laughton as King Lear in the mad scene, Stratford 1959. He wanted to play it too much and for too long and when the great moment came he failed – once again. (Sally Chappell/Victoria & Albert Museum)

His supreme ambition was to play King Lear. In preparation for the Great Day when it arrived, he learned the part, planned how he would play it, rehearsed it privately in solitude, dreamed about it, thought about it, and talked about it. It rapidly became an obsession. One day he would stride onto the stage to the shriek of trumpets and say *'Attend the Lords of France and Albany, Gloucester ... meanwhile we shall express our darker purpose ...'* And then one day in 1959 he was invited to play it at Stratford-upon-Avon. The omens were good: the sensible and sympathetic director was Glen Byham Shaw and the company included Vanessa Redgrave, Albert Finney, Ian Holm and Robert Hardy. On the first day's rehearsal, he asked permission to rehearse without the script. He'd known every word for thirty years and it would help him if he could just let the magical words flow. Permission being granted, he then proceeded to treat the company not to a low-keyed, cautious, first-rehearsal walk-through, but to a complete and superbly considered performance; it was powerful, passionate and deeply moving, a tour-de-force. 'This is going to be the greatest Lear we shall ever see,' said the company in wonder when they finished that day's rehearsal. And so it would have been if the critics had seen it there and then. But there were six long weeks of rehearsals and having struck his bull's-eye he couldn't keep it up. When you're at the top, the only progression is down and so it was. Day after day he was forced to go through the performance and it became dull and stale by repetition. Boredom and frustration set in and as the first night approached, sheer terror took over. This sad story had its climax on the first night which has been described by different members of that company. The first night audience was packed and studded with celebrities, all eager and curious to make odious comparisons. Fanfare of trumpets, the stage fills up with the Court, more trumpets and on sweeps Laughton looking magnificent. He climbs up to the throne, turns round, opens his mouth to say his first line – *and can't*. He has forgotten it. His mind is a total blank. He is paralysed with fear. Three actors standing nearby generously prompt him but the gesture is useless for he cannot hear what they say, their voices make up an indistinct trio of sound. The play has ground to a halt. Suddenly, with admirable presence of mind he points to the prompt corner. 'Yes dear?' he says, and the prompter's voice rings out loud and clear for all the audience to hear. *'Attend the Lords ...'* 'Thank you,' he interrupts and having remembered the line the play can now continue. The play proceeds without further incident and Laughton manages to get through it, but the evening has had a knife-edge tension and the performance has suffered immeasurably. It is a colossal disappointment to the critics, the public, the company and to Laughton himself. In later performances, things did, of course, improve, but history, most cruelly and unjustly, is made on first nights. Laughton never really got over his disappointment. He had wanted to play Lear too much and for too long, and therein lies bad luck.

It's interesting that the same situation crops up in a famous pre-war French film about an old actor's home *Le Fin du Jour* in which Michel Simon plays an old actor who gets his big chance. This actor had understudied Sacha Guitry for over a thousand performances at the Comédie Française in *L'Aiglon* but had never had a chance of playing the part and he is bursting to do so. A lifelong obsession. Now, at seventy, he is brooding resentfully over the past. Then the Comédie Française arrange a special charity matinée of this same play at the Actors' Home but the leading man is taken ill and the company doesn't carry an understudy. What's to be done? The old actor volunteers eagerly, is pushed into the costume and make-up and bundled on stage in front of a packed audience. And what happens? He can't remember a word. The other actors try to prompt him. Useless. Then he breaks down, crying through his make-up and muttering, 'I knew every word of it once ... I'm too old now ... every word ...!' (Michel Simon's acting in this poignant scene was really heart-breaking.) He then has a heart attack and dies. The second-rater who is finally forced to face the truth about himself. The perpetual understudy who never played the part.

Some producers consider that first night parties are bad luck – noisy, horribly expensive and not much fun because the tension, while the fate of the play is being debated by the critics, plays merry hell with people's nerves and tempers. Many people consider it very bad luck to wait up for the notices in Sardi's (in New York) or at the Ivy (in London) and to then have them read out aloud to the

Richard Huggett as Reggie in *Getting Married*, one of Shaw's few boring, bad plays, in which he gave a 'ridiculously caricatured, grotesquely unfunny performance' and nearly got himself assassinated!

company, backers and friends. If this is done in the complacent expectation of their being very good and they turn out otherwise it can be just a little embarrassing. Most actors can claim some memorable experience of this. It happened to me in Cape Town after I had opened in Shaw's *Getting Married* at the Hofmeyr Theatre and had given what I complacently thought was a very good, funny performance as Reggie. The party at the Negrita Bar was attended by dozens of actors, backers, friends and members of the local cultural administration. At 1.00am, the Afrikaans papers arrived and were grabbed by the company. As I did not speak a single word of that uncouth language, I asked for the notice to be read aloud. Our stage-manager, grinning broadly, obliged. *'Richard Huggett gives a grotesquely unfunny, ridiculously caricatured performance. If this is what passes for acting in the London theatre so much the worse*

Peter Stephens – did he possess occult powers of evil?

Jean McConnell in *The Immortal Hour* thought that he did!

for London. He should return to England as soon as possible.' The play did terrible business and I received an assassination threat from some SA patriots, who were doubtless angered by my grotesque and ridiculous acting.

Backstage superlatives are frowned on. To prophesy a great success and a long run before the notices appear is to ask for trouble. One old actor would go berserk if anybody said, 'Darling you'll be here for a year,' and there was one old musical comedy actress who never received backstage visitors for a week until the Sunday notices had appeared. Her speedy exit immediately after the performance into a waiting taxi was one of the sights of the West End.

From time to time stories leak out of actors and actresses who have occult powers and can make bad luck come to people who displease them; these stories cease to be mere superstitions and fall fairly and squarely into the realms of the supernatural. There was once an actor called Peter Stephens whose fleshy, beaky-nosed, rather eunuchoid appearance and personality made him specially well suited to parts which called for the projection of anything evil or sinister. In 1947 he was touring in a production of *The Immortal*

67

Hour by Clifford Bax. The star was an actress called Vera Lindsay who had married into the aristocracy, had retired from the Theatre and was now making a come-back. Peter Stephens took a violent dislike to her for reasons which were never made clear and got into the habit of making witty and malicious remarks at her expense whenever possible. One evening, after an unusually heated argument, he was heard to swear – half-jokingly, it was assumed – that he would deal with her. He went to his dressing-room and fashioned a little effigy of her out of a stick of make-up, painted her face on it and decked it with wisps of cloth he had taken from her dressing-room. Further identification was provided by her initials clearly written on the breasts of the effigy. Jean McConnell, who was the understudy, passed his open door and saw the effigy stuck with pins and sagging under the heat of the lights in a grotesque and horrible manner. Thirty minutes later she was informed by the stage-manager that Vera Lindsay was feeling ill and would therefore not be able to perform that night. The next day, suffering from what the doctor tactfully described as an undefined illness, Vera Lindsay left the company permanently and Jean McConnell played her part for the remainder of the tour. Bernard Archard who was in the company remembers that Peter Stephens was fascinated by witchcraft, talked about it a lot and clearly possessed an extensive knowledge of the subject. Nobody knew for certain whether or not he had occult powers and when questioned he would smile mysteriously and make an evasive answer. Nobody knew whether this particular incident was or was not a joke which just happened to turn sour, or whether Peter Stephens did practise the black arts. In fact, it will never be known for he is now dead.

† † †

An actor is the classical battleground between man's common-sense and his superstitious fears: many of these are absurd and irrational and anybody outside the theatre into whose hands this book may chance to fall might well be tempted to sneer. He should certainly not do so, for he does not know what an actor goes through before he gives his performance. This is something which nobody knows except the actor himself and his immediate colleagues. It is fitting that the outsider should be told since it is only with knowledge that he can achieve a sympathetic understanding. Let him be given a privileged glimpse into a place he has never been and never will be allowed – an actor's dressing-room on a first night. Let him see for himself just what an actor suffers in that vital half-hour before the performance.

It's a very big first night in a big West End theatre and there is the unhappy actor sweating unhappily away in his dressing-room. Let us call him Michael Plinge (Walter's grandson). Michael is aged thirty-four and has been in the profession for twelve years. He has had small parts in three mildly successful West End plays, and his career – augmented by a fair amount of television and film work – is at last beginning to take shape. The present production is a glossy revival of *She Stoops to Conquer* with a knight and a dame playing Young Marlowe and Kate Hardcastle, supported by a very distinguished company. The first night audience is glossier than usual and a large number of Very Important People have flown in from New York, Australia, Canada and even South Africa. There will certainly be a Broadway transfer, but whether the present company will go intact, or whether it will be only some and if so, then which – these thorny questions are as yet unanswered though rumours will circulate relentlessly throughout the limited run. Michael plays Hastings, a good supporting part, and it's his best yet in the West End. Everything depends on tonight he feels, and the fact that he has felt this no less emphatically on every West End first night doesn't diminish the urgency.

On Broadway, his opposite number would be called Rod Spelvin (nephew to the famous Uncle George). He is appearing at the Alvin Theatre in a new musical based on the Kennedy Family and it is called – how could it be otherwise? – *Assassination!* This project has been lovingly cherished by Broadway's top writing team until what they have generally agreed to be the Right Moment, and they've beaten all the rival teams by a narrow margin, for no less than six reputable authors had the same idea. Broadway's most dynamic leading lady has been coaxed out of her retirement to play Jackie, and by a unique stroke of showbiz genius, a singing TV cowboy star is making positively his first appearance on Broadway as

Kennedy. Rod Spelvin plays J. Edgar Hoover and he has one very good point number in Act Two, 'I'm going To Texas in the morning … get me down to Dallas on time'.

Rod is aged thirty, built on plumply fleshy lines with thinning hair and with a round amiable face. Casting agents invariably refer to him as a Zero Mostel type and have him on their files in that category, and while he is rather annoyed by this handle, however accurate, he is clever enough to have turned it to his advantage. Who is a more natural choice than Rod for those parts in summer stock and Bus n' Truck tours where Mr Mostel was unlikely to appear? Rod did his two years hard labour in the Broadway production of *Fiddler on the Roof*: he is not Jewish but looks it and deviously exploits the fact for all its considerable worth. He toured with *My Fair Lady* as Doolittle and with *The Odd Couple* as Oscar, thus laying the foundations of a career which began to really blossom at the Cape Cod Playhouse with his starring performance in, and as, *The Man who came to Dinner*. It was this which caught the attention of a prominent and inaccessible Broadway agent who promptly arranged for him to play Mr Mostel's part in *Ulysses in Nighttown* at a dinner theatre in Washington. Here he caught the budding eye of Louie Epstein who was setting up his Watergate musical and who noticed that Rod bore a distinct likeness to J. Edgar Hoover. This train of thought resulted in a meeting, then an audition and finally a contract.

Here he is in his tiny dressing-room which he shares with an old buddy, Marvin Q. Schwartz who was with him in *Fiddler*. Rod is very pleased with this for Marvin is fun to have around and doesn't talk too much. Rod has been in the theatre for two hours, fully dressed and made up, desperately trying to concentrate. The show has been on the road now for two months and it has been a difficult and exhausting time for everybody. Notices have varied between the lukewarm and the downright hostile which is a disturbing factor in a community where nothing less than unqualified hysterical praise will persuade the cautious customers to part with $30 for a ticket.

In common with every major production in the American musical theatre, it has been re-written mercilessly on the tour. New numbers have been written in and then after a few days have been cut. Actors have been sacked and replaced. The second lead, playing Oswald, walked out in Baltimore; the TV cowboy star had a nervous breakdown in Chicago missing twelve performances; and in obedience to an ancient and sacred tradition, the expensively-imported knighted English director was sacked in Boston. Four new Act One finales have been tried out and a fifth one was put in only last week. The show has been re-shaped, re-scored, re-numbered, re-everythinged almost out of recognition, the company has been rehearsing day and night, they are tired and confused, and Rod's chief anxiety at this moment is trying to remember what's cut and what's left. That witty line in Act One he's so fond of and which always got a laugh in Philadelphia, 'The President is making history, but can he consume it?' – was that cut in Baltimore or not? He checks with his script, now almost illegible with the mass of black and blue pencil marks. The line was cut in Chicago, replaced in Washington, cut again in New Haven and now replaced but transferred to Act Two for the Broadway opening thus providing the lead-in for Kennedy's new number *Bobby, They're Killing Me.*

Rod isn't particularly superstitious but he does observe one curious opening night ritual: he always goes down in the afternoon to a gay bar in Greenwich Village owned by an old army buddy from Vietnam. Hank is an artist and on these occasions does little instant cartoons of Rod on the backs of the menu cards. Rod has seven of these all round the dressing-room mirror. He has a pair of lucky cuff-links given to him by his first wife when they met in the Actors Studio years ago and which he always wears on opening nights. All round the dressing-room are photos of Hoover; when the show was announced in *Variety*, just about everybody Rod knew sent him a picture of, and cuttings about, his distinguished original.

On Broadway, the general rule forbidding backstage visitors before a performance is not strictly enforced; indeed, it hardly exists. Although curtain time is at 7.30 there is no question of the play starting for Clive Barnes hasn't arrived yet and is at that very moment in a helicopter thoughtfully provided by the management to transport him from Kennedy Airport to the theatre. The audi-

71

ence, furred, jewelled and dinner-jacketed, is still happily screech-
ing and screaming in the lobby and will be happy to continue doing
so for a very long time yet. Rod now has a series of visitors, starting
with his third wife, a pretty blonde, accompanied by her mother, a
fleshy blonde. They present him with a sprig of white heather, kiss
and hug him, and vanish. The press representative comes in with a
man from *The New York Times* and a photographer. Rod answers
politely the ineptitudes thrust at him. Finally, with much giggling
and laughing and screaming, a pretty little coloured girl from the
chorus called Blanche, accompanied by a party of friends from
another show, pushes her way in. She is the lucky recipient of the
Gipsy Robe and Rod touches it and kisses her, relieved that the
ritual is over and that he can now concentrate. At 7.26, Clive
Barnes breathless and apologetic, finally arrives, the audience is
coaxed to its seats and the show can go on. Rod is on at the
opening. He is not happy about this, not happy at all.

Back in London, Michael Plinge is sitting at his dressing-table,
naked except for a periwig and a pair of Regency striped boxer
shorts. All round his mirror are the telegrams and cards sent by his
family, friends and colleagues. Piled high on the table are the first
night presents he has received from the company, an unusually
friendly one, he is pleased to note. There is a bottle of champagne
with the compliments of the management, a silver tankard inscribed with the play's title given by the Dame, a beautiful framed
print of Rex Whistler's famous and highly scurrilous portrait of the
Prince Regent in Brighton from the Knight, a box of very expensive
liqueur chocolates from the Director, and a jeraboam of medium-
quality, insanely-expensive champagne from the Producer who
rather fancies himself as a connoisseur of wines. The other presents
include a wide variety of goodies to be eaten, drunk, worn, listened
to, read or just looked at. Since the sensible tradition still stands
whereby you give the same present to everybody in the company,
twenty-seven identical piles are standing in the different dressing-
rooms.

The dressing-room also accommodates his lucky mascots.
Michael doesn't regard himself as particularly superstitious, and
will deny it if asked, but the fact is that these little objects do give

him a feeling of reassurance and he would be very worried if one of them were lost. There is a 1933 penny picked up in a gutter in Brighton on the first day of his honeymoon: it is very rare and he has firmly refused all offers from fanatical numismatists. There is a tiny two-inch golliwog, given to him by his mother on his first first night in Lincoln rep. There is a medallion of St. Genesius, for he is a Catholic and he took this with him on a pilgrimage to Rome when he was a boy and it was blessed by the Pope. There is a silver threepenny bit which was used as a prop in his first West End play, four years ago, and most important of all there is a miniature framed photo of Irving, signed in the great man's illegible hand-writing. This was a present from Wingy, an old actor-laddie who befriended Michael in his first job at Lincoln and taught him much. The miniature had been given to Wingy (Wingfield C. Johnson to give him his full name and dignity) by Martin Harvey who had received it from Irving himself, so the Apostolic Succession, as Wingy used to say, was now complete.

The tannoy in the dressing-room suddenly comes to life. 'Good evening, ladies and gentlemen, good evening. This is your half-hour call. Half an hour please. Thank you.' The voice is as soothing as an air hostess but Walter is not soothed. He takes an eyebrow pencil and gently sketches very thin lines under his eyes to give them definition. A touch of red on the lips, a light dusting of the whole face with French chalk and the make-up is complete.

A low rumbled muttering is heard from the end of the room. It is his dressing-room partner, a big, muscular Cornishman, former boxing champion, former merchant navy seaman who has strayed into the profession as a stunt man with a passable singing voice and has, to everybody's surprise including himself, done rather well. He is a grumbler who grumbles incessantly about every conceivable thing and if there is nothing he will invent something. The third occupant is a pixilated little comic from Aberdeen who drenches himself in a very strong eau-de-cologne and twitters endlessly about his health. The fourth is a former Oxford don who has made a late entry into the profession. He would like to have directed the play which being a classic he regards as his own special property; instead he goes around telling everybody how they should act (every company has one). In the nicest possible way, of course, *'I say old boy, hope you don't mind, but you'll find it much better if you do it like this ...!'* He sports green tweeds, smokes a curved pipe and is generally regarded as a terrible nuisance. There have been no open rows and Michael, who is a peaceful person, hopes that there won't be, but he does sometimes wonder what he has done to be landed with the three biggest bores in the company and how long he can stand it? His contract runs for a year and if the play does likewise he is going to have problems.

The Company Manager, very smooth in an electric blue dinner-jacket and silver ruffled shirt-front, puts his head round the door. 'Good luck, gentlemen,' he says, and out he goes. The tannoy comes to life again. 'Fifteen minutes, please, fifteen minutes.' Twenty minutes to go. Michael now starts to put on his clothes; the white stockings, the white frilled shirt front, red-satin breeches, red velvet coat, black shoes with silver buckles, lacy cravat and three-cornered hat. He always leaves dressing till the last moment having heard that Bobby Moore used to do likewise (Michael is a keen follower of football.)

Other members of the company come in to wish him luck, in ones and twos. Michael privately wishes that they wouldn't for all this seems to be tempting providence, but he allows himself to be kissed, patted, hugged and generally stroked around. He is now bursting to pee and he goes down the stone corridor to the loo, but it is a false alarm, imagination rather than nature. Back in the dressing-room he hears the tannoy again: 'Five minutes, please, five minutes.' Christ! Only ten minutes to go and suddenly he realises that he can't remember his first line. In vain he searches the corner of his memory but it won't come. In panic he grasps the script lying open on his table and hastily turns up the relevant page – yes, there it is, how *could* he have forgotten it? Never in four weeks of rehearsals or fifteen previews did he have any trouble. He starts to mentally go through his big speech in Act Two but halfway through his memory falters and there is nothing but blankness; the whole part seems to be slipping away from him. He takes the Irving miniature and the threepenny bit and the golliwog and places them inside his pockets. Although the 'beginners please' has not yet been

74

called he now leaves the dressing-room and walks down the echoing stone steps to the stage. As he walks he starts to recite his lines, remembering one of Wingy's best pieces of advice, *'Run yerself in, laddie, start acting the minute you leave yer dressing-room'*. The stage is empty and he now embarks on a complicated good luck ritual. He walks round the empty stage concentrating as far as possible on nothing; he touches the front curtain; he touches and kisses the wooden struts behind the scenery; he whispers a slightly revised version of a childhood prayer of supplication, *'Matthew, Mark, Luke and John, bless the stage that I lie on.'* The end of this ritual is very curious: he holds out his hands in front of him and then slowly brings the two thumbs up and presses them against his forehead, concentrating on nothing but saying 'not bloody likely.' Wingie had passed this onto him. 'Concentrates the mind most wonderfully, laddie,' he used to say cheerfully, 'and with a quote from *Pygmalion* which is a very lucky play, you're off to a flying start.'

Already he is feeling better but the feeling is short-lived. The stage is now filling up with the company, lounging around uneasily, exchanging whispered small-talk with nervous hilarity and taking up their positions for the opening on and off the stage. And then comes the moment which every actor dreads – the raising of the safety curtain with a long, slow drawn-out hiss. The sound of the audience which was formerly a distant rumble is now a deafening roar, the howling of caged animals shrieking for blood with only a thin velvet and brocade curtain between all 950 of them and the twenty-eight unhappy actors. He remembers with alarm that his own party is sitting in the fifth row of the stalls consisting of his wife, his parents, an old actress-friend now turned film casting director, his agent and his agent's Jamaican boyfriend. But it is not them he is worried about for their goodwill can be taken for granted. It's the critics and other managements, the producers and directors of films and TV, in fact all those boss figures on whose collective goodwill his future depends. 'Places please,' says the Company Manager from the prompt corner. Michael retreats to the darkness of the wings: his teeth are chattering, his legs shaking, his heart pounding so loudly that surely everybody in the theatre can hear it; he is sweating all over like a bad attack of malaria; he feels sick, he is starting a headache, there is a pain in his throat and he can't speak above a whisper and now he really is bursting to have a pee so he dashes to the little backstage loo but once again it's a false alarm. When he returns to the stage the curtain is just about to go up. The roar of the audience is suddenly cut off like an electric light switch leaving behind a glacial silence more terrifying than any noise, and now he has once again forgotten that bloody opening line: he goes to the prompt corner and, ignoring the angry resentful look of the stage manager on the book, he refreshes his memory. Michael has exactly seventeen minutes before he is to step onto the brightly illuminated stage, and as he waits he asks himself if all the fame, fortune and success in the world can possibly compensate for these agonies, and wonders – as everybody has done throughout theatrical history – just *why* he had to become an actor.

Poor Michael. Is it any wonder that he should be superstitious?

2 · Superstitions in the Opera, the Ballet and the Cinema

The theatre is as sane and sensible as a provincial vicarage in comparison to the irresistible lunacies of opera. That is a fairy-tale world of extravagant emotions, imbecile plots and melodramatic behaviour. It seems inevitable that those who work and live in this world should be affected by it, and so they are. Not that any operamaniac would have it otherwise, for the outrageous behaviour of opera's deities is a small price to pay for the enormous pleasure they bring to their worshippers. The opera world is difficult and confining. Up to a point everybody can act and everybody does, but singing requires years of special training before a singer can even begin his career, and even after that the active life is limited. Whereas actors can continue their careers into their nineties and drop dead on the stage, singers must think of retirement at an age when an actor is still in his prime. It's a very strange life singers lead. Years of expensive training followed by years of flying and sailing round the world confining their activities to the six international opera houses which really count, their repertoire limited to the dozen or so operas which suit them. As they grow older their repertoire shrinks until retirement and teaching loom glacially before them. An operatic singer is exceedingly vulnerable to the ills of the flesh. The voice, that infinitely precious instrument, must be cuddled, coddled, cherished and cosied lest the slightest chill or

It was a lifetime's dream that I should appear in the Royal Opera House, Covent Garden, which is just about my favourite theatre in the world. It didn't matter what they asked me to do as long as it was something interesting. And my chance came, in *Moses and Aaron*. This photo was taken in the grossly overcrowded communal dressing-room.

breath of ill wind should spoil it and compel them to miss the performance. Walking on such a delicate tight-rope of health, and with a life so limited and so dangerous, it is surprising that singers are not more superstitious than they are.

There are fewer general superstitions in the opera world because, I suspect, singers are always too busy and too ubiquitous to have time to brood, but most singers have a lucky mascot, talisman or amulet and even a brief survey of operatic history will produce some intriguing items. Elizabeth Soederstrom travels a whole menagerie of glass animals with her, very expensive, very fragile, which must be placed in exactly the same position on her dressing-room table and God help any dresser or intruder who breaks one. Caruso carried a number of little charms strung together on a golden ring in the pocket of his costume and he would go mad if anybody wished him good luck. Seeing that the charms were placed in the pocket of his costume was his valet's most important duty and the only occasion on which Caruso's patience and good temper broke down was when this was forgotten. Tebaldi sets up dozens of dolls and little teddy-bears on her dressing-room table and Eugene Pavarotti always picks up bent nails and keeps them, for the V-sign is traditionally as good luck in opera as it was for Winston Churchill and the war effort. Melchior had a mezuzah, which is a gold case embellished with the Star of David picked out in diamonds and rubies, traditionally carried by rabbis and used in the ceremonies of Yom Kippur. Melchior had a very deep attachment to his, not because he was Jewish, but because it once saved his life. He had left his hotel in Canada to drive to the airport to catch a plane for New York where he was due to sing. On the way he discovered that he had forgotten to pack his precious mezuzah and insisted on returning to the hotel to collect it. As a result he missed his plane, but the plane crashed over the Rocky Mountains and everybody was killed.

Animals figure prominently amongst singers' lucky mascots. Tito Brignoli, a tenor who was very active in America during the nineteenth century, kept a stuffed deer-head. Not only did he invariably take it to the theatre, he further insisted that it be placed on the stage and it was the stage manager's task to find a suitable place for it. It was noticed by startled operamaniacs that the Café Momus, the square in Seville, the Countess's drawing-room, even Florestan's prison cell, were all dominated by a very large deer's head which cast a stern, unsmiling stare on the scene. Over the years audiences and singers and staff became very attached to it so when he died, the deer's head remained until it was destroyed by fire, much mourned by everybody. Offenbach had a very curious mascot: it was a conductor's baton which had been fashioned out of a croupier's rake given to him at the Casino in Baden-Baden where he had once enjoyed a very lucky evening and had won a vast sum of money. Thereafter the baton lay on his desk and piano when he was composing and it was with this that he conducted his operas. The sensational success he enjoyed with his best known operettas after he had acquired his lucky baton was always attributed to this. W. S. Gilbert would never have regarded himself as a superstitious man – from a soldier who embodied the nineteenth century's view of logical, rational man, such a thing would be a deplorable admission of weakness – but he did attach a certain occult power to the Japanese ceremonial sword which hung above the fireplace in his Kensington house. Savoyards all know the famous and well-documented story of how it fell with a clatter into

79

the fireplace on a windy day and thus triggered off the chain of creative thought which led to *The Mikado*. This was the greatest success he and Sullivan were to enjoy and the fifteen years which followed and which produced *Ruddigore*, *The Yeoman of the Guard*, *Utopia Ltd* and *The Gondoliers* were golden years indeed. The ceremonial sword was placed above his writing desk, the better to cast its benevolent influence, and though temptingly large sums of money were offered to him, Gilbert never parted with it. One night, thieves broke in and stole it and not all Gilbert's money, influence nor the combined efforts of the police could recover it. From then on his fortunes declined: his next opera was *The Grand Duke* which was a total failure and this was the last he and Sullivan wrote together for shortly after that Sullivan died and their unique partnership was at an end. Sullivan's lucky mascot was a handsome middle-aged American lady called Mrs Ronalds. She was his friend, his confidante, his constant companion and she brought him good luck. She was with him in his Victoria Street flat when he was composing and as she had a fine voice, an extensive knowledge of music and was a composer herself of popular ballad songs, he came to rely on her judgement. It is not known just how far she influenced the music he wrote for the operas, but it was a matter of considerable comment that she influenced the performance. On first nights and gala nights with Royalty present, he conducted and she always sat in the stage box where he could see her. When the audience was applauding each number and screaming for encores, it was her decision. If she smiled, he would allow the encore; if she didn't, then he wouldn't. She introduced him to another of her friends, The Prince of Wales, and through him to that colourful group of hell-raisers, high-livers and fornicating extroverts known as the Marlborough House set. Mrs Ronalds used to sing *The Lost Chord* the ballad by Sullivan which Victorian England had taken to its heart; the Prince carried on the Royal tradition of musical philistinism by declaring that this was the supreme musical achievement of his life. Mrs Ronalds continued to bring good luck to Sullivan throughout his life; posterity must be grateful to her.

There were some curious first night rituals. Caruso, being very religious, would say the whole rosary in the privacy of his dressing-

Caruso, who hated anybody to wish
him good luck. (Robin May Collection)

Jean de Reszke liked to sing on a
tiger-skin rug. (Robin May Collection)

room. Luigi Ravelli, a rival tenor of note, would sing to his dog and
await his verdict; if the dog growled approvingly and wagged his
tail, he would go happily to the theatre; if he didn't, then Ravelli
would go but not happily and his performance suffered. Jean de
Reszke would place on the floor of his dressing-room a tiger-skin
given to him by Sarah Bernhardt and would pace up and down on
it singing his part softly to himself. Kirsten Flagstad put her trust in
Yoga exercises which did, it must be admitted, keep her body and
voice in astonishingly good shape throughout her long and glorious career. Carl Ebert, who produced the Glyndebourne operas
before the War, would rap the stage-floor with his knuckles, whereas Wagner went further, he would kneel down and kiss it.

Swedes have one very peculiar superstition which is not observed
by singers of any other nationality. Before they go onto the stage,
they regard it as exceedingly lucky to be kicked on the bottom. It
has been suggested that the reason for this odd form of masochism
is that it is a willing sacrifice to the Gods to ensure their goodwill, as

81

Catholics used to mortify themselves on Friday. Melchior invariably suffered this mild indignity from his wife and there is a hilarious account of the Swedish mezzo, Gertrude Wittergen making her début at the Met in the late 30s. On her first night there in *Aida* her Swedish dresser was ill and she was reluctant to go on the stage until this little ritual had been performed. As she spoke no English and the stage staff no Swedish she had a problem. She was obliged to indicate her requirements in mime, a language which is traditionally open to misunderstanding. It seemed from contemporary accounts that her attempt to explain to a couple of uncouth, gum-chewing Brooklyn stage-hands just what she wanted them to do to Amneris right there and then in the darkness of the wings, caused some confusion: it was a scene worthy of the Marx Brothers, and since a scene not unlike this did occur in that classic *A Night at the Opera* it is tempting to suspect that the author did hear about it. It seems that the message did penetrate, the kick was administered in the right place, albeit with a trifle more enthusiasm and vigour than she had expected, and a slightly bruised and breathless Amneris finally took her place in the Temple of Ra.

Melba, though in every respect a tough, hard-headed, unsentimental Australian, did have two lasting superstitions: she thought it was very good luck to be paid in cash before a performance, having once been left stranded by an unscrupulous management with a worthless cheque. From then on she would not take one step onto the stage until her five hundred golden guineas had been counted out in her presence, locked in a trunk, her maid installed on top of it and the dressing-room locked and bolted until after the performance. The other one was a belief, doubtless influenced by stories of the African tribes in the Gold Coast and the Aborigines in the Australian desert, that seminal fluid was not only health-giving and life-enhancing but particularly good for the vocal chords and kept them fresh and young. It is believed that she took daily doses of this throughout her career on performance nights *and managed to obtain it at source*. There was, apparently, no shortage of willing donors – stage-hands, truckdrivers, hotel bellboys and male colleagues in the company. No first-hand confirmation of this is forthcoming, but if it is true then the ritual was certainly very effective,

82

Melba. She believed that seminal fluid, taken at source, would make her sing forever ... and she wasn't far wrong. (Robin May Collection)

for she continued to sing right till the end of her long life; even at seventy her voice retained a quality which the critics, by a strange ironic twist, would always describe as fresh, pure and *virginal.*

The Evil Eye is an ancient Italian superstition; this is what witches and people in league with the forces of evil are supposed to possess and with which they can bring about bad luck to their victims. Every Italian singer in history has gone in mortal fear of it and their memoirs are full of references to it. Offenbach was supposed to have it, though this may well have been circulated by his anti-Jewish rivals in the French opera and in any case didn't stop managements from accepting his operas and orchestral players from performing under his direction. Patti once conceived a violent hatred for Madame Gerster, a Hungarian mezzo with whom she once sung in *Norma.* She believed that Gerster had the Evil Eye, and every hitch, every piece of trouble was laid at her door. Once, when they took their curtain calls together, and Gerster was cheered more loudly than Patti, she exploded with wrath and slapped her rival's face. The audience turned very nasty and booed the temperamental Queen of Song who thereafter refused to have anything to do with Madame Gerster. Claire Kellog, an American soprano who enjoyed considerable success at Covent Garden in the 1860s wrote with great bitterness about her traumatic début there in *La Traviata.* Everything went wrong from torn costumes, missing jewellery, spilt face-powder to falling scenery. Small, irritating little bad luck things happened to everybody in the company and from time to time as the evening limped on, she noticed the company making the traditional sign which wards off the effects of the Evil Eye. After the performance the mystery was solved. It was the Russian-born mother of the popular actor, Richard Mansfield who was sitting in the stage-box. Her eyes were large and dark and baleful, and her personality was formidable, but whether the eyes were evil or not was never discovered.

Italian singers are more prone than any other nationality to attributing bad luck to the presence of a single evil person, known as a *iettaturo.* This jinx-laden performer can be a chorister, a principal, a member of the audience or somebody on the stage staff. Gigli invariably carried little sacks of garlic, fatal for social life but won-

Claire Kellog, she suffered a traumatic experience during *Traviata* thanks to the Evil Eye. (Sally Chappell/Victoria & Albert Museum)

derful for salads and repelling the powers of evil. He would distribute these little bags round his person, his house and his dressing-room, his costume, and would even try to persuade others to carry them also. Another famous Russian singer placed his faith in little bags of human excrement which he believed would frighten off evil spirits; they did, but they also frightened off everybody else as well. But there is a magic talisman which effectively cancels out the effect of the Evil Eye and it is a complex device consisting of a hand, a horn and a hunchback. A popular good luck card in Italian opera circles will show these three. Any deformity is attributed to diabolical influence and Tettrazini would never sing if by chance she met on her way to the theatre either a one-legged man, a cross-eyed person or a hunchback. Since most opera companies employ at least one hunchback to give colour to the chorus and crowd scenes, he would be told to keep well out of the way on the nights the great singer was around. However, most singers believe a hunchback brings good luck and to be kissed by one brings even better, which perhaps explains the extreme popularity of *Rigoletto*. There is an impressive list of unlucky operas, of which *Tristan* is perhaps the earliest. Wagner was very superstitious about it, his own special favourite from his middle period; in the century since it was first performed it has had a strange jinx on it. There were many difficulties in getting it produced at all and although it did go into rehearsal in Vienna in 1859 for performance at the Stadtopera, it was finally abandoned by the company as being unsingable and unstageable; this verdict seems inconceivable now but it did then represent a powerful body of influential musical opinion of the time. It was partly due to the inadequacy of the tenor who was due to sing Tristan and partly due to the failure of the conductor to give an even adequate account of the exceedingly complex score, a score which had been composed during a very nerve-wracking period of domestic strife with his wife, debt, financial worries and self-doubt. It was six years before a presentation could be arranged, in Munich in 1865 under the command and supervision of Ludwig II of Bavaria, Wagner's patron and fairy godfather. There had been endless delays, postponements and setbacks but on 10 June it was ready. Two disasters took place on that day: the first was the arrival of the bailiffs to turn Wagner out of his house and seize all his furniture, the result of a lawsuit brought about by a Frenchwoman who had lent Wagner a large sum of money five years earlier. Only the prompt action of the Bavarian treasury spared him the public humiliation of being made homeless. The second was much more serious – an accident affecting Malvina Schnoor. Malvina and Ludwig Schnoor, her husband, were the original Tristan and Isolde, two singers of exceptional quality who embodied everything Wagner could possibly want for these immensely difficult parts. On the day before the opening, Malvina took a vapour bath and promptly lost her voice. Postponement was inevitable and Wagner's many enemies were loud in their triumph. The performance finally took place three weeks later on 10 June in front of the King and 600 guests. For the first time Bavarian music-lovers were hearing music which was really new; they did not understand it and their reception was cold. Only the King understood and loved it and commanded two more performances. They were destined to be the last for a long time because two days after the third, Ludwig Schnoor died of rheumatism. His last words were 'Farewell, Siegfried', a part he had been promised and which he would definitely have sung if he had lived. He was the first Tristan and possibly the greatest. It was years before Wagner could bring himself to conduct the opera or even permit its performance.

Ludwig II was abnormally shy, very neurotic and superstitious about a number of different things. He disliked people and considered it bad luck to be too close to them, hence the fairy-tale castles which he constructed where he could live alone in total solitude. This had a predictable effect on his theatregoing; when Wagner composed *The Mastersingers of Nuremberg* and announced it for production, Ludwig insisted on having the first performance for him alone. Nobody else was to be allowed inside the theatre lest their coughs and shifting might distract him. *Mastersingers* was a huge success not only with the King but with the public who were later admitted, and thereafter it became a good luck ritual with Wagner to have the first performance given for the King alone. When the Festspielhaus opened in Bayreuth for the opening performance of *The Ring of the Nibelungen* it was arranged for Ludwig to be there alone to enjoy in solitude what was in effect a preview. Richter conducted, Ludwig Betz sang Wotan and Wagner sat with the King in the Royal Box. The performances were hugely successful though there were a few trifling mishaps – the River Rhine overflowed its banks a trifle too enthusiastically, Valhalla burned down rather more than anybody anticipated and the dragon had lost his head. This had been ordered from Nathans in London who enjoyed an international reputation as a theatrical costumier and property maker. But as Bayreuth was then unknown, a clerk in the mailing department sent it by mistake to Beirut just on the coast of North Africa.

Lest anybody be tempted to sneer at the ignorance of the Victorians it must be firmly stated that exactly the same mistake was made by an employee of the Decca Recording Company in 1951. He received an urgent request for a box of recording tapes from the engineers in Bayreuth and sent them to Beirut. The recording was not made because the tapes did not arrive in time. The opera in question was *Tristan and Isolde*.

If Ludwig's love of theatrical solitude was regarded by his court and people as a form of madness then there was a good deal of method in it. Wagner can be best appreciated in an empty theatre with no audience to distract you as I discovered in the summer of 1965. Having just appeared at Covent Garden in *Moses and Aaron* and having made some very useful contacts on the staff and administration, I was given privileged access to the dress rehearsal of the four parts of *The Ring* on four successive mornings. My seat in the Grand Tier overlooked an empty house and the cathedral hush, being so impressive, added immeasurably to the impact of the music which I was hearing for the first time. Never did I ever hear *The Ring* again in such superb conditions.

There are a number of unlucky operas, all very popular and constantly being performed. *La Forza del Destino* was commissioned by the Russian Imperial Court and first performed in St. Petersburg but was very coldly received from an audience of hostile Russian composers and their supporters. A number of fatalities have taken place during *Forza*: Ettore Bastianini, a famous nineteenth century baritone, was taken ill with a fit of convulsions and had to retire from singing, whilst Pietro Cimara, a conductor, died of a heart attack whilst conducting a performance in Milan. It was during *Forza* that a chandelier fell into the crowded stalls and during another performance that the theatre burned down with many fatalities. Toscanini always regarded it as his unlucky opera and throughout his long career always refused to conduct it; it seemed that when he had played the 'cello in the Rome Opera House orchestra, a number of small accidents had happened during *Forza* – he broke a string, he was knocked over by a cab whilst on his way to a rehearsal, and to cap it all, one of his colleagues in the orchestra suddenly went mad, rushed home and killed his wife with a breadknife. The most widely publicised of all the *Forza* disasters was the tragic death of Leonard Warren on 4 March 1960 whilst in the middle of the aria 'Soerre in Questore'. He collapsed on the stage and died in the wings while the understudy was rushed on and the opera continued. It was Hollywood's favourite backstage cliché bought to life. 'What a way to go, the end all theatre people dream of,' shouted the headlines the next day. More than any other opera, *Forza* fills opera singers with superstitious fears. At the mention of the name, they cross themselves and grab whatever lucky mascots are to hand. Many refuse to perform in it and some will even refuse to see it.

Other operas on the singer's black list include *The Tales of Hoffmann* because the composer died before he finished it, *Turandot* for the same reason and because a great fire, causing much loss of life and damage, broke out at the Ringtheatre in Vienna where it was staged. Puccini died at his desk while writing the final scene of *Turandot* and the final duet was finished by his friend, the composer Alfano. Also on the list is Halévy's *La Juive*; Caruso became ill during a performance of this once-popular opera and died shortly afterwards, Martinelli tried it and he too became ill and from then on the opera dropped out of the repertoire. John Brownlee, the Australian tenor, once missed death by inches when a chandelier dropped in front of him during a performance of *The Marriage of Figaro* and thereafter viewed the opera with caution. In England, Gluck's *Orphée et Eurydice* has bad luck associations ever since Kathleen Ferrier was barely able to finish her second performance at Covent Garden and died painfully of cancer a few weeks later (1953). Sophie Fedorovitch, who designed that production, also died a few weeks afterwards, and since then a number of famous English singers have firmly refused to appear in it.

But the most unlucky opera is ironically the most popular of all;

it has notched up more performances in its hundred years than any other and is constantly being declared by musicologists and critics as being the perfect opera, and a unique and imperishable masterpiece. *Carmen*. Everybody knows that the first performance was a failure, and if it wasn't quite the disaster which some of the more sensational musical histories have said, there is no doubt that its lukewarm reception from public and critics was a colossal disappointment to the composer. Bizet retired to the country to calm his shattered nerves, to nurse his *angina pectoris* and to study the notices which had the not unexpected effect of causing a total nervous breakdown. The plot, he learned, was incoherent and immoral, Carmen was a highly unsuitable person to be the heroine of a romantic opera (whoever heard of an opera-comique being set in a cigarette factory?). The music had no melody – a verdict which seems incomprehensible to us now – and musical opinion was divided between those who thought it was too Wagnerian and those who thought it wasn't Wagnerian enough. And since when did an opera-comique have an unhappy ending? This was Bizet's reward for six months inspired hard work. In fact the situation was not quite as bad as he imagined. Word of mouth was performing its usual miraculous cure: as one performance followed another, the audiences grew larger and more enthusiastic, but whether Bizet knew this in his retreat and whether he would have been reassured if he had, history does not relate. Within three months there had been twenty-three performances which, by any standards, spells success – when did a modern opera do as well in present times? – But on the evening of the twenty-fourth performance, 2 June 1875, a rather curious and disturbing incident occurred in Act Three when Carmen sees her death and that of Don José in the cards. The singer was Marie-Gallié who was believed to have psychic powers. When she looked at the cards, she burst into tears, collapsed over the table and had to be led off stage, sobbing and unable to finish. She said that she had seen very bad news in the cards, something which had nothing to do with the opera but it would have its effect on all their lives. She refused to say any more and went home, pale and silent. The following day the Director of the Opera, M. Camillie du Locle, received a telegram; Bizet had died very suddenly of a

Gallie-Marié, the first Carmen. She saw death in the cards.

heart attack. Carmen had claimed her first real-life victim.

Singers have ever since had a superstitious fear of the opera believing that on its first performance in a new production or a new opera house, something will go wrong. Fanchon Thompson, making her début at the Met, suffered a disastrous lapse of memory and had to walk off the stage thus bringing the opera to a complete standstill. Toni Ravelli, a famous tenor of the 1880s, suddenly went mad in Act Three and tried to kill his Carmen, the American Minnie Hauck, with a knife. He was jealous of her success and in the interval rushed round the theatre shouting, 'I will kill her, I will kill her.' He was eventually calmed down and the fourth act proceeded without incident. Ravelli was replaced for further performances and it is no coincidence that he retired from the operatic stage shortly afterwards.

Calvé. Lost her knickers in front of Queen Victoria, who was not amused . . . ! (Sally Chappell/Victoria & Albert Museum)

The embarrassment which every woman fears did occur to Calvé regarded as the greatest Carmen of her time which was the nineties. It was a Royal Command Performance at Windsor Castle in front of Queen Victoria who had a great admiration for the singer and had announced her intention of decorating her after the performance. In the middle of Act Two she lost her knickers; they fell to her feet but with admirable presence of mind she kicked them into the wings whilst resourcefully not missing a note. Alas, her professionalism was wasted; the old Queen was deeply shocked, neither smiled nor applauded at the end and retired early without presenting the medal.

It was at the Met in 1905 that a high wooden bridge at the back of the stage collapsed in Act One throwing dozens of choristers and extras onto the stage with bruises, cuts, contusions and a couple of broken limbs to mark the occasion. In Padua in 1920 the Russian singer, Anita Clinowa, miscalculated the distance she had to stab her Don José with the dagger, missed and struck her other colleague, Dancairo, blinding him for life. An outdoor performance in Verona was ruined by a tornado which broke up the scenery into matchwood and caused a stampede amongst the audience which resulted in a dozen fatalities. The latest disaster connected with the opera was the appointment of a charming Swede, Goeran Gentele, to the directorship of the Met following the long reign of Sir Rudolf Bing. Gentele planned to inaugerate his tenure with a new and exciting production of *Carmen*. Preliminary conferences were held with his production team; the principal parts were cast, the designs were approved, and Gentele left for a month's holiday in Italy before returning to start rehearsals. Six days later he and his wife and his two daughters were killed in a car crash. Carmen had claimed yet another real-life victim, and, as the opera is irredeemably popular and nothing will stop singers from singing it, there will doubtless be plenty more.

The Broadway theatre superstition about starting thirteen minutes late does *not* apply to the Metropolitan Opera. There the curtain commendably rises on the dot of the advertised time and latecomers are positively not admitted, but are allowed to watch the performance on closed-circuit television in one of the lobbies. I wonder how many of the opera houses in the world where this civilised rule is enforced realise that they owe it to the late Sir Thomas Beecham. It was he who created such a fuss when latecomers insisted on chattering through the overture to *Don Giovanni*, that he turned round, stopped the orchestra and abused them loudly and, it was reported, obscenely. Next day it was headlines all over the London newspapers (May 1933) the rule was announced and thereafter enforced. At the Met, a different superstition seems to prevail. It is good luck to see the operas on the instalment system, because a bird's-eye view from the tier of the house reveals an interesting fact: the pockets of empty seats change from act to act. It was then revealed that New Yorkers were in the habit of arriving punctually but leaving early to go to dinner or catch the second half of something else. Alternatively, they would see Act One, leave throughout Act Two for dinner somewhere and return for Act Three. It was during Act Three one evening that I found myself sitting next to such a party. My immediate neighbour was a shrivelled little monkey-faced matron who might have been William Bendix's great-grandmother – and possibly was. She kept up a continuous whine of petulant criticism, 'Oh, this goddam shee*yit*, why ya bring me heee*yah*, I hate this more'n I hate the toothache, ect ... .' It was like the moan of the airconditioner and no less irritating. Finally, I turned to her and said with what I hoped and intended was the most exquisite politeness, 'Oh *please*! Could you *possibly* hush, I can't hear the music?' whereupon she turned, looked incredulously at me and snarled, 'you hush your fucking self, who the hell do you think *you* are!' The opera was Goeran Gentele's ill-fated *Carmen*.

† † †

Good luck wishes in the operatic world are more repulsive and less hygienic than in the theatre. In Germany they spit three times, or they recite the sound which spitting is traditionally supposed to make which is *toi-toi-toi*. It is in Germany that *Hals und bein-bruch* (break-a-leg) originated. In France they also spit and say something even more distasteful, *merde-merde-merde* which delicacy forbids me to translate. In Italy it is *in bocca di lupo* which means 'in the mouth of the wolf' and the translation of what they to each other in Russia is 'to the Devil with your Grand-daughter'. In all cases the basic principle is that these will frighten away the evil spirits, and that if you wish evil, then good will come. It's an interesting theory, and one can only devoutly hope that it is borne out by the practice.

In Germany it is bad luck to get your hair cut during the rehearsals if it is either a new opera or a new production of an old opera, another example of the Sampson myth in operation: hair is strength and inspiration and you need all you can get. This led to an unexpected crisis at Glyndebourne when a group of German choristers recruited from Berlin and Stuttgart and Munich refused to get their hair cut when rehearsing for *The Marriage of Figaro* and the periwigs had to be made a little larger to accomodate them. In Austria you must never walk onto the stage with your overcoat and hat on, you must never use the backstage lift during a performance – good sense this, though; supposing you were trapped by a power cut just before your entrance – and if you drop your score, you must stamp your foot on the ground before you bend down to retrieve it, and some singers will never bend down for any reason – somebody else must pick it up for them.

In setting up and preparing for an operatic performance it is the good luck custom to place the furniture in position first and the scenery second. This is because the furniture is very big and it would not be possible to get it onto the stage otherwise. While it is waiting the furniture is stacked up downstage in front of the footlights, and it is considered very bad luck to sit on it. This is due to the ever-present possibility of the iron safety curtain falling unexpectedly and with lethal effect. The curtain is very heavy, it descends with terrifying speed and frequently without any warning other than a serpentine hiss. Ron Mullenger, who stage-managed a season of opera in Belfast, remembers a man being killed in this way and a number of other mutilations and near fatalities. In fact it was only his prompt action that saved a local stage-hand from having his hand chopped off by the rapidly descending curtain.

Animal excreta has a valuable good luck property in operatic circles. In the final week of technical dress-rehearsals of *Moses and Aaron** at Covent Garden in 1965, the camel, on hire from Whipsnade Zoo, deposited his candid opinion of Schonberg on the stage. This occasioned high hilarity from the four hundred people on the stage, but a good deal of angry mumbling from the stage staff who could not decide which of their various unions should

*For a detailed description of the rehearsals and performances of this revival, see *The Saturday Book* 1967.

deal with it. The TUC had sadly neglected to form a Camelshit Association and the rehearsal was stupidly held up while the matter was being debated. It was a very exalted member of the musical staff who finally lost his temper and grabbed a shovel.'Enough of this bloody nonsense,' he shouted as he leapt onto the steeply sloping ramp of the stage, '*I* will clear it up,' and he did. This whole incident was regarded by the older singers as a very lucky omen, an opinion justified by the huge and unique success of the opera which was fully sold out for all its six performances and received notices, acclaim and peripheral publicity about which press-officers can only dream.

† † †

Ballet dancers work harder than anybody else in the theatre and thus have little time for introspection, neuroses and occult fantasies. Their work schedule and the physical strain it involves in keeping their bodies in peak condition and their performance up to standard, would make a rugby international or a coal miner wince. Classes all morning, rehearsals all afternoon, performances most evenings, it's a hard gruelling life from nine in the morning until well after ten at night. There is no relaxation even on those exhausting one-night stand tours with which ballet companies augment their incomes and their reputations. An actor or a singer can sleep all morning, and laze around all day before going to the theatre where sometimes no more is required of them than a number of speeches or a couple of arias followed by a late-night supper with his friends. An actor's work, though frequently nerve-wracking, is not physically exhausting (though parts like Othello and Peer Gynt are) but a dancer's life is a very hard one. It is also a very short one, an average of twenty years, for by the time a singer is coming into his prime, the dancer is already thinking of retirement. Ballet is a very young art. Apart from *Giselle* which dates back to 1841, ballet as we now know it started with Tchaikovsky and Petipa in Russia in the late 1880s and for all practical purposes it started here in the West in 1910 with Diaghilev and his Russian Ballet. Seventy years is not really long enough for an art form to have acquired its own legends, traditions and mystique, nor has it. The balletic world is

96

astonishingly and healthily free of superstitions.

Investigation has, however, produced a few intriguing items: dancers always spit onto the ribbons of their ballet-shoes before tying them, for spittle represents strength and good luck. You must never hook a tutu downwards for this is bad luck: it must always be upwards for then your career will go upwards and from dancing third cygnet you will end up dancing Princess Aurora. Black safety pins are unlucky and so are lilacs which must never be included in floral tributes. More than one prima ballerina has refused a bouquet when the offending flower was seen lurking in the middle of all those roses and carnations. But the ballet *Lilac Garden* is very popular and successful provided that the flowers on the stage are not real. It's considered good luck to prick your fingers and draw blood when you're sewing on your ballet shoes: this represents a sacrifice and (literally) a blood offering to the Deities, like Catholics giving up meat on Fridays as we once did, or ancient Spartans sacrificing their children on the exposed sides of the mountains. Dancers preparing their shoes for performance have strange rituals: some break the stiffness by cutting the soles with a knife, some by bending them in the hinge of a door, some by taking out the inner sole, or slitting open the upper and extracting the cotton padding. But whatever is done, it's bad luck to prepare more than two shoes at a time, for this is tempting providence. Some dancers are regarded as lucky mascots by their colleagues and it is known that one dancer will allow only another dancer to hook up her tutu. Dancers often knock the stage floor three times for luck and it has been reported that some of the Royal Ballet dancers go down and kiss it, but then the stage-floor at the Royal Opera House enjoys a world-wide notoriety for its dangerously uneven surface.

Dancers are superstitious about their artificial curls: the dresser must not handle them and the dancer will herself take them back to the wardrobe for overnight storage after each performance. Hersey Piggott, a dresser at the Royal Opera House, once collected the curls from the dressing-rooms and thus provoked a storm of anger from the wardrobe-mistress. An alien hand, she was firmly told, must never, *never* touch them.

Diaghilev, like so many Russians, was deeply superstitious, but

97

the belief which really haunted his life was the bad luck of the sea. He had been told by a gipsy that he would die on water and for that reason he avoided sea voyages whenever possible for they were torture to him. But as his seasons of Ballet in London were so successful and important, he was forced to take a great many trips across the Channel. He would always go down below to the saloon and sit huddled miserably in a chair with his back to the sea, muffled in a blanket covering his beaver-fur overcoat, his hat pulled down over his eyes so he could not see the invariably calm sea. Though not religious he would clutch his icon of St. Nicholas and mutter prayers in an angry whisper. After an hour of inaction he would start to rage against the English, their inedible food, their ghastly weather, their unattractive girls, the ignorant philistine public, even the language did not escape censure, which he likened to the barking of dogs and frogs. Only when he safely landed at Dover did he relax and then it was sunshine and smiles. In fact, he didn't die by drowning as he had feared, but the gipsy's prophesy did come true. He died in Venice in 1929 which by extension can be described as being on water. He is buried there.

Pavlova was regarded by her superstitious company (mostly English charmingly disguised with Russian names) as being a source of good luck. For years of touring, nothing ever went wrong: no earthquakes, storms, revolutions or crashes ever happened when the Pavlova Company was circulating round the world. They never had a rough Channel crossing in spite of adverse weather forecasts. They believed that she was under some mysterious sort of divine protection and with her shrewd awareness of public relations and company morale, she encouraged this belief. The nearest they ever came to disaster was in America when the train carrying them had to cross a very shaky bridge and it did finally collapse but only after they had safely crossed to the other side.

Pavlova was superstitious about strangers in the wings, regarding them as harbingers of bad luck. If she saw one, however distinguished or in whatever authoritative company she would walk off the stage and refuse to continue till they had left the theatre. She was superstitious about curtain presents; she would not allow anything but flowers to be handed up at the end of the performance. On one occasion a statue of the Madonna and Child was brought onto the stage and presented to her. When the curtain finally descended, she ran to her dressing-room, weeping loudly, which was regarded by the apprehensive company as a very bad omen. Once in Berlin she was presented to the Kaiser after a performance. As she bent down to kiss his white glove, she left there a trace of scarlet lipstick. The Kaiser made a joke about it, saying that he now had blood on his hands, but Pavlova was deeply distressed by the incident. Shortly afterwards, the War started and nothing would convince Pavlova that the lipstick was not a bad omen, and that she herself was in no way responsible for the carnage that followed. The date of that sinister little incident, as she realised with alarm, was 13 October, 1913. Her final performance in England at the Golders Green Hippodrome, was marked by a big laurel wreath. She took it home and stayed up all night with it, surrounded by candles. She forgot to say goodbye to her swans in her London home, Ivy House, and two months later, in January 1931, she died in Amsterdam.

All her life she had been superstitious about a short ballet which had been arranged for her, *Danse Macabre*, from the Saint-Saens music. After its first performance, which was enthusiastically received, she declared that she felt frightened and nervous, and in spite of incessant public request, she never danced it again nor allowed any of her company to do so. Naturally, its association with death would be alarming. The only other ballet which has distinct bad luck associations is the *Rite of Spring*. It had its world première at the Théâtre des Champs Elysées in 1913, clearly an unlucky year for the ballet. Stravinsky's music was horribly new to the conservative ears of the Parisian public and Nijinsky's choreography was incomplete and in the eyes of many, totally obscene. The performance was one of the best documented theatrical disasters of the century, when the audience started to hiss, boo, shout and scream from the beginning, with fights and face-slappings breaking out all over the house, the police were called in to eject the hooligans, Stravinsky rushing in panic backstage to find Nijinsky screaming abuse at the dancers from the wings and Diaghilev in tears all over the Champs Elysées. There seems to have been a slight jinx on the ballet; there have been very few attempts to revive it, its complex rhythms and atonal dissonances are still a formidable stumbling block to all but a few very daring choreographers, and the few that have been mounted have not been successful, with the possible exception of Kenneth MacMillan's for the Royal Ballet.

Nijinsky was superstitiously attached to the ballet *Spectre de la Rose* and was very hostile to any suggestions that anybody else should dance it. Even if he had no actual control over the copyright – which was Fokine's – the ballet had been created for him and was always associated with him. It had been, one of his greatest successes and to let lesser feet touch it was to court disaster. Happily no lesser feet did touch it in his lifetime and revivals of it since his death have shown how dependant it is on its creator. His costume covered with rose petals was a lucky mascot and although he was offered a fortune in cash by his admirers for just one rose petal as a souvenir, he always refused. To have parted with just one would have been bad luck. Nijinsky liked money just as much as anybody else, but his rose petals were sacred. In fact, they were gradually sold off, but the culprit, who did it without Nijinsky's knowledge, was Vassiliev, Diaghilev's bodyguard.

† † †

The cinema is even shorter-lived than the ballet, for all practical purposes no more than sixty glorious years, but since the actors and actresses were recruits from the theatre bringing with them their own traditions, since the tycoons who created the art form were mostly semi-literate peasants from the slums and ghettos of Eastern Europe and since the industry started, flowered and matured in the enclosed, hothouse world of Hollywood, the cinema is not without superstitions.

Lucky mascots abound, and from time to time, the fan magazines publish little articles about them. They tell us that Bette Davis cherishes a box of theatre programmes of the plays she appeared in at the Cape Cod Playhouse during her early theatre years in the 20s. Joan Crawford invariably preserved in her dressing-room a red belt she had originally worn in the Molnar play *The Guardsman* which had brought her good luck and a contract. Van Johnson has a pair of red socks and always wears them in his films – red appears to be a lucky colour in Hollywood. Gregory Peck has a stiffback script-holder given to him by David O. Selznick when he appeared in *Duel in the Sun,* the first film they made together: ten years, twenty films and thousands of miles later, the script-holder, though torn and tattered, was still functioning and still lucky. Kitty Carlisle, Moss Hart's wife, always wore a tweed suit for film tests even in the height of the Californian summer. Greta Garbo put her trust in a rope of real pearls which went with her everywhere: nobody, not even her trusted Swedish dressers, were allowed to touch them. Humphrey Bogart had a selection of mascots – a silver cocktail shaker given to him by a famous bridge-player called Joseph Elwell who was subsequently the victim of a mysterious unsolved murder; an Egyptian scarab set in gold which was given to him by a jeweller when Bogart was in his shop buying a wedding-ring; and, most mysteriously, five German helmets. Leslie Howard had a lucky gold sovereign which had an interesting history. Years ago, in his early years in the London theatre, he had been very hard up, almost broke, and down to this last sovereign. He was very reluctant to sell it as it had been given to him by his father, but hunger was a strong persuader and he finally decided that he must. At the crucial moment he was saved from this drastic step by the unexpected offer of a part which led him to fame and fortune. He resolved never to spend the sovereign no matter how poor he might one day be, nor did he. It was in his pocket when he was killed in the aircrash over Portugal in 1942.

Some rather peculiar behaviour is reported in the fan magazines. Dyan Cannon once refused to cut her hair since her good luck, she claimed, dated from the day she let it grow, another example of the Sampson myth: it was right down to her waist before she finally consented to have it trimmed to a reasonable length. Godfrey Cambridge never bends down to retrieve dropped money or a bar of soap if he happens to be in the shower. Spencer Tracey never returned to collect a forgotten errand, for this was bad luck, while Jeanette Macdonald, when braiding her hair, always started with her left hand: in addition, she would never bend down to button up her shoes, she would always bring the shoe up to the chair. Dorothy Lamour considered it bad buck to drop an umbrella and then pick it up herself, somebody else had to pick it up and if there was nobody she would leave it. Phil Silvers considered it bad luck to meet a white horse on his way to the studio, and if he did then he would go back home and change his spectacles. Tyrone Power considered it bad luck to eat baked potatoes on a Friday, but he was a Catholic and we Catholics have never been quite sane on the subject of Fridays. Lionel Barrymore had a dread of Rubinstein's *Melody in F* which a violinist friend had once played just before his death by heart attack. Boris Karloff's great success had been the Monster in *Frankenstein*; from then on he always used the same dressing-room, walked down the same corridors to get to it, entered the studio by the same gate, ate his lunch at the same table in the commissary, insisted on having the same dresser, the same make-up man and the same canvas chair on the set.

Certain people have been lucky for others: for years John Wayne regarded Ward Bond as lucky and made sure he was in all his pictures until Bond achieved independant fame in a very popular TV series. David Niven entertained similar feelings about his old wartime friend, Michael Trubshawe and likewise employed him in a number of his post-war films. Elinor Glyn, the author of those controversial and deeply erotic novels *It* and *Three Weeks*, made herself a very powerful force in Hollywood. With her striking, red-haired beauty, her distinguished bearing and her aristocratic manner, she had no trouble in convincing the tycoons that she was a person of immense importance. Louis B. Mayer was so convinced of this that he believed she possessed occult powers, and refused ever to make an important decision without consulting her. Should this actress be put under contract? Should this actor play this part? Should this property be bought for filming? Madame Glyn would advise him. Over the years her influence was considerable and many careers either blossomed or were nipped in the bud following a discreet word from Madame Glyn. She claimed that she received her occult powers from a vase which was supposed to talk to her and tell her what to do.

Alfred Hitchcock had a very unusual and striking lucky mascot –

himself. He was of the opinion that he brought good luck to his films if he was in them, however briefly, and the opinion seems to be justified. His films are enormously successful and became classics in his own lifetime. Those magic words 'Alfred Hitchcock presents' are a guarantee not only of superbly polished filmmaking but also first-class entertainment. He was the only director who got star-billing above the title, who was more important than any star he cared to employ, and made successful films without any stars at all. For as long as anybody could remember he made tiny personal appearances in his films which were eagerly awaited by his admirers and the subject of much delighted speculation and discussion – crossing a crowded street (*Psycho*), walking down a pavement (*Rear Window*), carrying a double-bass case out of a bus (*Strangers on the Train*), a neon sign outside a skyscraper (*Rope*), a face in a newspaper advertisement (*Lifeboat*).

† † †

Even in its short lifetime the cinema has managed to produce not so much an unlucky film as an unlucky story. Cleopatra has exerted a powerful fascination over the imaginations of producers, writers and actresses: in sixty glorious years many films about her have been produced, some based on existing stage plays, some have been originals, but all except one have been disastrous. The pattern is predictably the same: Mr Z, a producer, decides that a multi-million spectacular will solve his, and his studio's, problems: Miss X sees herself in the part. The film is budgeted to money beyond the dreams of de Mille, dozens of superstars and mini-stars are signed up, some to speak but a single line. Asps are auditioned. The publicity drums scream and shriek out their glad tidings. The producer exceeds his budget by untold millions and, in spite of the impressive display of talent in every department, the result is a boring mess with only a few oases of interest in the desert of boredom. Cecil B. de Mille's *Cleopatra* (1935) was laughed off the screen at its last showing at the Starlight Film Club which isn't surprising in view of such gems of Hollywood History dialogue as 'Poor Calpurnia, the wife is always the last to know!' delivered with barely concealed mirth by Claudette Colbert. When Gabriel Pascal produced his film of Shaw's very uncinematic play *Cæsar and Cleopatra* in 1944, he successfully bankrupted the British film industry and killed all chances of other Shaw plays being filmed for many years (*The Doctor's Dilemma* was the next, some fifteen years later). It resulted in great tensions and clashes between those involved, some of whom never spoke to each other again, and although the acting from a cast which was the cream of English acting was individually superb, the film was very badly directed – by Pascal himself which everybody agreed was a mistake – and it amounted to two and a half hours of unadulterated tedium. For Vivien Leigh there was tragedy as well as boredom: while she shivered on the location desert at Denham studios, she miscarried and lost the baby which she and Laurence Olivier were expecting. Though she was not superstitious, it seemed clear that there was a curse on the subject.

This chapter is no place in which to give a blow by blow account of the Burton/Taylor *Cleopatra* except to say that more than one newspaper showbiz columnist headed his article 'The Curse of Cleopatra'. The start in England with Peter Finch and Stephen Boyd, the cancellation of the film due to bad weather, the transfer to Rome, the happy substitute of Burton and Rex Harrison, the endless delays, the difficulty of finding a suitable script (Mankiewicz was reduced to writing each evening the scenes he was to shoot the next day; throughout the film he seldom remained more than one day ahead) and finally the cost which soared up to $37,000,000 and elicited the most savage notices of the decade from critics who were waiting eagerly for the kill.

Happily, this did not deter Charlton Heston from directing and starring in a long-cherished project to film Shakespeare's highly cinematic play. With a hand-picked supporting cast and all the right locations, he produced a film which was totally faithful to Shakespeare, received respectful notices, played to empty houses in London and failed to find a distributor in America.

There are other unlucky film subjects. Lawrence of Arabia was a figure who fascinated film producers during and after his lifetime and it was Alexander Korda who first set up a film of the *Seven Pillars of Wisdom* in 1935 to star Walter Hudd, an up-and-coming young actor who had played a part very like Lawence in Shaw's *Two True To Be Good*. The publicity and excitement was enormous and Lawrence promised his full co-operation. Korda took his actors and film unit to the Jordan desert and some marvellous footage was shot. Suddenly Lawrence was killed in that famous motor-bicycle accident and for reasons which have never been properly explained the film was abandoned. It was a shocking disappointment for everybody, particularly Walter Hudd who saw his chances of truly international stardom snatched away from him. Although he lived to do some very distinguished work in films (*Major Barbara*) and stage (the 1950 Old Vic season) he remained to his death a very difficult and embittered old man. In the post-war years, Anthony Asquith set up a new version of the story with Dirk Bogarde playing Lawrence. This too went out to the desert and was likewise abandoned under speedy and rather mysterious circumstances. It was left to David Lean and Peter O'Toole to lay this jinx forever.

The other unlucky subject is Diaghilev/Nijinsky. Many attempts have been to set up a film of their enthralling relationship and achievements, the first being Charles Laughton and the young Anton Dolin in 1938 to be produced by Alexander Korda. Partly due to Korda's truly Hungarian inability to make up his mind, Laughton's nervous insecurity about everything he did and the slightly restricting existence of Nijinsky himself in England, the film was abandoned. In recent years Ken Russell has tried to set up another version with Paul Scofield as Diaghilev and Nureyev to dance and act Nijinsky, but backing was not forthcoming. In the eyes of many producers the subject is offbeat, non-commercial, and deeply suspect. It was Herbert Ross who broke the jinx. Unhappily, his film, *Nijinsky* (1980), contrived to please neither the film-goers nor the balletomanes.

† † †

Fans are often regarded as bad luck. Not, of course, the armies of enthusiasts who besiege the stage doors and pester their divinities for autographs in the street, but fan clubs, those highly organised societies with monthly letters, mailing lists, badges and membership branches all over the world. Fans like these are jealous, possessive and demanding: if the stars want to change their hair-styles, their clothing or their performances, if they wish to play comedy instead of drama, or to do Shakespeare instead of musicals, or to marry somebody unsuitable, then the loudest opposition will come from the fan clubs. In the bad old heyday of Hollywood, fans wielded a terrifying power over their divinities and many of the stars would not make any decision affecting their work until the fans had been consulted. Fans are avid for sensation and scandal; messy divorces, nervous breakdowns, contract-breaking and hell-raising are all grist to their mills. They are consumed by a terrible death wish and nothing less will satisfy them. 'They want me to die,' said Judy Garland with a flash of alarming foresight, 'they *want* me to die and they'll kill me if they can!' and obligingly she died, to the crocodile tears of her fans who had encouraged her drunken tantrums, her drug-ridden unpunctuality, and all the excesses of her unprofessional behaviour. Many stars have had a superstitious distaste of the whole sordid business and have refused, beyond coaxing, to have a fan club. Of course, the club can exist without the approval of the star but without some co-operation in way of an annual personal appearance at the fan club tea party or an occasional letter for the magazine, the club will not survive for long.

† † †

There appears to be a jinx on the part of Jesus Christ, and many actors consider it bad luck to play it; it's surprising how many actors can confirm this from their personal experience. Charles Houston, the English actor, is a case in point: in 1960 his career was shaping up nicely – leading parts in films and television and stage which were not only bringing in good money but giving him a good reputation. Then he played Jesus Christ in an old mediæval play which was filmed for television. The supporting cast boasted such names as Rupert Davies, Edward Woodward, Ewen Solon and Patrick Troughton. The performance was much admired and Charles Houston received a crop of excellent notices and then his career, instead of flowering, took a sudden nose-dive. The television offers suddenly stopped and three very important films in which he had good parts were all cancelled – the ill-fated *Cleopatra* was one of them. *He did not work for eighteen months.* It will be remembered that Jeffrey Hunter who played the part in a long-since-forgotten epic *King of Kings* died shortly after, and that Warner Baxter's career went into a decline after he played it in a famous silent version in the late twenties.

If there is an unlucky film, then it must surely be *The Exorcist.* The subject might well have caused alarm for the religious and the nervous, for it is the only film to date which deals with deadly seriousness and accuracy with the theme of diabolical possession and in the process spares the audience no physical detail however repulsive. It's history would have made Dracula smile: it was reported that everybody in the film was ill at some time, that the sets were all destroyed by fire involving cripplingly expensive rebuilding, that Jackie Magowran, the Irish actor, who played the sarcastic film producer, died mysteriously of a heart attack before they could film his death scene in the film, and that the sceptical producer, William Friedkin, was finally converted to a belief in the supernatural. With all these accidents, the eight weeks shooting schedule was dragged out to an agonising nine months. There is doubtless some compensation in the fantastic commercial success of the film which has broken all US box-office records and required no less than five West End cinemas to satisfy the demands of London filmgoers, (*The Godfather* had to make do with only four). It was threatened with legal action; it was denounced from TV studio to pulpit. The self-appointed moral guardians ran around like hysterical children screaming for it to be banned, thereby confirming the film publicity's chief pronouncement – that it had a disturbing effect on the feeble-minded, who should not be encouraged to see it. The full story behind the filming of *The Exorcist* will hopefully be told one day in all its fascinating horror, but it would seem that once again, as with *Macbeth*, bad luck and financial success go together, and that it is dangerous to dabble too deeply and too revealingly with the Devil's works.

3 · Theatrical Ghosts

The English theatres are happily well populated with ghosts for these old, creaking buildings provide the right atmosphere for their activities and a comfortable and suitable home for them. Most of these ghosts are benevolent, pleased to see visitors and view with apparent approval the entertainments and developments which they could never have anticipated in their lifetime, though it is interesting to speculate what the ghost of Mrs Siddons would think of *Oh, Calcutta!* or the ghost of Charles Kean of *Oklahoma*. Without doubt, the oldest ghost, the most famous, the most frequently seen and consequently the best documented is in the Theatre Royal, Drury Lane (known affectionately as the 'Lane' to theatregoers). The ghost is known as The Man in Grey and it must be stated firmly that he has no connection with Lady Eleanor Smith's famour Regency novelette, nor with the delightful and very successful film of the same name.

The Man in Grey has one curious habit which places him in a very different category from most other ghosts: he is a daytime ghost and only appears in the morning and afternoon. In addition he confines his activities to the upper circle; he appears at one end, goes through the bar at the rear, walks along the back of the circle and then vanishes into the opposite wall. In the rehearsals of a new show, he has occasionally been seen sitting down or standing at the rim gazing down at the stage, a silent, immobile grey figure. He had even been known to appear at matinées with an audience present. On these occasions not everybody sees him; some do and some don't, according to whether or not they're receptive to psychic phenomena. He has been seen by cleaners, attendants, barmen and various members of the theatre staff who have been up there. Most people do not realise that he is the ghost and assume that he is one of the actors or perhaps a costumed attendant, but if people go to the upper circle in the hope and expectation of seeing him, then he will not appear. Royal visits from the Queen, visits from TV companies doing a documentary on the theatre, radio writers, journalists and members of the Society for Psychical Research, all these are doomed to disappointment. The Man in Grey, though not shy of people, dislikes vulgar publicity and is no respecter of Royalty.

Nobody knows who he is or anything about him. Was he an actor? On the grounds of probability, it is thought he probably was not, for ghosts tend to haunt the place where they spent their lives and what is an actor doing spending his time in an upper circle? There is a theory that he was a young man-about-town who was in love with one of the actresses, spent his time watching her from the circle, antagonised her lover or her husband and was killed in a duel. For over two hundred years he has been seen and in 1850 there was a discovery which cast an interesting light on the matter. The theatre was being altered to accommodate more seats and a group of workmen, knocking down the right-hand wall of the circle found a little chamber. What they saw was worthy of any Regency novelette and a good example of life following literature: it was a skeleton (male) with a dagger stuck in the ribs, golden guineas on the floor and some playing cards. The skeleton was taken out and buried in consecrated ground just round the corner from the theatre; it was given a funeral service and the coroner's court brought in an open verdict.

I saw him once after a matinée of *No No Nanette* in the autumn of 1973. I had returned to collect my programme which I had forgotten. The circle was empty except for a man sitting at the other end in the front row gazing at the stage. I took no notice of him though I did notice that he wore a three-cornered hat and I assumed that one of the company had come to the front of the house and there was to be a rehearsal somewhere. As I collected my programme, I noticed that he stood up and walked up the stairs towards the exit on the other side of the theatre. He was of medium height, he wore a long grey cloak and a sword and his face was square-shaped, and finely chiselled. I left the circle, thinking no more of it, and half way down the stairs to the street, I suddenly realised that this was the famous Man in Grey, and that what I had seen perfectly tallied with the description I had read in various books and articles. I cursed myself for being so stupid and dashed up to see if I could catch a closer glimpse of him, but when I arrived panting back in the circle, he was gone and the circle was empty. Investigation has produced one intriguing fact – ten feet is about the closest anybody has come and anybody who tried to get any closer fails, for he just quietly vanishes.

He is a lucky mascot for if the show is going to be a success he will make an appearance during the rehearsal, and frequently during the prolonged dress rehearsal and throughout the run. The companies of *Oklahoma*, *Carousel*, *The King and I* and *My Fair Lady* all saw him and he has always been greatly loved and cherished by the companies and theatre staff. But if he doesn't appear, then the show will be a failure: he was, alas, conspicuously absent during the rehearsals and brief runs of *Pacific 1860* and *Plain and Fancy*.

The Man in Grey is not alone at the Theatre Royal. He has a number of colleagues who also appear from time to time there. The most striking of these, in both senses of the word, is a gentleman (one presumes it is a gentleman though with ghosts one can never be sure) who has never yet been seen but is tangible. Very tangible indeed. He is clearly a former actor because he confines his activities to the stage and the dressing-rooms and contrives to make his presence felt in many different ways. On first nights he goes to the dressing-rooms and helps the suffering actors on with their clothes. Many such, struggling with recalcitrant cloaks and dresses have felt a pair of hands help them; buttons and zips are efficiently done up, coats and jackets are gently placed on shoulders, dresses tied and ribboned at the back. In every case the actor or actresses says 'thank you' to what he imagines is the dresser, then turns round to find the dressing-room empty. The experience, they have all firmly stated, is a little puzzling but not frightening. The ghost produces an atmosphere of friendliness and affection. In the wings, the actor or actress is standing shivering nervously, waiting for the entrance. Suddenly they feel a reassuring pat on the back or a kiss on the neck. They turn round to acknowledge this gesture to find nobody there. The ghost clearly knows what we all go through on first nights and is anxious to help in any possible way. But his help is not limited to off-stage. The American actress, Betty-Jo Jones who was in the original *Oklahoma* company in 1947, told the theatre's publicity director, W. Macqueen Pope (author of many informative theatre books) that one evening she was playing a small scene upstage. It was a comedy scene, she herself was young and inexperienced and in addition, the wide-open spaces of the Lane are death to comedy. Suddenly she felt a pair of hands grip her and steer her, firmly but gently, down to the footlights. This is where she was forced to play out her scene, much to the bewilderment of the others on the stage. She was later asked for an explanation but nobody believed her when she told them what had actually happened. The second night the same thing happened; she was standing upstage ready to start her small comedy scene when the hands propelled her down the footlights and the scene which had been coldly received started to get laughter. The following night it happened again and with the confidence borne of experience she played her scene and was rewarded with a round of applause. From then on she invariably played that particular scene downstage with great success and the unseen hands were never felt again.

According to W. Macqueen Pope in his book *Pillars of Drury Lane* an actress called Doreen Duke experienced the unseen hands but over a much longer period of time. She felt them when she stepped onto the empty stage to audition for a part in *The King and I*. The hands were gentle and reassuring; her nerves vanished, she gave a good audition and got the part. Throughout the rehearsals the hands were in evidence, patting and stroking her in moments of tension, and on the first night they were there too, giving her reassurance when she most needed it.

Not that his activities are always so benevolent. Occasionally he

111

kicks actors in the seat of their trousers and quite violently, some-times in the wings, sometimes even on the stage. This seems to be confined to bad actors, or good actors giving bad performances when miscast, which isn't quite the same thing. This happened to Mr Beerbohm Tree in the 90s when he was giving a soliloquy from Falstaff at a Shakespearean Gala Matinée at the Lane. The kick was felt, and furthermore *seen* to be felt by a packed, royalty-studded audience, though it must be admitted that the sweating Mr Tree cleverly passed it off as part of the performance, a brilliant piece of comic mime. The incident was later reported to Sir Henry Irving that the Drury Lane ghost had kicked Mr Tree during his Falstaff soliloquy. 'That settles it,' said Sir Henry with gleeful sar-casm, 'the ghost isn't an actor, he's a critic!'

The ghost has had many further moments of mischief. Tony Britton who appeared in the 1973 production of *No No, Nanette* remembers a couple of amusing incidents: 'I actually had the tail of my jacket pulled when on stage and the other night he goosed a chorus girl within a few feet of where I was standing, and it *wasn't* me, honest!' Gloria Stuart of the *Oklahoma* company remembers that one Friday night when she had been paid she locked the money into a drawer in her dressing-room table, and locked the room before going onto the stage. She was absent for fifteen minutes with both keys in her pocket. When she returned after the performance the drawer was still locked but the money had gone. She searched the dressing-room high and low and then fetched the company manager. Together they searched the dressing-room again and then the money was discovered – in her handbag. Nobody could have got in, it was clearly not the work of mortal man, so it just had to be the ghost up to his tricks again. It was reported to Harry Price, ghostwatcher extraordinary who promised to investigate, saying that it was clearly a case of psychic transference, a familiar trick with poltergeists, if poltergeist it was.

Who is he? Who is the actor who knows about the art of comedy, is kind to beginners and has a violent, mischievous sense of humour? Experts have considered the matter and the most popular theory is Joseph Grimaldi, the most loved and most successful comedian of the Regency period, whose great career centred round the Lane. He would certainly have administered punishment to a posturing actor: he would undoubtedly have steered a talented but inexperienced young girl to a favourable position: he would have been delighted to have hidden a pay-packet, and beyond question he would have goosed a chorus-girl.

Other ghosts have been seen in the theatre. In 1900, two old ladies were sitting in two gangway stalls during a sparsely attended matinée. They noticed an old man sitting at the end of the row next to the wall. He was dressed in early nineteenth century clothes, had white hair, and a square, pale face. Their attention was distracted by the play and when they looked back he had vanished. This startled them because he had not passed them, nor could he have climbed over the seats to the exit and there was no other way. Later, they compared their memories with a portrait in the Garrick Club and discovered that it was Charles Kean who had died some thirty years earlier. In 1937 an actor called Clifford Heatherley appeared briefly as Henry VIII's ghost in a musical called *Crest of the Wave* by Ivor Novello. Soon after the opening, he died during a mid-week matinée and instructions were given that, until a replacement could be found, the short scene would be cut. That night the ghost of Henry VIII did appear and it was not the understudy. The horrified and astonished company were prepared to swear that it was Clifford Heatherley himself. In 1960 during the run of *Camelot*, Elizabeth Larner returned to her dressing-room in the interval to find a tall stately lady in the armchair. She assumed that it was a new dresser but when the lady rose revealing a dark eighteenth century dress and cloak and then proceeded to vanish through the wall, she realised that she certainly wasn't. Her description tallied with the portrait in the National Gallery. It was Mrs Siddons whose uniquely distinguished career as England's greatest tragedienne had centred round the Theatre Royal.

The ghost of Ivor Novello is supposed to haunt the Palace Theatre, London. This is where his last musical *King's Rhapsody* was playing when he died of a heart attack in 1950 and the theatre is always associated with his memory. Nobody claims to have actually seen him, but his spirit has been felt as when a young actress recently auditioning for a part in *Jesus Christ Superstar* prayed out loud to him as she stood trembling in the wings. Her reward was not only to get the part of Mary but also his dressing-room.

Sir Alec Guinness was supposed to have seen the ghost of Shakespeare sitting in the stalls on the first night of his ill-starred 1951 *Hamlet* who supposedly got up and walked out in the middle of the performance. The press played this story up in a big way and it has since appeared in magazines and books dealing with the occult. I wrote to Sir Alec for confirmation and discovered from him that the whole story rose from a little misunderstanding. What he said to his fellow-actor in the interval was not that he had seen Shakespeare get up and leave but that he had seen somebody *looking* like Shakespeare. The mysterious stranger turned out later to be Somerset Maugham.

The ghost of Dylan Thomas has recently been seen at the Bush Theatre. This is a little fringe theatre formerly a BBC rehearsal room and it occupies premises above the Shepherd's Bush Hotel. A documentary play about Thomas was being rehearsed by the author, actor Michael Mundell, and six colleagues. One evening after a late-night rehearsal they locked up and remembered that they had been observed by a man who had stood silently at the back of the theatre. They went back to fetch him but he wasn't there and there was no trace of him anywhere and all the exit doors were locked. He was described later as plump, podgy-faced, about forty and with dark curly hair, a description which perfectly fitted the Welsh poet. The Shepherd's Bush Hotel was where Thomas used to go regularly for his drinks after working at Lime Grove Television Studios round the corner.

The ghost of William Terriss haunts London's Adelphi Theatre in the Strand. He was the darling of the late Victorian theatre, a handsome, charming lively actor who had learned his trade in Irving's company at the Lyceum and had enjoyed a highly privileged position there. Irving was very fond of him and allowed familiarities and impertinencies from him which were unthinkable from anybody else. Ellen Terry, in her letters to Shaw, said that, 'Terriss could do no wrong, the Chief lets him get away with anything.' There was one occasion illustrating this, which was told and retold throughout London's clubs and green rooms, the night he stole Irving's limelight. In those star-ridden and totally undemocratic days, the star actor performed in the unwinking glare of an individual spotlight which followed him round and concentrated on him even if he was doing nothing, while the supporting company would act themselves into a stupor in the dim twilight around him. (This truly abominable custom has long since been abolished in England but sadly survives in America with the big musicals.) The supporting company would grumble but the custom was sanctioned by centuries of theatrical tradition and there was really nothing they could do about it. Terriss thought otherwise. He went to Irving and asked if he could have a spot once in a while. Irving refused. Terriss renewed his request. Irving refused again. The defeat rankled and one evening he took action. The play that night was *Louis XI*, a mindless melodrama by one of Irving's tame pets, whose worthlessness was redeemed only by Irving's extraordinarily malevolent performance of the evil hunchbacked king (a dry run for his famous Richard III) and the rivetting death scene which ended the play. Terriss, in the small part of Louis's bastard son and successor, was doomed to stand motionless by the death bed while Irving writhed and groaned and screeched in his death agonies. One evening he went to the light-operator. 'The Guvnor says to put the spot on me,' he said. The man was incredulous; such a thing had never happened in all his years at the Lyceum, but Terriss, who was nothing if not persuasive, eventually convinced him that the order had indeed come from Irving. That night Irving played his death agonies in darkness while Terriss, registering nameless emotions, stood bathed in light and enjoyed himself hugely. Afterwards, the storm broke; Terriss, his guilt established, was summoned to Number One Dressing-Room for a either a severe reprimand or dismissal or possibly both. In fact he got neither; accurately assessing the situation he flung his arms open and assumed an expression of deep contrition. 'I'm sorry, Guvnor,' he said, 'but you see, *it was the only chance I had!*' It was a crafty piece of flattery for the implied compliment was not lost on Irving who smiled, and relaxed. 'Don't do it again, m'boy,' was his answer and with that the incident was closed.

A few years later, in 1890, Terriss left the Lyceum and went into management on his own. He took a lease on the Adelphi and launched a season of popular romances and melodramas. Seven years of financial success and popular acclaim followed. The girls and middle-aged women welcomed his arrival on the scene of the commercial theatre and although the term was not to be invented for another twenty years, he was, in fact, the first matinée idol. He was also a very good actor, critics liked him and older theatregoers, while sometimes shaking grey heads over his choice of plays, responded to his charm and personality.

And then in 1897, he decided to present a melodramatic thriller called *Secret Service*. In the company was an actor called Richard Prince, who was that very sad person, a very bad actor who believed himself to be a very good one. His status in the company was a very humble one, little more than a walk-on with a couple of unimportant lines but he fancied himself in the leading part and considered himself better than Terriss. He even learned it and asked permission to understudy it, but the company manager sensibly decided that he was not good enough even for this – one day he might have to play it and the public deserved something for their money. The rejection hurt Prince very much and he began to brood miserably on his predicament. This is where the situation took a very unhappy turn: he confided his feelings to his fellow actors. He told them that he was a great actor and that he should be playing the star part and that he felt that only Terriss's obstinacy stood in his way of success. His colleagues, with unbelievable cruelty and thoughtlessness, encouraged his delusions and even added to them. Terriss was jealous, they said. He knew that Prince was a better actor and he was scared of giving him his chance for fear that his own status might be imperilled. If it wasn't for Terriss he, Prince, would be a star, and girls would queue up for his autograph and he too would be invited to dine with Royalty and he would have his photo in front of the theatre. In dressing-room and pub they talked to him and fed his self-pitying fantasies. Doubtless they considered it a huge joke and in all fairness to them (their names are unknown but the responsibility for what happened is largely theirs), they did not intend it to be taken seriously and could have had no possible suspicion of the effect it was having on the unhappy Prince nor of its outcome. The psychological torture continued week after week. Nightly, Terriss received his standing ovation and nightly Prince writhed in jealous fury in the wings, watching the charlatan and imposter (as he had privately denounced him) receive the applause to which he was not entitled. Only Terriss stood in his way to success. Terriss must go.

What aggravated the situation was that Terriss, being totally unaware of his feelings, was extremely kind to him. Terriss, like all the actor-managers of the day, looked after his company with a benevolent paternalism. He sent them presents on birthdays and wedding anniversaries, took them out for supper and pre-performance drinks, chatted to them amiably in the wings and made it clear that he regarded them as friends and not merely employees. Prince was no exception. Terriss sent him a birthday card, invited him out to supper at Rules Restaurant and even invited him, with a couple of others, to Sunday lunch at home. From Prince's point of view, it was insufferable that he should endure such patronage.

It was the night of Friday, 16 December 1897. Terriss had been enjoying his usual pre-performance pint of champagne and dozen oysters at Rules with his son-in-law Seymour Hicks who had married his daughter, Ellaline and was appearing in *The Gaiety Girl* at the Gaiety Theatre opposite the Adelphi. The parted for their respective theatres at seven, Seymour Hicks down the alley way to the Strand and Terriss along the dimly-lit Maiden Lane to the stage-door of the Adelphi. Just before he reached it, Prince leapt at him and stabbed three times with a knife which he had, it was later established, bought only that afternoon. Terriss sank to the ground bleeding profusely from a chest wound and was carried inside to his dressing-room by the theatre staff. Seymour Hicks, hearing shouts and screams ran back, heard the news, rushed inside the theatre to find his father-in-law lying on the couch with his leading lady, Jessie Milward, weeping loudly and cradling the dying man in her arms. Just before he died he was heard to whisper 'I shall come back,' and a minute later, 'Can any man be so foolish as to believe that there is no afterlife?'

Prince had remained at the stage door flourishing his knife. The police arrived and had no trouble in seizing him and dragging him off to Bow Street Police Station round the corner. He was tried, found guilty of wilful murder and since he was clearly insane, sent to Broadmoor Criminal Lunatic Asuylum. By a curious twist of fate, the theatrical success he so keenly desired was later achieved for he became the leading light of the prison drama group and amongst the plays which he presented and starred in was *Secret Service*. Throughout his forty years imprisonment, he never gave any trouble and died in 1937 at the age of 81 and was greatly mourned by his colleagues.

During the following years, a great many strange things happened at the Adelphi. The ghost of Terriss kept his word and did come back, not once but many times. Many people have seen the tall, well-dressed man in frock-coat and top hat with walking stick stand outside the stage door, walk through and down the corridors, pass through the locked door into the dressing-room which he formerly occupied. The stage-hands see him standing in the wings, the electricians see him walk across the footlights into the empty auditorium, the tickets-ushers see him go through the empty lobby into the street. He never does anything, he never speaks or even stops. He just passes by and vanishes. Inevitably, it is assumed that his a member of the company, or a member of the theatre staff with an old fashioned taste in clothes. Only when they see a photo of Terriss do they recognise him, or when they enquire from older members of the theatre staff who then tell them who it is. Various disturbing occult happenings have been reported ... lights which come up and down, changes in temperature from very hot to very cold within the space of a single minute, green lights hovering above dressing-room tables, and a lift which behaves in a very peculiar manner with nobody in it.

More disturbing is the behaviour of the couch in Terriss's former dressing-room which has been known to bump up and down, to roam round the room while strange footsteps and rappings are heard in the empty corridor. More than one leading lady occupying Dressing-Room No. 1 has experienced these alarming things. But most disturbing of all is the appearance of Terriss on the platform of Charing Cross Underground Station where in his lifetime he would frequently wait for a train, after a convivial meal at Rules, the last train which was in those days considerably later than it is now.

From time to time various peculiar occult incidents are reported and discussed in pub, club and green room. Hersey Piggot, a well-known West End dresser, once worked at the Piccadilly Theatre in 1970 dressing Sarah Miles who was playing Mary Queen of Scots in her husband's play *Vivat, Vivat Regina*. She had a series of beautiful and dazzling costumes and one very quick change, from a cream-and-red creation to a dark brown riding habit. Three people were involved in this change which had to be done in slightly under a minute. To make it possible, Hersey used to unbutton it in advance, and before she left for the theatre at night, she would put it thus in the wardrobe in Sarah Miles' dressing-room. One night, when the quick change came, she discovered to her annoyance that the buttons were done up. The change took a little longer that evening. Hersey enquired angrily round the stage-staff but nobody knew anything about it. The following night it happened again; suspicion naturally fell on the cleaners but they too denied all knowledge. That night she and Sarah Miles placed the unbuttoned dress into the wardrobe, locked it and then the dressing-room and took both keys with her. Nobody could have gone in but nevertheless the dress was buttoned up as usual when they arrived at the theatre the following evening. Clearly something supernatural was in the air, but what? Or who? Sarah Miles had a sad theory. 'It must be the ghost of Mary Queen of Scots haunting me,' she said laughing. 'Perhaps she doesn't like the play – or my performance!' This aggravation continued for a week and then finished and there was no further trouble.

Another piece of clothing which provided a rather more disturbing occult experience turned up at the Duke of York's Theatre during the run of a play called *The Queen Came By*. It was a little black bolero jacket originally made for a production of *Charley's Aunt* before World War I and hired from one of the big West End costumiers. It became known as The Strangler and there was undoubtedly a curse on it. A number of women in the company wore it in their turn and each time there was unpleasantness. Firstly, the play's star, Thora Hird, complained that it was too tight, even though it had been comfortable at the original fitting, and that it became tighter every time she wore it. Three other women wore it and all of them experienced not only a feeling of tightness and suffocation but a sensation of fear and trembling as if something exceedingly nasty was about to happen to them, such feelings vanishing the minute they took it off. A fourth, Mrs Frederick Piffard, wife of the producer, discovered to her alarm that she had red weals all over her throat as if somebody had been trying to strangle her. The matter was reported to occult-minded friends who arranged to have a seance inside the theatre with the jacket placed before them. The mystery was solved: from the proceedings, a clear picture of the terrible events emerged. The coat, it seemed, had originally belonged to a young actress who had aroused the jealous hostility of her boy-friend; he had attacked her in the theatre one evening, strangled her, placed her body in a barrel and thrown it into the river, another remarkable example of how evil lives on after death not only in places and people but also in objects. Peter Underwood, whose well-researched book *Haunted London* is probably the definitive treatment of the subject, discovered that the jacket subsequently became the property of a Californian gentleman named Lloyd. He, his wife, their daughter and a number of others all tried on the jacket and all of them felt faint, frightened and strangled.

No less alarming was the incident at the Theatre Royal, Margate, a late eighteenth century gem and one of the oldest theatres in England. Bernard Archard remembers acting in a play there, supposedly a comedy; there was one particular line which he and his colleague in the scene though was very funny but they never got a laugh. Nightly, they would try different inflections, different facial expressions, different bits of supporting funny business. All useless. The audience obstinately refused to laugh. One evening, in desperation, they decided to stay behind after the performance for an extra rehearsal. Privacy was essential, so when the company had gone home, they locked up the theatre, searched everywhere to check that there was nobody around and no chance of anybody sneaking in, and then went onto the stage. By the light of a single

120

Bernard Archard, he was frightened out of his life by ghostly laughter in an empty theatre.

working bulb which cast eerie shadows on the bare wooden boards, they ran the scene. When Bernard Archard said the line, with an entirely new inflexion he'd just thought of, a loud and long laugh suddenly echoed throughout the theatre from somebody, apparently, seated in the front of the dress circle. 'The effect was indescribably frightening,' he later said. 'We dropped everything and ran to the circle but there was nobody there. We searched the theatre from top to bottom but it was empty and all the doors were locked.' Considerably shaken by the incident, they decided to abandon the rehearsal and went home. The following evening the recalcitrant line *did* get a laugh, a very good one, and so it continued to do every night they played the comedy. Supernatural approval of his comedy timing had clearly given Bernard Archard the confidence he needed, but who was it who laughed?

The popular theory is that is must have been the ghost of Sarah Thorne, the elderly Victorian matriarch who mananged if for a period of years in the mid-nineteenth century and who also founded a drama school. Many people working there have seen a dim grey figure glide down a corridor, or stand in the corner of what is now the dress circle bar but which used to be her office. The gaunt acquiline features they can dimly see match up neatly with the portrait of her standing in the theatre lobby. The odd behaviour of the theatre lights has also beeen laid at her door. One evening in the middle fifties, Stanley Mills, the stage-manager locked up the dress circle where the lighting switchboard was kept, locked up the theatre and went home. In the small hours of the morning the police summoned him. It seemed that the front and back doors of the theatre were wide open and the theatre was flooded with light. On investigation it was discovered that although the light switches had all been turned down to ON, the door of the lighting switchboard was still locked. It was all very strange and it was generally decided that a supernatural or occult force was the only explanation.

Sarah Thorne had certainly chosen a very suitable venue for her activities and her perambulations as I discovered when I played there for a season of weekly rep in the winter of 1954. It had a truly delightful atmosphere where any ghost would feel at home ... creaking wooden corridors, a crazy, crumbling attic which was my dressing-room accessible by a ladder, cobweb-filled cellars, a warren of rooms, passages, and unexpected little nooks and niches weaving their tortuous way round the place. One afternoon I came early to the theatre. There was an excellent Bechstein piano in the pit and I wanted to make a little music and thus put myself into the right mood for that evening's performance of *Ring Round The Moon*. I changed into the Butterfly Collector's check suit and went to the pit and started to play. I remember that I started with the D Flat *Etude* of Liszt and followed this with a Schubert *Impromptu*. Then I started to play the E Major Study of Chopin, the popular one which is (regrettably) known to some as a wartime swing-tune under the title of *So Deep Is The Night*. I had played a few bars and suddenly the temperature which had been cool but not cold, suddenly became very cold indeed. It was as if somebody had opened a door on a freezing night. I looked around but all doors were closed and in any case it was a fine spring day. Shivering, but unsuspicious, I continued to play. Then I heard a voice saying very quietly just behind me, 'No, not that.' I turned round very quickly but there was nobody there. The stalls were empty. I looked nervously around but there was no sign of anybody. I shrugged my shoulders thinking I must have just imagined it and continued to play the same piece. Suddenly the temperature dropped even lower and I started to shiver and I had the strongest feeling that somebody was standing right behind me. I began to feel frightened and then I heard the voice again saying, with a touch of real urgency, 'No, NO!' Once again I turned round and once again there was nobody but this time I distinctly saw a formless shapeless light hovering over the stalls about ten feet away from me. I was too frightened to run away or make any move, I just stood there shivering, my eyes glued onto this shapeless dim light. Then the idea suddenly came into my head that I was in danger unless I started to play again and something different. By a supreme effort of will I forced myself to sit down at the piano and I started to play, this time the second movement of the *Pathetique* Sonata. It was a happy choice for within the space of half a minute the temperature not only returned to normal but actually became warmer than it had been, as if somebody had switched on the heating. I stopped trembling, my feelings of fear vanished and were replaced by a surge of happiness and pleasure. I finished the movement and then looked round. The light had vanished, the presence had gone, but did I hear, or did I only *imagine* I heard, a soft voice saying, 'Thank you'?

I can offer no sensible explanation for all this. Whether this was the ghost of Sarah Thorne or not is a matter for speculation but for lack of any other claimant (and none has been seen or felt), she must take the responsibility. From this, one gathers that she liked Beethoven and hated Chopin but why this tender, lyrical piece should have aroused such fierce emotions, it is impossible to say. Perhaps in her lifetime she associated it with the death of somebody close to her, or some tragedy in the theatre. Maybe it was used in a play which had been a disastrous failure (this can affect you for life; to this day, and for that reason, I can't listen to the overture to *The Force of Destiny* without shuddering) or maybe she herself was playing it when something terrible happened. Whatever the reason, the piece seems to have a definite curse on it inside that theatre, and while I was there I never touched the piano again.

The other invisible ghost is in the Haymarket Theatre Royal. This is one of the most beautiful theatres in the world, old, atmospheric, rich in tradition and success, full of long creaking wooden corridors, hidden doorways, a warren of carpeted staircases leading to hidden offices and dressing-rooms. A unique and enchanting theatre where it is a pleasure and privilege to play and work. The ghost is seldom seen. He opens and shuts doors. He walks up and down the corridors when the theatre is empty. He will sometimes cast a shadow as he walks. He will sometimes enter the dressing-room on the stage level and sit down and just gaze at the occupant who might be resting, entertaining his friends or preparing for the play. Peter Barkworth who occupied this dressing-room, Number One, which has a connecting door onto the stage (no longer used), felt an unseen presence on a number of occasions when he was resting between the performances after a mid-week matinée. It was decidedly eerie when he rested with the lights out so he always kept them on. Others who have had this room have stated that on occasions they felt that someone was in the room watching them.

The ghost is Mr John Buckstone, longtime manager of the Theatre from 1853-1878. He was Queen Victoria's favourite manager as the Haymarket was her favourite theatre. Many times he sat with her in her Royal Box and the first recorded appearance after his death was in 1880 when he was seen sitting in the Royal Box. Many people during the last century have seen him, firemen, stage door keepers, cleaners, and commissionaires. The experience of a wardrobe mistress can be taken as typical. The play was *Hadrian VII* with actors dressed up as cardinals and popes and other colourful characters. One evening the wardrobe mistress was ironing in her room and she heard a knock. 'Come in and sit down, dear,' she said, 'shan't be a moment.' She assumed it was an actor come to fetch a piece of his costume and was a little surprised when there was no answer. She turned round and there was a man in mid-Victorian costume which was not the period of the play. 'What are you wearing?' she said, 'what's all this about?' The man turned and smiled and then moved away out of her sight and when she looked out into the corridor it was empty. Later, she was drinking in the Buckstone Club which lies in the basement of a house opposite the stage door. Hanging on the wall of an inner room was a large engraving of the man she had seen. The resemblance was startling. It was Mr Buckstone.

The ghost of Mr Buckstone is above all a friendly one and Peter Underwood who has gathered a great deal of fascinating information on the subject in his book *Haunted London* is of the opinion that happiness and love over a long period of time in life can produce a ghost after death as is clearly the case here. Mr Buckstone loved his theatre and was greatly loved by his actors, many of whom have had very kind things to say about him in their memoirs and reminiscences. Mrs Stuart Watson, the former chairman and managing director, had an office which used to be Buckstone's dressing-room. It is here that the feeling of his presence is strongest – his footsteps on the carpet, his hand opening the door, and on occasions his hand to rummage about a cupboard or to turn the pages of a book which was once his. 'I'm no longer frightened of him,' she used to say to enquirers. 'He was happy here and if I feel he's in the room I'll make him welcome. I wouldn't do anything to hurt or scare him.'

† † †

American Theatres don't provide such a happy home for ghosts as they are all so new, the oldest being Ford's Theatre in Washington, little more than a hundred years old, where as every American schoolboy knows, Abraham Lincoln was shot. Nevertheless, a few ghosts do survive into the twentieth century. The Belasco is undoubtedly haunted by the ghost of its namesake and creator, David Belasco, that supreme arch-poseur who decorated his rooms like a monastery and habitually wore a monk's habit. Actors from time to time have seen him sitting in his favourite stage box, dimly visible behind the curtains, his white hair, bald head and monk's cowl easily recognisable. And at eleven o'clock at night, when the theatre is empty the lift can be heard whirring and creaking its way up to his rooms at the top of the theatre. Yet the lift is lying at the bottom of the shaft, its cable long since snapped, rusty and immobile. At nights when there is nobody there, laughter can be heard, singing, footsteps, door opening and shutting and – most

125

eerily of all – the front curtain mysteriously rises, hovers and then lowers.

A number of other rather sinister happenings have been recorded. From time to time, the ghost of a tightrope walker can be seen in the Palace Theatre in New York swinging away from the dress circle rim. People watching through the peephole in the curtain before the audience is admitted have seen him, seen the death fall and heard a shrill cry of pain and fear. It happened in the 30s and his name was Louis Borsalino, part of a vaudeville acrobat team called The Four Casting Pearls. He was taken to the Flower Hospital and died shortly after. The tragedy cast a distinct gloom over the theatre thereafter and it is regarded, understandably, as a sign of very bad luck if you see his ghost or hear the ghostly death-scream.

Jay Fox, director and choreographer, has recorded a very peculiar occult experience. A few summers ago he was setting up a musical version of the life of Harry Houdini. From the start, he remembers, everything went wrong; there were money problems, backers backed in and then backed out and it was difficult to raise the necessary money. Casting problems abounded with the right people accepting and then walking out in favour of better-paid jobs, plus the perennial difficulty of finding performers who could sing, dance and act all equally well. There were script problems, with a long, complex life to be honed down into a two-and-half hour show, plus technical problems of how to put on the stage, without too much risk to the star, all the terrifying feats which Houdini actually did. The early rehearsals took place in a little theatre in the country and these were hectic traumatic days. One day, it was suggested that they use a ouija board to see if they could establish some sort of contact with the Fates, to find out if there was any help they could get from the Other World. They did so and the message came back loud and clear '*I'll send a sign*'. After the depression and gloom this lifted their spirits and rehearsals continued in an atmosphere of optimism. One evening they decided to decorate the outside of the theatre with strips of tinfoil. A wind came along from nowhere which mystified them for it was a sunny day. The strips of tinfoil were rearranged and to their astonished

126

eyes began to form themselves into the shape of a big 'H'. Houdini. Harry Houdini was trying to get in touch and trying to tell them that everything was going to be alright and that he was taking a personal interest in the project. The opening performances took place in a private house called Wheatleigh owned by an old lady called Stephanie Barber. During the performances, a trunk used for Houdini's escape suddenly revealed a large 'H' painted on the front. It had not been there before and nobody had any idea who had done it. Another sign. The performances were a great success and made a lot of money, though, unhappily, it has not yet arrived on Broadway.

The old Met was a house which attracted every sort of human excess as an International Opera House rightly should, and it should, and did, provide the right atmosphere for a ghost. During the final years of that wonderful old echoing gilded house, there was a stately old dowager who occupied a seat in what Americans insist on calling the Parterre and which the English have always called the Orchestra Stalls. She sat at the end of the row and provided an endless distraction for her immediate neighbours by loud tut-tuts of disapproval, shakes of her over-bejewelled head, clucking and audible comments of disparagement whenever the current soprano was singing her aria. She invariably vanished after the first act never to reappear until the next evening, leaving behind an empty stall. One evening a woman sitting nearby became seriously annoyed. Her attempts to shut the woman up being unsuccessful, she went to the Head Usher and reported the facts to him. The Head Usher was deeply embarrassed and was unable to suggest a satisfactory method of dealing with the nuisance, whereupon one of the Directors of the Met took the lady aside, bought her a glass of sherry and explained to her in confidence that this was the ghost of the late Mme Frances Alda, the ex Mrs Gatti Cazzaza (former director of the Met) who apparently made it a practice in her lifetime of turning up whenever any of her favourite operas were being performed for the express purpose of making life difficult for the soprano, and found she was unable to stop the habit after her death. She was seen many times by the old-time regulars of the old Met, but has not been seen in the new building in the

Lincoln Centre. It has been suggested that the prices are too high.

Fifty years ago, a women ran down the centre aisle of the Avon Theatre, Utica, NY, and shot the pipe organist dead. It seemed that the man had been cheating on his wife and she took the time-honoured way out of the problem. From then on, until its demolition just after the War in 1947, the theatre was haunted. Night-porters and passing dustmen would testify that the organ would rise out of the pit at midnight and play itself with no human hands on the keys; the theatre would be filled with sinister organ music which would stop as soon as somebody entered the theatre. From then onwards, it was exceedingly difficult to find coloured people to work in the theatre in any capacity, and many superstitious whites would also refuse employment. Mrs Ruby L. Betts, who worked there shortly after the murder, is of the opinion that the whole affair could have been an elaborate practical joke on the part of the local electrician. As this is true of so many hauntings, the matter remains undecided.

As already mentioned every American schoolboy knows – and a few English ones also – that Abraham Lincoln, the sixteenth President of the United States of America was assassinated at Ford's Theatre, Washington on 4 April 1865 by a none-too-successful actor from a famous theatrical family, John Wilkes Booth. The facts, should any schoolboy not know them, are that he broke into the Presidential Box, emptied his gun, a Derringer, into Lincoln's head, and made his escape by leaping over the rim of the box onto the stage and running diagonally across it, out of the stage door and into the street. He was later found hiding in a barn and was shot to pieces by the vengeful military.

The theatre was never demolished but it fell into disuse a few years later and was allowed to stand empty for a whole century, a classic example of the primeval curse in action. But in 1968, the Ford's Theatre Society restored it both as a museum of assassination souvenirs and theatricalia, and partly as a working, practical theatre. Does the ghost of Booth haunt the theatre? Logically speaking, if there is a ghost, it should be Lincoln's who was killed there rather than his assassin who died several miles away. Certainly there is an occult presence. Many have felt and heard it. Once again there emerges the familiar pattern of footsteps in the empty theatre, lights coming on and off, curtains rising and lowering without human hands, strange voices, laughing and crying. One stage-hand was so frightened by these, while changing to go home, that he ran out into the street wearing only his underpants. He was not arrested.

Supporters of the ghost theory find some confirmation in one rather peculiar fact. The spirit of evil definitely does survive even a century of disuse and darkness. When Booth ran zig-zag diagonally across the stage, scattering terrified actors on both sides he left behind an occult aura which has been felt. Actors standing on, or even close to, this occult line have been affected in very definite and disturbing ways. They feel sick and nervous: they tremble, they forget their lines, they even forget where they are and what play they are supposed to be doing. Hal Holbrook, performing his famous Mark Twain recital, and Jack Aaronson in an evening of Herman Melville, have both testified to a sudden and terrifying drop of temperature as they crossed the line of evil. A photo of the empty house taken just after the assassination by Matthew Brady reveals a transparent figure standing inside the Presidential Box. Pamela M. Larratt, who has recounted these enthralling facts in the *Players Club* magazine, says: 'To the show business end of the theater, the suggestible horror of it all seems a welcome idea. To the untheatrical the question of Booth's ghost is something they don't want to contemplate.'

† † †

The strangest occult experience in the annals of Broadway happened to Guthrie McClintie. He has described it with a wealth of colourful and circumstantial detail in his excellent memoirs, and the story – which is a good one – has been told and re-told and has doubtless gained in the telling. The facts are simply as follows: he was a starving young actor in 1909 who had left his home and family in Seattle to take up a theatrical career strictly against the wishes of his father, a man who was as strict in his outlook and prejudices as Mr Edward Moulton-Barrett, a gentleman who was to play a not unimportant part in McClintie's later life. He enrolled in the New York Academy of Dramatic Art and found excessively cheap lodgings at $3.50 weekly in the apartment of a Texan gentlewoman, Mrs Heinsohn.

When he finished his course he embarked on a long period of further training – being out of work, continually frustrated and nearly starving, a familiar and indispensable part of an actor's experience. With him it was a little worse than with some, he worked only five weeks in the first year which is a very low figure even for 1909; the two productions concerned toured briefly but didn't get to Broadway, another familiar story. One day he was sitting in Central Park feeling very sorry for himself when he learned from another youthful actor, similarly circumstanced, that the great Winthrop Ames was casting for a new musical, *Prunella*. Ames was then at the height of his fame as Broadway's richest, busiest and most powerful producer, and to work with him was regarded not only as a privilege but also a lifelong meal-ticket. He went without further delay to the Ames office only to learn that the great man was out of town, but that his manager, Mr Foster Platt, would deal with applicants in his place. Platt was a tall, thin, forbidding personality who took a sadistic relish in intimidating the young actors who appeared before him. The interview was bleak, embarrassing and unsuccessful; Platt said that there was nothing he could offer and indicated that the meeting was over. McClintie was shaking with nerves and confusion as he stood up and in attempting to shake hands he accidentally knocked over a bottle of ink which spilt all over the desk and its papers. 'Get out, Mr McClintie,' shouted Platt in a cold fury, '*Get out at once!*' Out he went, trembling in distress and mortification. He went to a nearby hotel, sat down in the lobby and without thinking of the possible consequences he wrote an angry letter to the absent Winthrop Ames. He was in a fighting mood, the letter seethed with bitter invective and it was – as he later recalled – a masterpiece of invective. He accused him of treating his actors badly, of neglecting keen young American talent in favour of foreigners (Ames's pro-British policies were notorious on Broadway) and of employing ill-mannered, underlings like Mr Foster Platt. As a postscript he offered his services and generously dwelt on his views on theatrical production. When he had written the letter, which covered several pages, his temper had cooled off considerably, and he decided not to post the letter – yet. He put it in his pocket and returned to his lodgings. When he arrived he put the letter in a drawer and forgot all about it.

Five weeks and two dozen unsuccessful interviews later, he returned home, tired and depressed, to be greeted by Mrs Heinsohn in a state of great excitement.'Come into my room,' she said, 'the table wants to speak to you.' Mrs Heinsohn had the old widow's usual keen interest in the occult; she dabbled in table-rapping and spiritualism and passed onto her friends what she sincerely believed to be messages from the spirit world. That evening, the table had rapped out McClintie's name. He went with her and the seance began. It took a long time but the message which the table eventually rapped out made little sense at first: 'Mail that which you have written your entire future depends on it.' What had he written? He didn't know, he couldn't remember. And then he realised. It was the letter still lying in his trunk upstairs. He rushed to his room, took the letter, addressed and stamped it, ran out into the street and posted it. Three days later he received a letter from Winthrop Ames himself, inviting him for an interview. The upshot was an offer to stage manage at $25 weekly, a new play *Her Own Money* to be directed by the ink-splattered George Foster Platt. This lead to further engagements with Ames who finally put him on a permanent contract as his personal assistant. Fourteen months after he entered on the place and dignity of his new position and with a strangely ironic twist, he found himself occupying the same ink-splattered desk as Mr Foster Platt. Ten years later, Ames offered him money with which to produce a play on his own. He chose *The Dover Road* which was a huge success, so in 1924, after eleven years, he was an independent producer. A little later he married the most beautiful, admired and talked-of young actress, Katherine Cornell and thus one of the great inter-war theatrical partnerships was formed. They moved into a beautiful house on Beekman Place and before long he found himself one of the richest men on Broadway. And all because of a letter written and posted in – of all lucky years – 1913!

He lost touch with Mrs Heinsohn, the unconscious architect of his success, but she did not lose touch with him. Once again the occult powers she possessed, came to his aid. In 1932 he was attempting to produce and direct his wife in *The Barretts of Wimpole Street*. The play is regarded as a modern classic and it is difficult to realise how little faith the American theatre had in it. No less than twenty-eight Broadway producers turned it down before McClintie bought it; after a week Cornell decided that the part was not for her and asked to be released from it, and in the anxious process she went down with a bad dose of 'flu. It was a very tense worrying time for him as not only his professional reputation was in the balance but a great deal of his money. He was on the verge of giving it up when a mysterious telephone call came from Mrs Heinsohn who had long since moved out of New York into some unspecified place in the country. 'Don't worry about a thing,' she said firmly, and without preliminary explanation. 'You're going to have your greatest success ever,' and with that she rang off. Puzzled, depressed, but hopeful, he decided much against his better judgement to go ahead with the production. His better judgement turned out to be distinctly at fault, for *The Barretts of Wimpole Street* was a huge success and gave them both their greatest theatrical triumph to date. The rest is history.

The last episode in this very odd occult experience was in 1937 when he was producing *Jezebel* starring the irrepressible Tallulah Bankhead. A phone call from Mrs Heinsohn put the whole matter into perspective. 'Miss Bankhead will never play the part, you're wasting your time, and the show will be a flop. Forget it!' This time he decided to ignore her, his better judgement telling him that even table-rapping has its limits, but once again his better judgement was at fault. Tallulah had to leave the play with a bad peritoneal infection (even her diseases were exotic; nobody had caught *that* since Valentino) and the part was taken over by Miriam Hopkins. It ran for a week and gave McClintie one of the few real failures of his distinguished career.

He enquired after Mrs Heinsohn and made many attempts to find her for future reference, but he never saw her or heard from her again.

4 · The Curse of Macbeth

These superstitions between them cover an impressively wide range of human insecurity and incredulity. Not all theatre people will believe in all, but most will believe in some, for there are superstitions to suit all tastes. But these are merely the *hors d'oeuvre* before the joint; there is one superstition so old, so all-consuming, so intimidating, that just about everybody in the theatre believes it, however cynical, materialistic or hard-boiled he is, and who can blame him for the evidence is well-nigh overwhelming, and indisputable? This is the superstition about *Macbeth*.

Macbeth is the unlucky play of the theatre and has for four hundred years carried in its wake a truly terrifying trail of disaster and bad luck. The play is cursed and the curse is so strong that it is considered very unlucky to quote from it while inside a theatre. Actors are frightened even to mention it by name: if it must be discussed, and this is in itself is not encouraged, then it must be done in a roundabout way and over the years an interesting vocabulary of evasion has gained acceptance. It is talked about as *That Play*, or *The Scottish Play* or *The Unmentionable* or *The Caledonian Tragedy* or *The Comedy of Glamis* or *Harry Lauder*, references which must surely bewilder any backstage visitor. The bad luck extends to anything which has ever been used for a production of *Macbeth*, and it is not unknown for an actor to refuse to wear a cloak or helmet if he learns that it was once worn in *That Play*. In the old days of the travelling Shakespeare repertory companies, the scenery of the plays would be largely interchangeable, but the costumes, furniture and settings for *Macbeth* were kept strictly apart. Never, under any circumstances, would a *Macbeth* throne be used for *King Lear, Othello* or *Hamlet*, however hard-pressed the manager was for money, transport or space. The bad luck also pursues the text if it is quoted in any other play: any playwright who allows his character to say 'What bloody man is this?' or 'When shall we three meet again' or 'Is this a dagger I see before me?' is asking for trouble and usually gets it. Unfortunately, *Macbeth* has more quotes than any other Shakespeare play: all are beautifully apt and popular and have passed into the language to the extent that many people do not realise their source.

Why should *Macbeth* be the unlucky play? It is, admittedly, a tragedy and full of blood and violence, but that is true of *King Lear, Othello, Troilus and Cressida, Anthony and Cleopatra, Julius Cæsar*, and *Titus Andronicus*. Macbeth is a multiple murderer but then so is Richard III. There are ghosts but then there also are in *Hamlet*. there are witches but these were an acceptable and intermittent ingredient of Elizabethan and Jacobean drama. But on the subject of witches the truth begins to emerge dimly on the horizon.

Macbeth is the murkiest, gloomiest and most despairing of all the classical tragedies. The story of a weak and foolish man, who seeks supernatural aid to satisfy a ruthless ambition, reeks of corruption. It is a play entirely obsessed and pulsating with wickedness and it generates such a powerful aura of evil that even to read it at night can make a sensitive person tremble, as Mrs Siddons found to her cost: to see a good production of it can be a truly unnerving experience as any theatregoer can confirm. There are evil characters in Shakespeare's other plays, Iago, Edmund, Claudius, but these are neatly offset by characters of real shining virtue, Desdemona, Cordelia, Ophelia, and the plays have plenty of sunshine and blue skies to lighten the darkness. But there is no sunshine in *Macbeth*; the representation of goodness in Malcolm and Lady Macduff is inept and ineffectual because goodness was not a quality in which Shakespeare was interested while writing this play. So what is left is a tragedy which is in effect entirely black.

This is not on account of its blood and gore which can be duplicated in a dozen contemporary plays, but its particularly sinister atmosphere. And this is the point: it is the only Shakespeare play in which witchcraft, black magic and satanism not merely play an important part, but provided the vital pivot on which the entire plot depends.

Why *Macbeth?* The answer lies in the circumstances in which the play was written and those of its first performance. It is thus necessary to consider briefly the state of the theatre at the turn of that century, its relationship with its royal sovereign and the position which Shakespeare occupied in the contemporary hierachy.

Queen Elizabeth had been a passionate lover of all the arts, and of the theatre in particular. Legend has it that she had so enjoyed the character of Falstaff in the two parts of *Henry IV* that she had commanded Shakespeare to write a play in which the fat knight was to be shown in love: the play was written, rehearsed and presented at a Garter Feast at Windsor Castle all within a fortnight to the Queen's evident satisfaction. It is, in fact, one of Shakespeare's least satisfactory plays, but the royal gesture was greatly appreciated. There can be no doubt that the flowering of the theatre in its most golden age was largely due to her enthusiasm and support, but in the last years the position had deteriorated badly. The aged Queen was racked with painful diseases, tormented by unsatisfactory love affairs – the Essex disaster had cast a black cloud over her final years – plagued by affairs of state, perpetually worried by money troubles and in no mood for theatre-going. Royal command performances which had been so profitable and frequent had been cut down to only three a year: payment was ten pounds a performance, a sum which was considered by Shakespeare to be adequate but by no means generous.

The social status of actors was dangerously equivocal. They may have enjoyed royal patronage, but the theatre had its enemies who would have been only too happy to have closed the theatres permanently and clap the actors into prison. The law still officially classified them as rogues and vagabonds and if found pursuing their art they could be publicly whipped and placed in the stocks overnight.

This did not often happen but the possibility was always alarmingly there. Playwrights worked under a very severe system of censorship: under the domination of Edward Tilney who was Master of the Revels from 1579 to 1610 and thus covered the whole of Shakespeare's career, playwrights could go as far as they pleased with sex, but had to be very careful with politics and religion. Bawdy was permitted: blasphemy and sedition were not. If an author offended in either of these matters he could be fined ten pounds, have his hand chopped off or be sent to prison.

More disturbing for Shakespeare and his company, the artistic supremacy which he had enjoyed for so long was no longer unchallenged. There were rival companies of note some of whom enjoyed great success and many command performances: the Admiral's Men were greatly admired for they included in their number such shining talents as Alleyn, Henslowe and Marlowe.

And then in 1603, Queen Elizabeth died and was succeeded by James VI of Scotland, son of Mary, Queen of Scots. He now became James I of England and this proved to be a decisive moment in the history of the English theatre. To explain this, it is necessary to consider the nature and personality of the new king.

His childhood and upbringing would have made a Freudian textbook. His mother was eight months pregnant with him when she saw her lover cut to pieces before her eyes. He was an only child and suffered to the full the loneliness and misery of royal isolation. He was taken from his mother in infancy and he never saw her again, being subsequently entrusted to a team of regents and tutors. His education was in the chilly narrow world of John Knox's bigoted hellfire religion. He grew up with a morbid interest in witchcraft and an obsessive fear of the Devil. Witchcraft was a real and ever-present social problem and it is difficult for us in the twentieth century to understand the terror which it inspired. James knew that King Duff of Scotland had been threatened by the notorious conspiracy of the Witches of Forres; that witchcraft was responsible for the terrible storms which delayed the arrival of his bride, Princess Anne, from Denmark and that a large number of witches had confessed to him that the Devil had incited them to do this against the foreign ungodly princess. He knew that a terrible

136

epidemic of witchcraft had nearly destroyed him and that hundreds of witches had been burned (over fifty were burned in England in his lifetime). The urge to tell is sometimes irresistible and in 1595 he wrote down his thoughts on the subject and published them under the title, *Dæmonologie*.

He was homosexual and his early marriage to the silly, frivolous Anne of Denmark was a purely domestic and dynastic convenience. Life was dangerous for the Stuart Kings: there had been three murders in their line and James was never entirely safe from physical violence, surrounded as he was by an aggressive and warring nobility. He grew up to be excessively squeamish of any sort of physical violence, and with a deep horror of naked steel. All his life he wore a quilted doublet to guard against the sharp thrust of the stiletto.

But this nervous, sickly, tormented, sexually-divided neurotic turned out to be a passionate theatre lover. Never having seen a play, for Scotland was culturally still in the dark ages and with only the gloomy sermons of John Knox to provide popular entertainment, James was unprepared for the full impact of Shakespeare's verse, the warmth of his comedy and the colour and splendour of his company's productions. He and the Queen were fascinated by all they saw; they commanded endless performances until they had seen the entire Shakespearean repertoire. The company had never before been so busy travelling up and down the country to entertain the King in whatever stately home he happened to be staying.

All this had a number of material benefits and a number of long overdue improvements in the company's social and financial position now took place. In 1603 Royal Letters of Patent were taken out: the company were now known as the King's Men, and ranked in his household as 'Grooms of the Chamber'. They were given his special protection and had a special license to perform in whatever university, town or village they chose without hindrance or obstruction from local authorities. They were awarded a place of honour in the Coronation procession and other state occasions and a special suit of clothes to wear in them. The number of command performances was increased from three a year to fifteen, and payments were doubled from £10 to £20 for each performance, with generous allowances and bonuses of up to £30 whenever they had been inconvenienced by the plague.

The accession of James I was the best thing which could have happened to Shakespeare, and it is no coincidence that the bulk of his greatest plays were all written at this time (he never wrote another comedy after *Hamlet*). Now he had financial security, popularity with the public, the respect of his colleagues and rivals and, most important of all, a quick-witted, discriminating and sophisticated court audience in constant attendance and expectation who could appreciate, far more than the public at the Globe Theatre, just what he was trying to do. Only with all this can a creative genius give of his best. Shakespeare buckled down and within five years produced *Measure for Measure, Othello, King Lear, Anthony and Cleopatra, Coriolanus* and *Macbeth*.

Macbeth was written and first performed in 1606 and although some have stated that it is an earlier play dug up for the occasion, there is enough evidence in the text to place it in this year beyond doubt. The reference by the Witch in Act One Scene Three to the master of the *Tiger*:

> A sailor's wife had chestnuts in her lap
> And munched and munched and munched ...
> Her husband's to Aleppo gone, master of
> the *Tiger* ...

was clearly based on a well-known nautical exploration which caused a good deal of excitement in the summer of that year when Sir Edward Michelbourne returned on his ship also named *The Tiger* after a disaster-studded voyage of three years. The porter's reference to equivocation in Act Two Scene Two,

> Faith, here's an equivocator that could swear in
> both scales against either scale who committed
> treason enough for God's sake yet could not
> equivocate to heaven.

can only refer to the notorious execution of the Jesuit Father Gar-

138

nett in the spring of 1606 who had invoked the doctrine of equivocation in his defence. The theme of royal assasination and the dialogue between Lady Macduff and her son on the subject of traitors,

SON:	What is a traitor?
LADY M:	Why, one that swears and lies.
SON:	And be all traitors that do so?
LADY M:	Everyone that does so is a traitor and must be hanged.
SON:	Who must hang them?
LADY M:	Why, the honest men.

these are obvious references to the Gunpowder Plot which had shaken the country only the year before. In addition there are references to *Macbeth* in a number of contemporary plays published and performed a little later, *The Knight of the Burning Pestle*, and *The Puritan Widow*.

So much for the date. The occasion was the state visit of the Queen's brother, King Christian of Denmark, his first since his appearance at the Coronation, three years earlier. Christian was a robust, likeable, popular man with a great interest in the arts and in sport. He was also a talented architect and had designed the first public theatre ever built in Copenhagen. He was fond of his sister and James had always liked his brother-in-law. The visit was thus as much of a domestic reunion as a state occasion.

The visit was to take place at the beginning of August and had been arranged in June. Suitable entertainment must be provided: Christian was known to like the theatre and a new play was a long-standing tradition for the delight of foreign visitors of note. Sometime in early July, Shakespeare would have been summoned to the office of the Comptroller in Whitehall Palace acquainted with the facts and asked to provide a new and suitable play for the occasion.

This commission must have given Shakespeare some considerable thought. The last royal commission he had received had been five years earlier in 1601 when Queen Elizabeth had requested a play suitable for the entertainment of the newly-appointed Italian ambassador, Count Orsino. Shakespeare had very quickly concocted *Twelfth Night*, an amiable and harmless piece of romantic nonsense which had been a huge and lasting success with the court audience, partly because he had named his leading romantic hero after the guest of honour, and partly because the character of Malvolio was a shameless portrait of Sir William Knollys, Master of the Royal Household, and the most hated figure in the court. He had naturally been present at the performance and had seen with horror his *alter ego*, doubtless played by Burbage, costumed and made-up to resemble him. During the letter scene, the court had been reduced to a hysterical uproar of delight. Shakespeare doubtless remembered the unhappy man's humiliation with satisfaction.

But something very different would be needed for the forthcoming festivities. The Danes were reputedly very different in their tastes and outlook from the frivolous, pleasure-loving Italians, and a Scottish King was a very different thing from an English Queen. James was not difficult to please, but a play written specially for him had to draw a careful line between theatricality and political discretion: there had been a drama of treason and violence called *Gowrie*, written shortly after his accession by an unknown author. It described in documentary terms an actual conspiracy in which James had narrowly escaped death at the hands of treacherous friends. The council had seen a private performance: it was felt to be too dangerous and was never presented. Later a comedy called *Eastward Ho* was written by a team of authors and presented by the Children of the Queen's Revels who performed in their theatre at Blackfriars. In this they ridiculed the Scots and even required a boy actor to mimic the King's speech and accent. The players were disbanded for the season and the authors were sent to prison. James had not been amused.

There is evidence that Shakespeare went out of his way to please his Royal Patron to an extent he had never done before or was to do again. The play would be set in his native Scotland and would be about a Scottish king. There would be a brief glimpse of five other Scottish kings as they paraded through the satanic vision of the cauldron. One of James' ancestors, Malcolm, would be portrayed sympathetically. Banquo, one of those supposed Stuart ancestors, would be praised with phrases like 'dauntless temper of mind,' and 'wisdom that doth guide his valour,' and there would be a number of flattering references to James' wisdom, his peace-loving intentions and his reputedly divine powers of healing the sick. More important, the play would be short, for James did not like long plays and was liable to fall asleep or even to leave before the end – and the royal guest did not speak or understand a word of English. James would not want to be reminded too vividly of the dangers of regicide so the deaths of Duncan and Macbeth would take place off-stage. Most important of all, the play would deal dramatically and seriously with witchcraft, the subject in which James had an obsessive, terrified interest and on which he was an acknowledged expert. And because of this, the relevant scenes, Shakespeare decided, would have to be authentic.

It was a very unfortunate decision.

† † †

In one sense the commission came at a bad time for he was exceptionally busy in the summer of that year. There were the daily performances at the Globe and the extra performances at the week-end in the private houses. There was the complex and endless rehearsal schedule if the repertoire of up to twenty plays was to be kept up and the high standard maintained – their noble patrons were liable to request a particular play at a moment's notice and it had to be ready. And in addition to all this he was working on his longest and most ambitious play yet, *Anthony and Cleopatra*: a number of striking textual similarities make it clear that he did work on the two plays simultaneously.

Reluctantly putting aside ancient Rome and Egypt, he turned his attention to mediæval Scotland. He had little more than a month in which to write and rehearse it but he was a quick worker and the mark of the true professional is that he can produce his best work under pressure. *Macbeth* shows all the signs of having been written in a hurry: it is one of the shortest plays he wrote: there are no sub-plots, no superfluous characters and scenes, just the intense concentration on the one all-important theme; there are a surprising number of loose ends in the story line and one astonishing gap –

141

why, for example, does Lady Macbeth not have her death scene? And although the white-hot inspiration carried him through to the end to produce one masterpiece which has been unfailingly popular with actors and public alike, a certain brevity and scrappiness of the scenes in the final act indicate that he was working against time.

Shakespeare would have drawn his plot from Holinshed's *Chronicles* and it is interesting to note that the account therein of Macbeth's life and activities distorts history in every possible way. Duncan, far from being the gentle, noble character he is shown, was a dreaded tyrant and Macbeth killed him, not in his bed at night, but in fair battle near Elgin. Macbeth reigned for all of twenty years and was a wise, enlightened and popular king who made a large number of excellent reforms and pilgrimaged to Rome. He was eventually killed by Malcolm who was an even worse tyrant than his father. Shakespeare's play is, in fact, a gross libel on the dead king.

Shakespeare would undoubtedly have done his homework well when it came to the witchcraft scenes. He would certainly have read *Dæmonologie*: like most royal writings, it is tedious and amateurish, but Shakespeare would have found it a useful pointer to the King's state of mind on the controversial subject. He would have read Reginald Scot's *Discovery of Witchcraft* published in 1584 and which caused great offence and controversy by being a spirited defence of witchcraft. But for the actual text of the Witches' scenes, Shakespeare would not have had to go further than his own memories of his boyhood in Warwickshire. Witches were a very vital force in Tudor England. Shakespeare grew up in a countryside where they lived and practised, where people believed in them and their powers, where they were ducked in ponds, tortured, humiliated and killed in dreadful, unspeakable ways. He would certainly have known some in the Warwickshire villages where he lived and played: he would have heard of their spells and incantations, these being the living tradition of country life with which he grew up. In his natural and praiseworthy desire for authenticity he went a little too far when he wrote the witch's brew in Scene Three whose repulsive ingredients make up the cauldron's potion:

Fillet of a fenny's snake
Eye of newt and toe of dog
Wool of bat and tongue of dog
Adder's fork and blind-worms sting
Lizard's leg and owlet's wing
Scale of dragon, tooth of wolf,
Witch's mummy, maw and gulf,
Of the ravin'd salt-sea shark
Root of hemlock digg'd i' the dark,
Liver of blaspheming Jew
Gall of goat and slips of yew
Sliverd in the moon's eclipse
Nose of Turk and Tartar's lips
Finger of birth-strangled babe,
Ditch delivered of a drab
Cool it with a baboon's blood
Then the charm is firm and good.

All this is not a figment of Shakespeare's vivid and bottomless imagination: it is taken from an actual black magic incantation which he would certainly have known about during those years in which he lived in Stratford.

After a time gap of four centuries one can only speculate as to what was in Shakespeare's mind when he did this. Did he or did he not know just what he was doing? Did he, like many enlightened men, dismiss witchcraft and all that appertained to it as superstitious nonsense? Or did he have a healthy respect for it? We shall never know. But he was trespassing on forbidden ground: it is not safe to tamper with the forces of evil or use them for frivolous purposes: an appeal to the powers of darkness will not go unanswered. Nor did they in this case. For in using a real black magic incantation, Shakespeare placed a curse on the play which has dogged it for four centuries.

The first performance took place on the evening of 7 August 1606 in the Great Hall at Hampton Court. Macbeth was played by Richard Burbage, the company's leading actor and a tragedian who enjoyed a very great popularity with the public on the strength of his performances as Hamlet, Richard III, King Lear and Malvolio. His handsome, bearded face stares quizzically at posterity from his portrait and gives no indication that he was, alas, short and fat; but these physical handicaps were of little account beside the splendour of his voice, the nobility of his bearing and the strength and dignity of his acting.

Separating facts from legend is difficult when writing about Shakespeare, for one is constantly brought up to face the sad realisation that there are so few facts: but one has emerged. It seems that the Curse did not waste any time before making its presence felt, for on this night of all nights, the boy actor who played Lady Macbeth – his name was Hal Berridge – was suddenly taken ill with a fever, and at such short notice that the only possible substitute was the author himself. Since he had written the play and had directed the rehearsals, it could be hopefully assumed that he had more than a passing acquaintance with the text, and with its four brief scenes, Lady Macbeth is the shortest leading part he ever wrote.

The man we have to thank for this piece of vital information is that charming old gossip, John Aubrey. He was born seven years after Shakespeare died but he loved the theatre and theatre people and knew a number of the King's Men in their old age and their sons. In his many writings he reported faithfully everything he heard from them and whereas seventeenth century gossip cannot be accepted completely, it should not be totally ignored.

One can only sympathise with Shakespeare and his company when confronted by this appalling crisis, and it needs no great effort of the imagination to visualise the panic and nervous distress which would have thus descended on them. Anyone who has been involved in a theatrical first performance knows how painful is the occasion: when it is a royal event the tensions are considerably multiplied. One can easily see the hasty re-allocation of parts, the hurried extra rehearsals in the Great Hall, the inevitable delay in starting and the knife-edge tension on which the whole performance would have taken place. Theatrical tradition has suggested that there were other disasters that evening, but unfortunately tradition has not been specific; but a play performed in a dark gloomy hall lit only by candlelight which involves fire and blood, ghostly apparitions and realistic scenes of witchcraft, bloodstained fights, murders and battles acted by a small team of tired, overworked and under-rehearsed actors is bound to have its fair share of trouble.

Trouble did, however, come from another and unexpected source. Shakespeare's well-meaning attempts to please the King seem to have failed sadly, for there is evidence that James was not at all pleased with the play. Since Shakespeare was not one of the royal intimates, he would not have known about the King's squeamishness and allergy to the sight of cold steel. And here was a play with more deaths, stabbings, murders, fights and battles than any he had written. And there was James, trapped in his seat as guest of honour sitting in the front of the audience close to the action and forced to witness sights which were so unpleasant and distressing; death and murders were portrayed in the Elizabethan theatre with a grossness and realism which we would now find disgusting; blood and guts from the butcher's shop would be spilled over the stage in large quantities. The realism and authenticity of the Witches' scenes would undoubtedly have upset him, and the murder of Duncan would have been an unfortunate reminder of the perils of his own life, for regicide had been and would continue to be a popular pastime for fanatics.

Royal disfavour had one immediate effect on the play – it was banned for five years. Between 1606 and 1611 there is no record anywhere of *Macbeth* being performed either in public or in private. The first known performance after the première was in 1611 in the Globe Theatre and it was witnessed by a theatre-loving lawyer and astrologer, Simon Forman. The Hecate scenes had been added, there was music and dancing and Macbeth and Banquo rode onto the stage on real horses. Forman's account is of great interest and value, as it is the first written account of a performance of the play. After that, *Macbeth* seems to have disappeared from the repertoire. The Globe Theatre was burned down shortly after and with it all the scenery, properties, costumes and manuscripts which had kept the company going so long and so successfully. Shakespeare himself died in 1616 and his world slowly disappeared to make room for the elaborate and spectacular masques which the Jacobean and Carolingian audiences so greatly loved and a world in which he, even if he had lived, would have had no part.

Macbeth vanished from the theatre for nearly fifty years for there are no records of any production until it appeared again in 1667 extensively rewritten by Sir Henry Davenant to suit the irredeemably trivial tastes of Restoration playgoers and barely recognisable as the play Shakespeare wrote. With music by Matthew Locke and songs, dances and divertisements and what appears from contemporary accounts to have been a flying ballet, it emerged as a charming light opera which was seen and admired by that indefatigable theatre-goer, Samuel Pepys:

'... to the Play-House where we saw *Macbeth* which is one of the best plays for stage and variety of dancing and musique that ever I saw ...'
(Diary. April 19.1667)

Converting a tragedy into a musical seems to have had a slightly discouraging effect on the Curse for it appears that it went underground during the Restoration and there is little record of trouble during the last years of the seventeenth century. But at the turn of the eighteenth, a strange wave of puritanism swept through the land and once again the theatre came under fire. Most active and voluble in this attack was the reformer, Jeremy Collier who wrote a pamphlet, *Dissuasive from the Play-House* (1703) in which he bitterly attacked those playwrights who used music 'to disguise their obscene prologues and unchaste wits' and thereby made their entertainments more attractive to the public than church services. The play which aroused his most bitter anger was *Macbeth* for how could an interminable sermon on morality compete with Hecate and three Singing Witches at Covent Garden? In that year, 1703, after a long absence from the stage, *Macbeth* was revived in its musical version, the management having characteristically defied

146

the press, the Deity and augery in order to provide the public with what it confidently described as a wholesome and enriching entertainment. The moralists gloomily and gloatingly prophesied disaster and for once they were right. While *Macbeth* was still playing, the worst storm in England's history occurred: fifteen hundred seamen were killed, a million pounds of damage was done in London and the City of Bristol was totally destroyed. The moralists were triumphant and Jeremy Collier announced that the hurricane was an expression of God's anger at a playwright who 'mock'd the great Governour of the World who alone commands the wind and the seas.' Queen Anne declared a day of fasting and humiliation to appease God, and the theatres closed down for a full week.

Davenant's musical comedy trimmings are another example of the extraordinary bad luck which has dogged *Macbeth*. More than any other Shakespeare play, *Macbeth* has suffered at the hands of hack-writers who believed that they could improve on the original and that the play must, on all accounts, be re-written. After Davenant, it was David Garrick who improved it and attempted thereby to restore the play to its tragic stature; his famous revival of 1744 placed him firmly in the front rank of popular tragedians. He cut out many of Davenant's improvements and being a frustrated playwright he could not forbear to write in that very death scene which Shakespeare had taken so much trouble to avoid, producing in the process some of the most ludicrously inept blank verse in the history of the theatre.

> Tis done! The scene of my life will quickly close!
> Ambition's vain delusive dreams are fled
> And now I wake in darkness and guilt.
> I cannot bear it, let me shake it off.
> It will not be, my soul is clogged with blood.
> I cannot rise! I dare not ask for mercy.
> It is too late; Hell drags me down.
>   I sink.
> I sink, I sink, my soul is fled for ever … o! Oh!

An actress who, although it gave her the greatest success of her career, was to believe firmly in the intrinsic evil of the play and for whom it was a nightly ordeal to appear in it, was Mrs Siddons. She was a young and inexperienced actress of twenty-one when she first played in it touring in the West of England in the winter of 1775. Owing to a sudden illness in the company she was told only the night before that she was to play Lady Macbeth. She had never played the part before and there were to be no rehearsals. Horrifying as this may sound to contemporary theatre people, it was taken for granted that in the popular classics the company knew their allotted parts and that further rehearsals would not be necessary. It was an old custom and beginners had to sink or swim. Mrs Siddons took the play to her room and prepared to stay up all night learning it by candlelight. 'I went on with tolerable composure in the silence of the night,' she later wrote in her memoires, 'till I came to the assassination scene. The horrors of the scene rose to such a degree that made it impossible to get further. I snatched up a candle and hurried out the room in a paroxysm of terror. My dress was of silk and the rustling of it, as I ascended the stairs to go to bed, seemed to my panic-stricken fancy like the movements of a spectre pursuing me. I capt my candlestick and threw myself on my bed where I lay without daring even to take my clothes off.'

The following night she played Lady Macbeth for the first time and gave what she admitted to be the worst performance of her career. The evil generated by the play still gripped her and she was pale, nervous and ineffectual. She did not know the lines and the number of prompts she received was phenomenal. The audience showed its displeasure in the customary rowdy eighteenth century provincial manner and her embarrassment and mortification was complete. Never again, she vowed, would she play Lady Macbeth with inadequate rehearsal.

An actor who refused for years to play it and was finally persuaded much against his will was the English actor, Charles Macklin, (1700–93). He was Garrick's contemporary and his only serious rival. He was half Irish and half Jewish, years before it became fashionable to be either; he combined the aggression of the first with the sensitivity of the second. His performance of *Macbeth* was

148

badly received by the critics and by one in particular who was sufficiently ill-advised to end his review with a malicious rhyming couplet:

I must confess I never knew
A Scottish king sound like a Dublin Jew!

Seething with anger, Macklin charged into the coffee house where the author held court and gave him a thrashing. He was arrested, spent the night in custody and appeared before the magistrate in the morning. The magistrate was not a theatre-lover; Macklin was heavily fined and severely admonished. But worse was to happen a little later. He had a violent argument with an older actor in the theatre green-room over a costume. Macklin hit him over the head with his cane, but the silver tip accidentally gouged out his eye and he died instantly. This took place during a performance of *Macbeth*. The judge was a great theatre-lover and apparently accepted Macklin's plea that he had acted under unbearable provocation and that he hadn't meant to kill him anyway. Macklin was not hanged, imprisoned, nor branded on the hand. He was merely required to pay a fine to the dead man's family.

The full text of the play as Shakespeare had originally written it was not restored to the public until Kemble revived it in 1794 at Drury Lane with Mrs Siddons, his sister, and with the text came back the Curse, and throughout the nineteenth and twentieth centuries, *Macbeth* has had a very turbulent history of accident. Cynics will point out that if the play is disaster-prone, then there are sensible reasons for this. They will state that the play is immensely popular with actors and audiences and, with the possible exception of *Hamlet*, is revived more than any other Shakespeare play; that it is the shortest of all the Shakespeare plays and that the twenty-two scenes are all very short which means a quick succession of scenery and lighting changes. They state that most of the play takes place at night which means dim lighting and sometimes total darkness; that there are more duels, fights, murders and battles than in any other Shakespeare play. These disbelievers will triumphantly say: if you have up to thirty actors wearing the heavy and traditionally awkward costumes and armour used for the play, rushing up and down the stairs, rostrums and bridges of the inevitable permanent set and in the dark, then by the simple law of averages there are bound to be a number of accidents. This is indisputably true: but when all this has been said; when the Curse is dismissed angrily as superstitious nonsense and the disasters as so many coincidences, when it has been firmly pointed out that if you believe in the bad luck then it will come, you are still left with an appalling amount of disaster which simply cannot be explained away.

Four hundred years of death, doom and disaster offer an intimidatingly large field of investigation. During the seventeenth and eighteenth centuries the information, coming largely from the occasional memoire and diary, is naturally a little sparse. During the nineteenth century, with the arrival of the popular press, the documentation is noticeably better; but with the present century and with so many of the actors involved still happily alive to describe their experiences with the play, it is possible to recount them with a wealth of colourful (if contradictory) detail. Where does one start, for there is an *embarras de richesses*? To take the reader through every production of *Macbeth* in chronological order would be to produce a tedious and repetitive encyclopedia rather than a selectively readable slim volume. But a random choice from the last fifty years has produced some deeply interesting and disturbing case histories.

A typical one is the famous 1937 revival at the Old Vic with the thirty-year-old Laurence Olivier playing the part for the first time following his sensational triumph in the entirety Hamlet at the beginning of the year. The director was Michel St. Denis who had enjoyed a distinguished and controversial career in Paris with the avant-garde theatre and had recently settled in London. He had started a drama school and had directed John Gielgud in André Obey's *Noah*. This revival of *Macbeth* was his first Shakespeare play. The invitation had been extended to him at the insistence of Tyrone Guthrie who not only had a very heavy production schedule himself but was anxious to bring in new ideas and new blood to the Old Vic and rescue it from the dusty insularity which had inspired one wit to describe the theatre as 'La Tragédie Anglaise'.

Laurence Oliver's first *Macbeth* in 1938 at the Old Vic. Not an ideal
Christmas attraction as the intelligent schoolboy indicated.
(Angus McBean)

The invitation had been fiercely opposed by Lilian Baylis, the
matriarchal founder and director of the Old Vic, who disliked and
distrusted foreigners and feared the evil influence they might possibly have on *her* actors and *her* theatre (her love was both jealous
and possessive).

It became speedily obvious that what seemed an excellent idea in
theory wasn't going to work out in practice. The great difficulty
was the unforeseen language barrier: Michel St. Denis spoke a little
fractured English and few of the company spoke enough French.
The chief sufferer in this was his Macbeth. Olivier was tackling for
the first time what is arguably Shakespeare's most difficult part and
he urgently needed help, advice and encouragement. The directors
spirit was certainly willing but the language was weak. Long dis-
cussions in garbled English, torrential French and mime on the
inner meaning of the play, the historical background and the
deeper motivation of the part were no substitute for hard theatrical
instruction. St. Denis' ideas seemed to be original when you could
understand him, but throughout the company there was a nagging

151

suspicion that the French had never really liked or understood Shakespeare, and that St. Denis was concerned only with the play's visual possibilities rather than its true theatrical meaning. Michel St. Denis was the most tiresome of all theatrical birds, the experimental perfectionist with a dozen different meanings and subtleties for every line, but very little practicality.

The production was immensely complicated and made extensive use of masks, weird symbolic lighting, multiple scene changes and all the outward manifestations of that continental expressionism which has always been deeply suspect in the English Theatre. The production might have succeeded if he had three months to rehearse and an unlimited budget, but in those tightly scheduled Old Vic seasons, rehearsals were for only three weeks and there was very little money: the company was virtually self-supporting and the budget was pitifully small, top salary being ten pounds weekly.

The company was nervous and unhappy and the troubles started without delay. St. Denis and his friend, Vera Lindsey, who played Lady Macduff, were travelling away from a party when the taxi braked suddenly to avoid a collision; they were thrown violently forward and crashed their heads against the glass partition resulting in some very nasty bruises and cuts. The next day when they appeared at the theatre, bandaged and stitched and pale, one of the company sighed deeply and said for all to hear, 'Oh dear, the bad luck has started already.' Michel St. Denis did not understand the remark and it had to be explained that *Macbeth* has a history of bad luck. He shrugged his shoulders and continued to puff at his pipe but there was a distinct feeling in the company that he was seriously worried, not only by the Curse but the probable effect it would have on the company morale. Company morale deteriorated still further the next day when Lilian Baylis' little dog was killed by a passing motor-car. Like many lonely old spinsters she lavished all her accumulated affection on the animal and its death affected her very deeply.

By the end of the third week the production was under-rehearsed, far from ready and it was quite obvious that it could not possibly open in time. The first night was on the Tuesday but when the dress rehearsal started on the Sunday before, it was discovered to everybody's horror that the elaborate sets, which Motley had designed and for which such careful measurements had been made, did not fit. They were too big so they had to be taken back to the workshops and cut down to size. Then the accumulated effects of overwork and nervous strain took their further toll of Olivier who developed a bad cold and finally lost his voice completely and could speak only in a whisper. Postponement until Friday was inevitable, a drastic decision, for the plays followed every four weeks in those tightly scheduled pre-war Old Vic seasons and even a three-day postponement resulted in appalling inconvenience and disappointment. There were hundreds of loyal patrons who had regular bookings for every play. Lillian Baylis had never had to do it before, she hated to disappoint her public and she took it very badly. Since it was clear that St. Denis could not cope, Tyrone Guthrie was called in by Lilian Baylis to take over the production, to pull it together and get it on the stage within three days. This he proceeded to do and with characteristic generosity refused to take a credit in the programme or to allow the news to be leaked to the press. During these four days the company were worked morning, evening and night; morale was naturally low and it sunk still lower when Olivier was nearly killed. He was sitting in the wings talking to Vera Lindsey. He was called and rose to go onto the stage. Shortly after he left his seat, a stage weight weighing twenty-five pounds crashed down on to the seat from the flies, crushing it to fragments. He had missed death by seconds.

But worse was to come. Lilian Baylis had to go home early on the Wednesday and it was reported to the company that she was seriously ill. Everybody prayed for her recovery, prayed that these dreadful rehearsal weeks would conclude without further trouble, but it was not to be. When the company came to the theatre on the Friday for the final dress rehearsal they were greeted with the news they had all been dreading – Lilian Baylis had died of a heart attack in her home in Stockwell. She was sixty-five. It was the end of an era. Never again would that fat myopic figure in the red doctorate robes be seen in the stage box. For the company, Friday night's first performance was an unforgettably sad traumatic evening, they were sustained only by the knowledge that her last message had been an anxious enquiry that everything was alright at the Vic and her desire that the show should go on.

They played together magnificently and Olivier gave what he later considered the most passionate and emotional performance of his life. When he finally returned to his dressing-room he found a note from Lilian Baylis which her secretary had thoughtfully witheld until the end of the performance. 'Welcome return to dear Laurence Olivier. May you be as happy in *Macbeth* as in *Hamlet* last season.'

The notices were excellent and the press played up the Curse of Macbeth relentlessly in the popular papers throughout the four weeks run. The public, loving the play and intrigued by the melo-dramatic sensationalism of the whole matter, flocked to the Waterloo Road and filled the house night after night. It was certainly this factor which prompted Bronson Albery to transfer the production to the New Theatre for a three-week season before Christmas. It was a disaster. The pre-Christmas month is traditionally a bad time for the theatre and the West End public (very different then from the Old Vic public) was not interested in an avant-garde, cheaply-mounted *Macbeth* without big West End star names, and the production played to dispiritingly empty houses.

And so it ended not with a bang but a whimper, but even the saddest whimper can produce one amusing incident. Such a one did occur and thus provided Olivier with one of his favourite stories which he tells against himself and has generously confirmed for inclusion in this book. One afternoon, the matinée audience was exceptionally sparse with acres of empty stalls, but in the stage box sat a young schoolboy who was watching the play with keen, intelligent eyes. Olivier found this very encouraging: he acted up and directed his entire performance to the boy in the box. The rest of the company did likewise and never had a performance of *Macbeth* been thundered, screamed and howled with such intensity as was this to its youthful and appreciative audience-of-one. In the interval Olivier (with a touch of complacency), remarked to John Merivale, his Macduff, 'that boy will never see anything like this as long as he lives, it's an experience he'll never forget'. But when they all returned to the stage after the interval, the boy had gone.

154

Ann Todd and Paul Rogers at the Old Vic in 1959. (Old Vic Archives)

After Lilian Baylis' death *Macbeth* was not performed at the Old Vic for sixteen years, and it was Michael Benthall's production with Paul Rogers and Ann Todd in 1954 as part of his famous five-year plan to do all Shakespeare, which brought the play back to the theatre. Frederick Marshall, the conductor, remembers that on the first night the portrait of Lilian Baylis, stern and disinheriting, suddenly, and without any apparent cause, crashed down to the floor breaking the glass and scattering it all over the room. She had died during the final rehearsals of *Macbeth* – was this her post-humous way of showing her disapproval of the play? The pro-duction had no real trouble during the Old Vic season but when they went on tour with it, the Curse struck hard. John Moffat remembers that there were two abortions and an attempted suicide in the company, the company manager broke both his legs in a car accident and an electrician in Dublin electrocuted himself causing first-degree burns, and amongst the physical accidents in the fights were several broken legs and a nearly-gouged eye. But it was on tour in South Africa that two very mysterious troubles dogged

155

them. Paul Rogers remembers that he wounded his leg and in spite of every medical attention it obstinately refused to heal, causing him a lot of pain and aggravation. As soon as he had finished with the tour and with *Macbeth*, the wound mysteriously healed up. The other incident took place outside the theatre in Cape Town when the scenery, props and furniture were being unloaded by local stage-hands and lifted by a very high crane through the scene dock and into the theatre – a lengthy process known in the profession as *the get-in*. A total stranger passed, paused briefly to watch and enquired which play was to be performed. '*Macbeth*,' said one of the stage-hands and the minute he had said it, a spear which was being craned up and poised high in the air with a bundle of others, dislodged itself and fell right on the stranger's head, killing him instantly.

Olivier's first contact with *Macbeth* had been nine years earlier at the Royal Court. Nothing had caused more speculation, amusement and alarm than Barry Jackson's announcement that his forthcoming production of *Macbeth* would be in modern dress. This was the first: soon it was to trigger off a series of modern dress Shakespeare productions, it became fashion, then it became a craze and then finally it came to be taken for granted and has now become a commonplace. But in 1928 it was an exciting novelty.

Sir Barry Jackson was one of the astutest theatrical brains of the century. He gave *Back To Methuselah* to the public, he started the Malvern Festival and his repertory theatre in Birmingham was to supply so many of the stars who enriched the theatre between the wars. But here he was to make one of his rare mistakes. There were casting troubles from the start, for the whole project was arousing pockets of fierce resistance in the theatrical establishment and nobody wanted to play Macbeth in a dinner-jacket. The likely actors were all mysteriously unavailable and only the unlikely ones were interested. In desperation he engaged Eric Maturin, a much-admired actor whose low-key realistic style was admirable in Galsworthy and other modern plays but was totally unsuited to Shakespeare. Maturin had never been in a Shakespeare and never even seen one and for some extraordinary reason this was regarded by Jackson and his colleagues as an advantage.

Not that they were looking consciously for a gimmick, not Jackson, nor H. D. Ayliff and certainly not Paul Shelving the designer. They believed honestly and sincerely that to liberate Shakespeare from all his gaudy trappings was to do him a great service; they believed – so the idea ran – that if the audience saw familiar, everyday clothes and settings on the stage they would thus be able to concentrate on the play without any distractions. An interesting theory but it turned out very differently in practice. Admittedly, the audiences were used to modern everyday clothes, *but not in Shakespeare,* and therein lay the rub. The Jackson triumvirate might have taken warning from the advance publicity which concentrated on the clothes to the total exclusion of everything else. It is doubtful if in the whole history of the theatre there had been so much eager speculation on what the actors would be wearing rather than on what they would be doing. Further warning might well have been taken from the fact that most of the papers, as well as their dramatic critics, sent along their fashion columnists to the first night.

The physical troubles started immediately. The sets had been constructed in advance and the actors had the unusual luxury of rehearsing in front of them rather than the usual empty stage. In the first week, they started to fall down and collapse onto the company who sustained some rather serious injuries. A month of rehearsal took place in an atmosphere of tension and gloom, everybody wondering as is always the case, what was going to happen next. It was a fire in the dress circle which mysteriously broke out during the Sunday before the opening when the theatre was closed. There was considerable damage, many seats were burned beyond use and a fireman was nearly suffocated to death. Miraculously, the fire was extinguished in time, and replacement seats were found before the opening.

It was as bad as the critics anticipated. Far from being an unobtrusive background, the costumes captured everybody's fascinated attention and succeeded in totally distracting the audience from the play. Shakespeare lost on points, he just didn't stand a chance. Macbeth in plus-fours wielding golf-clubs was a vastly intriguing novelty, and how could you take seriously a Lady Macbeth in a

You would be forgiven for thinking that this and the next four photographs are from an Ivor Novello musical, but you could not be more wrong. They are the only photos that survive of the modern dress, 1928, *Macbeth* at the Royal Court. (Sally Chappell/Victoria & Albert Museum)

cloche hat and a waistless beaded skirt (Molyneux), reclining on a chaise-longue, smoking a Balkan Sobranie from a long green cigarette holder, reading Richard Arlen's *The Green Hat* and listening to *Carmen* on a wind-up gramophone? But the loudest laughter was reserved for the soldiers in khaki uniforms and tin helmets carrying rifles and Bren guns as if they were on loan from *Journey's End* at the Savoy. With the three Witches dressed and equipped as charladies complete with buckets and mops, Fleance in an Eton collar, champagne and pêche Melbas in the banqueting scene, plus a dazzling display of white ties and tails, it was obvious to the first night audience that Shakespeare had been wilfully sacificed to a stunt, and Barry Jackson was honest enough to admit the failure of the experiment in his curtain speech. The only person who came out of the sorry mess with any credit was Olivier himself, then turned just twenty-one. He played Malcolm in a dinner-jacket for the banquet-

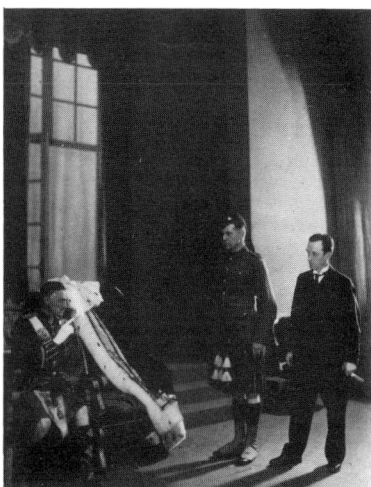

Above left: Mary Merrall and Eric Maturin as the Macbeths. Above right: Eric Maturin as Macbeth, Douglas Payne and Ernest Stidwell as the Two Murderers. Below left: Eric Maturin as Macbeth. Below right: Laurence Olivier as Malcolm.

ing scene, silk dressing-gown and Charvet pyjamas for the murder, and a very natty check lounge suit for the England interludes. Whereas the others tried to make the blank verse sound like Galsworthy, he tried to make them sound like Shakespeare, and thus caught the eye of Basil Dean who proceeded to give him a taste of overnight stardom in, and as, *Beau Geste* at Her Majesty's Theatre a few months later. That this spectacular and much publicised production was a total disaster and was the beginning to the most frustrating year of his life, was nobody's fault and is, in any case, another story.

† † †

The disasters are not always physical: there are artistic disasters no less unpleasant and traumatic. It was also at the Royal Court Theatre that experiment of a rather different sort was the prevailing character of the 1966 revival. William Gaskill, one of the Royal Court directors, had invited Sir Alec Guinness to play Macbeth and he had eagerly accepted. It was not his first contact with the part: before the War, he had learned the part in four days when asked to replace an actor at Sheffield Rep who had been suddenly taken ill. Under the circumstances he appears to have done well but the opportunity of bringing thirty years' experience to the problems of the part was not to be turned down. There was, however, a condition attached: that a suitable Lady Macbeth be found. It has always been a very difficult part to cast, and it is highly unlikely that Shakespeare had any realisation of just what sort of casting problem he was bequeathing to posterity. Do you get a hag or a sex pot? A woman who can drive her warrior-husband to regicide by sheer force of personality must be a battle-axe but she must also be able to project some sort of sensuality to explain the domination. Sarah Siddons was a good example of the first and Sarah Bernhardt (also Francesca Annis in the Polanski film) a good example of the second. Clearly a combination of the two was the ideal, but who?

Their choice was to cause enormous controversy and bad feeling. Simone Signoret, the French film star, clearly combined sexuality with leadership. It had been Guinness' suggestion and Gaskill

Simone Signoret and Alec Guinness at the Royal Court in 1966.
(Thomson Newspapers)

liked it. She was approached and after a few initial misgivings, accepted it eagerly. She had never acted in Shakespeare even in France, and had never seen or even read *Macbeth* which was quaintly regarded by her colleagues as an advantage; in addition there was a slight language problem. Her English was fluent enough off-stage and had seen her happily through her big film success *Room at the Top*, but to make her stage début in Shakespeare in a foreign language and a foreign city with a co-star whose presence would inevitably guarantee the widest publicity argued either great courage or great foolhardiness. 'I must have been mad,' she said laconically to the press. Rehearsals took place in a strangely light-hearted atmosphere, 'we don't have to behave as if we are in a church even if it is a tragedy', she said sensibly. When Guinness and Gaskill were challenged to defend their choice of actress, Guinness pointed out the well-known theory, that the part of Lady Macbeth was inspired by Mary Queen of Scots who was French, and the play clearly reflected the murder of Darnley. It was a great challenge and Simone Signoret impressed everybody by her determination and hard work. She had a blackboard permanently installed in her hotel bedroom on which she wrote out the particularly difficult passages:

> What wouldst thou highly
> That wouldst thou holily
>
> Wouldst not play false,
> And yet wouldst wrongly win

Tricky alliteration and cross-rhythms which, as Guinness pointed out sympathetically, would twist the tongues of many experienced English actresses.

Within three days of opening the box office the four weeks limited run was totally sold out. The rehearsals dragged out in a blaze of publicity and the production opened on a very gloomy, foggy night – a very *Macbeth* night, as the press drily pointed out – 20 October 1966. The performance went smoothly and there were no accidents or physical disasters. Simone Signoret was clearly exceedingly nervous, though nobody blamed her, and it was noticed that Guinness offered a very gentlemanly helping hand in moments of crisis. But Ronald Bryden, then writing for *The Observer*, remembers that although it was difficult to understand everything she said, the audience, which had been very restless and coughing interminably, shuddered to a respectful silence whenever she appeared, a tribute not only to her film star fame but also her stage personality and charisma.

The notices were appalling: never had there been such unanimity, such an avalanche of abuse and vituperation. The closest examination of the Royal Court files reveals only two kind words. *The Daily Telegraph* described it as 'sound but emphatically plain' whilst Harold Hobson from the pulpit in *The Sunday Times* admitted that he had liked Simone Signoret's smile and enlarged on the point with his usual verbose and repetitive detail. Madame

Signoret was doubtless gratified to be that week's Hobson's Choice, but she shrugged her shoulders with truly Gallic *je m'en foutisme* and continued to face her nightly ordeal.

The critics denounced two experimental aspects of the production; the use of three West Indian actors to play not only the three Witches but also the murderers (increased to three) was dismissed as a pointless gimmick and greeted with a tornado of jealous anger by the coloured theatrical community. The set which consisted of an open, unfurnished stage surrounded by three sandy-coloured flats with bright unchanging lighting was regarded as dull and unhelpful. Certainly it cannot be denied that the lack of any visual appeal or aids did throw an even greater strain than is usual on the acting abilities of the company.

Gaskill's reaction was an instant declaration of war: he wrote a scathing letter to *The Evening Standard* whose critic, Milton Shulman had described the production as 'a pretentious shambles'. Gaskill protested against the cheap journalism which passed as criticism and announced his intention of banning the critics from all future Royal Court productions. In years to come similar threats were to be made by Royal Court directors but in 1966 it had the air of novelty. The battle raged furiously for weeks and relations between Fleet Street and Sloane Square reached their lowest-ever point. Gaskill was then invited to discuss the matter on television and was asked by Milton Shulman why he had selected a French actress who, whatever her talents and fame, couldn't speak English well enough to do justice to the part. 'Because in my opinion, no English actress is capable of playing it,' was his cool, calm reply. This was indeed putting the cat in with the pigeons and the result was predictably frenzied. From the angry letters to the press and the Royal Court office, and the headlines following them, there was the inescapable conclusion that the English theatre was thickly populated with Lady Macbeths, both potential and actual. Gaskill diplomatically qualified his statement by announcing that the four weeks season would be extended with Maurice Roeves and Susan Engels, who had been playing the Macduffs, promoted to the Macbeths. At the same time, Alfred Eisdale and Neville Blond, the chairman and deputy chairman of the Royal Court, announced that the ban on the critics was none of their seeking and they would continue to be invited. There was some talk of William Gaskill resigning in protest, but he was persuaded to stay, and once again peace reigned in Sloane Square. However, a projected film version of the play, to be filmed as a straight photographic record of the production by Peter Snell, who had recently filmed Frank Dunlop's no less controversial production of *The Winter's Tale*, was finally abandoned.

The cancellation of a film version is a theme which weaves its sad way through this story like a Wagnerian *leitmotif*. This was only one of the troubles which hit the Old Vic revival in 1933. Charles Laughton had always wanted to play Macbeth ever since he had been a fat, much-ridiculed schoolboy at Stonyhurst, and when Lilian Baylis invited him to join the company for the 33/34 season he readily agreed. Lilian Baylis had not wanted him, for she disliked and distrusted film stars, regarding them as parasites who would use her theatre for their own advantage and self-glorification. But Tyrone Guthrie, her artistic director, convinced her that Laughton would be a great asset in many ways. Apart from all artistic considerations, there were distinct financial advantages: the public would flock to see him and thus bring much needed money to the box-office. He pointed out that he had only been a film star for a few months and that his great success in *The Private Life of Henry VIII*, should not be held against him. His salary of £20 weekly – unheard of then at the Old Vic – would, he assured her, be amply justified by his success

At thirty-three, Laughton enjoyed international fame, but like so many film stars, before and since, he ached to get back to the stage where he felt he belonged. Few of his admirers realised how little actual stage experience he had enjoyed. Since he had left the Royal Academy in a blaze of glory clutching his Bancroft Gold Medal, only seven years had passed and only four of them in the theatre. The Old Vic Company included Flora Robson, Ursula Jeans, Roger Livesey and his own wife, Elsa Lanchester, so the support was good. So were the parts – Canon Chasuble, Lopakhin, Mr Tattle, Prospero, Angelo, Henry VIII and finally, Macbeth. Tattle and Chasuble were triumphs and it was quite evident that he had a

Flora Robson and Charles Laughton at the Old Vic in 1933.
A superb dress rehearsal and a disappointing opening performance.
(BBC Hulton Picture Library)

superb, unsuspected comic talent, but for the Shakespeare parts the critical reaction was very mixed. The press unanimously pointed out that he couldn't speak the verse, a fact of which he was painfully aware, but they did admit that something very compelling was flowing over the footlights. As expected, the public flocked to see him in his not inconsiderable flesh, and the houses were packed to the roof.

Then came Macbeth, right at the end of a long and exhausting season. This would be the climax, the acid test by which he would be remembered and judged. With Flora Robson as his Lady and Guthrie's imaginative but sensible production (Guthrisms hadn't started then) the omens were good. In his memoirs *A Life In The Theatre*, Tyrone Guthrie has described how the three weeks rehearsals proceeded in an atmosphere of great anticipation as Laughton's performance slowly took shape. Then came the final dress rehearsal on the morning and afternoon of the first night and he decided to Give His All. An older and more experienced actor would never have done this, but he had either never heard of the superstition or he decided to ignore it. By all accounts he gave such a magnificent performance that the company, shivering in excitement, said to each other, 'this is going to be the greatest Macbeth any of us have ever seen!'. Three hours later he gave the first performance but unhappily he had shot his bolt. He was tired, his voice was strained and the old superstition about the good dress rehearsal leading to the bad performance proved to be sadly true. He got through the evening without too much trouble and without any accidents, but this was clearly not enough. There had been one unfortunate textual slip when he said, malapropishly, 'Full of scorpions is my wife, dear mind' instead of 'full of scorpions is my mind, dear wife', which elicited an unwanted and disconcerting laugh. It was a terrible disappointment for everybody, and the atmosphere at the end in the dressing-rooms was like a funeral parlour. The audience had certainly applauded enthusiastically, but Laughton knew, as everybody did, that the evening had been a sorry failure. Guthrie rushed round to his dressing-room to offer what consolation he could, and found Laughton, still fully costumed and made-up, slumped miserably at his table and gazing

166

suicidally into the mirror. On these occasions, an actor is at his most vulnerable, and Laughton was a nervous, hyper-sensitive, deeply insecure man. It's always difficult to know what to say in these circumstances but Guthrie did what he could. Suddenly Lilian Baylis, wearing her Oxford University Doctorate gown, swept in like a red and black tornado. It was *her* theatre and this fat film star was one of *her* actors, so she clearly had to say something, but what? Her solution to this delicate diplomatic problem was exceedingly unfortunate. 'Never mind, dear, you did your best,' she trumpeted in her shrill Cockney voice, 'and I expect that one day you'll make quite a good Macbeth!' and with a nervous little titter she vanished. Laughton never forgave her and for the rest of the season he refused even to speak to her. He was convinced that she had said it out of malice, and ignored Guthrie's firm reassurance that malice was just not in her nature, and that such a monumental piece of tactlessness had risen out of sheer nervousness. The breach in their relations was very unfortunate, because Guthrie had persuaded Lilian Baylis to invite Laughton back for a second season, and that the parts should include Dogberry, Pandarus, Falstaff and Sir Toby Belch, pointing out that as these were all written in prose, his inability to speak verse would not matter. These parts would have given Laughton a heaven-sent opportunity to extend his rich and robust comic talent and his Falstaff would certainly have made theatrical history, but his anger with Lilian Baylis was so great that he refused.

Alexander Korda was interested in a film version of *Macbeth* using Laughton and the Old Vic Company; offers were made and plans discussed but Laughton refused. 'I've done some good things in this season and I've had one complete failure. Why should I put that failure permanently on record to haunt me and make people laugh?' he asked not unreasonably. He suggested a film version of *Measure for Measure* in which he had scored a real triumph as Angelo, but Korda was not interested.

The most tragic case of a film cancellation was Olivier's of 1956. In 1955 he had played his second Macbeth at Stratford with Vivien Leigh as his Lady and Keith Michell as Macduff in a production by Glen Byham Shaw. This was one of the few cases where the Curse

167

Laurence Olivier at Stratford in 1955. The greatest Macbeth the author ever saw or hopes to see. (Sally Chappell/Victoria & Albert Museum)

was known to have taken a holiday, for apart from a couple of little accidents in the duel scene (Olivier nicked the white of Keith Michell's eye during rehearsals, and himself nearly fell twenty feet from a high rostrum in one of the early performances), rehearsals and performances took place without incident. Olivier scored one of his greatest successes in this part and those few who were lucky enough to have seen it are agreed that it is indisputably the finest Macbeth our generation has seen. Keith Michell was a very dashing, passionate Macduff and Vivien Leigh brought an unsuspected vocal depth, dignity and dramatic tension to the Lady. Shaw's production was sensible, atmospheric, full of imagination and was in every respect a triumph for all concerned. A film version had been in Olivier's mind for some years and now was the time. It seemed the most natural thing in the world that he should thus complete the quartet begun with the immensely popular, prestigious and money-spinning *Henry V, Hamlet* and *Richard III.* Backers were found, a script was prepared, Olivier grew a beard, and a little preliminary casting was done round the Oliviers as the Macbeths. Then disaster struck: the backers backed out and the money was not forthcoming. Rank wasn't interested and the major American distributors decided that Olivier was not box-office. This smear had been pursuing him for some years and it was one of those maddening half-truths which it was difficult to deny *in toto.* Admittedly his last two films, *Carrie* and *The Beggar's Opera* had not been successful, in fact the latter had been a total disaster. But his three Shakespeare films had all made a profit over a period of years. This was not enough for the moguls of Wardour Street: they wanted large profits instantly. If Korda had been alive there would have been no problem but Korda was dead. Olivier travelled round hopefully looking for the money until two days before shooting was due to start in Scotland, before finally admitting defeat. The film was put up on the shelf and has never been taken down. This story, typical of the appalling stupidity and sheer wanton insanity of the film world, is enough to make any theatre lover weep. Thanks to all the faceless moguls, our greatest actor's greatest performance has been allowed to become a slowly blurring memory. Posterity's loss is incalculable, and if posterity spits blood at the thought, then nobody shall cry shame. It can be seen from this sad story, that the Curse works its evil in many strange and unsuspected ways.

One name suggested for inclusion in the Olivier film had been Paul Scofield, and few announcements caused more excitement than that of the 1967 *Macbeth* at Stratford. Paul Scofield had always wanted to play the part, and Peter Hall had always wanted to direct him in it; for both men, it was their first contact with the play. The company included Vivien Merchant, Ian Richardson,

Sebastian Shaw, Brewster Mason and Patrick O'Connell. Rehearsals started in early June for a mid-July opening and on the first day Peter Hall delivered a long talk to the company which is still remembered and quoted. He spoke about his interpretation of the play, his production ideas and what he hoped to contribute to the play and its tradition. He is a fluent and articulate man; speaking to the company is something he has always done very well (the *Figaro* company at Covent Garden in 1966 still speak admiringly of his initial talk to them); it clears the air, it puts everything into perspective and it builds up company morale. One of the most important points he made was about the superstition. He urged them to put aside all thoughts of bad luck; there was no curse on the play, it was all superstitious nonsense and if unfortunate things had happened then these had been pure coincidence. It was all in the mind, and if the company were sensible and hard-working the production would take place without incident and, he hoped, with great success. The company was deeply impressed.

For a month everything went according to plan. The rehearsals were stimulating and became progressively more exciting. The production was beginning to take shape and Scofield was mapping out a performance which in its broad outlines would clearly add to and surpass his previous Shakespearean laurels. From an actor who had triumphed in his historic performances as Sir Thomas More and Gogol's Government Inspector, much was expected and clearly much would be given. At the end of June the company had its first run-through. Excellent. It was clearly going to be the most exciting production any of them had ever been in.

A few days later the troubles started. A local man, employed in the theatre offices, collapsed in the Assembly Hall one day and died in hospital of a heart attack, and it was an indication of Peter Hall's success with his morale-building talk that this was not regarded as a sinister omen. But a few days after that, Peter Hall himself collapsed and was taken to hospital with shingles, a particularly nasty and painful affliction. He had for some time been fighting a running battle with bad health and nervous fatigue; three years earlier during the History Cycle he had had a nervous breakdown and this second onslaught was evidence that he had not properly recovered.

For six weeks he had to lie on his back in a dark and silent room; it was rumoured that he would go blind but this turned out to be, happily, a false alarm. In his absence the governors had to make a decision – to postpone or not to postpone. Since there was nobody else to take over the production and since Peter Hall himself was very anxious to see it to a successful conclusion, it was decided that a postponement was inevitable and desirable. Tickets were re-funded, the entire autumn schedule was revised and many thousands of overseas visitors were disappointed. In his absence the production was placed in cold storage; from time to time they would do a run-through under Paul Scofield's supervision but clearly little extra could be contributed.

Peter Hall returned in late July and was photographed outside the theatre smiling happily with Paul Scofield and Vivien Merchant. All seemed to be satisfactory but it was not so. He tried to galvanize the company into their former enthusiasm but it was not possible; the excitement and the fun had gone, and it became speedily evident that he was still not well. His physical energy, his enthusiasm and the flow of ideas had gone. The company morale sank very low. It went even lower when the costumes arrived; they looked magnificent but they were made of p.v.c. which is very heavy and hot. The final rehearsals and the opening performances took place in the middle of August during a heat-wave, and to this day the company remember the torture of those evenings sweating away in the punishing heat of the theatre. In fact it was only the regular supply of salt tablets which enabled them to get through a performance.

The notices were mixed though respectful. Audiences were on the whole very enthusiastic and the play did capacity business for the rest of season but the feeling of disappointment throughout the company was keen. American television wanted to film it and contracts were in preparation, but it was eventually decided to cancel it. 'The production just didn't work,' Peter Hall wrote to me years later. 'It didn't recover from its postponement and I, being ill, stuck rigidly to my original conception instead of modifying it. In the circumstances it seemed better not to film it. But I mean to do the play again.'

Anthony Tuckey's production at Liverpool in 1970. The camera flashed at the very moment when they were all cheering which accounts for the slightly operatic aura of this photograph. Bob Harris as the Bleeding Sergeant in on the stretcher in the centre.

Another man who is eagerly looking forward to directing *Macbeth* again is Anthony Tuckey, of the Liverpool Repertory Theatre. The first time was in early 1970 and the sequence of disasters was so extraordinary that a chill goes through the whole of the theatre whenever the play is mentioned. Before he started rehearsals he talked to a number of other prominent repertory managers who had previously directed the play. All, without exception, advised him to abandon the idea. He refused to take their advice. The troubles began in the second week. John Franklyn Robbins playing Macbeth was hit in the eye by a sword and the membrane covering the eye was broken, an accident which, though not very serious, did involve a complete rest. On the same day, Barbara Ewing, playing Lady Macbeth, went down with 'flu, Anthony

172

Macbeth back on after mishap

JACK LYNN, guest star and director of Chesterfield Civic Theatre, who was back on stage last night after being accidentally stabbed in the face during the final fight scene in Tuesday's performance of " Macbeth," in which he plays the title role.

The audience were unaware of the mishap. The part directs that Macbeth, fatally injured in the fight with Macduff, falls into the orchestra pit, out of sight of the audience, and Mr. Lynn was able to do so and also get back on stage for the curtain calls, though having to be supported by other members of the cast.

Subsequently, Mr. Lynn had six stitches inserted in the wound at Chesterfield R o y a l Hospital but— " bloody, bold and resolute," to quote the Bard — was insistent that the show, in the time-honoured s h o w business tradition, must go on.

Jack Lynn.

Tuckey took over Macbeth and Audrey Barr, one of the witches, deputised for the Lady. This left a gap in the witches scenes and an actress called Liz Gebhardt, visiting her husband in Liverpool, found herself at an hour's notice sticking her head through a trapdoor and choking to death in the smoke while she quavered one of the vision's lines. The 'flu spread and by the end of the second week there were five understudies playing. An urgent message was sent to Jack Lynn who had just played the part at Chesterfield, but as he was still suffering from severe head injuries sustained during his opening night duel, he had to decline. By the end of the third week, the company was together again and in good health. After a rehearsal on the Saturday, Anthony Tuckey wished them good luck for the final performance and said how glad he was that they had survived their troubles. Unbelievably, he spoke too soon. Bob Harris, the actor who was playing the Bleeding Sergeant, went out for a stroll at about 7.00 pm and carefully, adjusted his watch by a public clock: he had not been long in Liverpool or he would have known that this particular clock had *always* stood at thirteen minutes past six. He thus confidentally extended his walk and eventually returned to the theatre to be greeted with the horror-struck news that the play had already started twenty minutes earlier and that he had missed his only scene. The supreme irony was that the play got the best notices for years and played to full houses.

† † †

There are many who do not believe in this ancient superstition, and do not believe in *any* superstition; the concept of bad luck does not exist for them. Many of these are sufficiently sensible and diplomatic to keep their private thoughts on the subject to themselves; many are not. The Powers of Evil do not require that every actor should believe in them, but they do get very angry and aggressive if they are laughed at and made the target for mockery. It is necessary to respect them and it is even more necessary to respect your colleagues, particularly those with whom you share a dressing-room. A young actor might quote from *Macbeth* accidentally, which is very easy to do. He will inevitably be taken to task by some older actor, gently or, not so gently. What he must do is to perform a simple ritual of exorcism which is traditionally thus: to go out of the dressing-room, turn round three times, to spit and to knock on the door three times and beg humbly for re-admission. The alternative is to quote a famous line from *The Merchant of Venice*, 'fair thoughts and happy hours attend on you'. *The Merchant* is a lucky play and its text has a traditional exorcising effect on *Macbeth*. What the young actor must definitely *not* do is to laugh contemptuously and say that he doesn't believe in any of that superstitious nonsense and to continue quoting the play in defiance of all decency or commonsense. The story of *Macbeth* is full of tragic incidents where young actors (and some not so young, too), have deliberately defied augery and even insulted it with disastrous consequences. Diana Wynyard played Lady Macbeth at Stratford in 1948 with Sir Godfrey Tearle's Macbeth directed by Michael Benthall. She didn't believe in the Curse and made the sad mistake of saying so shortly after the dress rehearsal. Just before she went on for the sleep-walking scene, she decided that the way she had been rehearsing it, and the traditional way of playing it, was all wrong. Sleepwalkers did *not* walk with their eyes open, as they had always been shown. They walked with their eyes *shut*, and without telling anybody she went on the stage on the first night and put the theory into practise. The rostrum was wide enough for comfort and as she had been rehearsing on it for several days she thought she knew exactly how far it went and at what point it started to curve round. The first night audience gasped audibly with horror as she slipped from the rostrum and fell fifteen feet. It was a mark of her professionalism that she picked herself up and continued with the scene, and of her courage that, although bruised, bandaged and considerably shaken, she did not miss any performances. Ian Holm, playing Romeo at Stratford, remembers that he heard another actor quoting *Macbeth* in the wings. When he left the stage to make a quick change, he received an urgent message to 'phone his wife at home, and discovered that their young daughter had put her hand through a plate glass window and needed immediate medical attention. 'In fact it wasn't all *that* serious,' he said, 'but the incident certainly made me think!'

An actress in the cast of *Irma La Douce* was foolish enough to quote *Macbeth* in the wings while waiting to go on, and carried the folly still further by refusing to take seriously the concern of the actors in the wings. That evening the car in which she was being driven home, crashed and although neither she nor the driver were seriously hurt, she was badly shaken. Two days later she went down with food poisoning and had to miss a number of performances. Martin Jarvis, playing Hamlet at Windsor in 1973, remembers the evening in which an old colleague, one Joshua Plinge, started to quote from the play at great length just before his appearance. An hour later he suffered an agonising lapse of memory, and a long speech – which had previously given him no trouble whatever – suddenly vanished from his mind resulting in a very lively duet with the prompter. That same performance, Polonius suffered a stroke and had to retire from the company. The fact that my letter, asking if he had had any *Macbeth* experiences, arrived at the theatre on that very evening was just a sinister coincidence. Actors at the Old

Malcolm Keen at the Old Vic in 1934. The first of four Macbeths who appeared in one week! (Sally Chappell/Victoria & Albert Museum)

Vic remember a young actor called Andrew Plinge who quoted *Macbeth* during a performance of *The Merchant of Venice*, during the middle fifties. The sad, predictable pattern followed: the actors told him not to, he laughed contemptuously and refused to believe what he described as nonsense. Within a few minutes three actors suffered physical injuries in connection with a rather lethal piece of mobile scenery – broken toes, broken fingers and bruised shins. After the performance, young Plinge stepped out of the stage door and was promptly knocked over by a car. He wasn't hurt, only bruised and shaken, but he did then admit that there might be something in all the nonsense and from that time on he was careful never to quote the play again. Malcolm Keen was another actor who didn't believe in the superstition. He played the part at the Old Vic in 1934. He lost his voice shortly after the first night and had to be replaced by Alastair Sim. Sim was struck by a bad chill and had to go into hospital and it was the young Marius Goring who learned the part at short notice and played it for a few performances until he was finally relieved by John Laurie who played it for the rest of the run. Four Macbeths in one week is probably a record.

The staff of London's New Theatre during the run of *Oliver* remember with horror the night a young girl, employed as a temporary usherette was waiting in the front lobby for the show to finish and whiled away the time by quoting *Macbeth* 'tomorrow and tomorrow and tomorrow...'. She was severely reprimanded by a senior member of the staff, a cloakroom attendant. The young girl was, it seemed, suitably apologetic but it was too late. A few minutes later one of the actors rushing across the bridge in the final crowd scene, fell to the stage, fractured his skull and died instantly. His name was Claude Jones.

Mocking Shakespeare in musicals and revues is frowned on and never seems to be very successful, but mocking *Macbeth* is really dangerous. It was Charles Cochran who decided to include a Herbert Farjeon sketch about *Macbeth* in his wartime (1942) revue, *Big Top*. He wasn't superstitious at all even though the sketch involved extensive quotation and mis-quotation from the text of the play. Beatrice Lillie was the star and in this sketch she did indescribably funny things with her kilt, sporran, bagpipes and the inevitable rope of pearls. A few old actors were heard to mutter nervously but the hysterical laughter she drew from the wartime audience seemed justification enough.

Where shall we three meet again
The Vic, the New or Drury Lane?
What hags are those with their soup tureen
The middle one looks more like Basil Dean!

But a double tragedy was to follow. Within one week shortly after the show opened, an actor in the company, whose name really was Robin Hood, lost his father, and Beatrice Lillie received the tragic news that her only son, then serving in the Royal Navy, had been killed in action in the Far East. He was a tall handsome boy, the apple of her eye, and her bereavement and the effect it had on her are most movingly described in her autobiography.

Nicholas Hawtrey, an actor from Stratford, had always viewed the superstition with disbelief. His mother had at one time been the curator of the Ellen Terry house in Smallhythe which was also used as a theatre museum, and among the exhibits was her famous and magnificent Lady Macbeth costume which had been designed (and later painted as a portrait) by Whistler. Hawtrey was there one day when it was being moved to allow the house to be spring cleaned. A small jewel fell from the crown and he retrieved it deciding to adopt it as a lucky mascot. A diamond from Ellen Terry's *Macbeth* costume would certainly carry some status. For some years he cherished it but it bought nothing but bad luck and so much of it that he finally decided to return it to the Ellen Terry museum. He was still not entirely convinced so he put the superstition to a further test during the 1959 season at Stratford. Every night for a period of several weeks he quoted from *Macbeth* in his dressing-room and persuaded the other actors to do likewise, just to see what happened. His curiosity was quickly satisfied. There was a succession of small troubles, nothing very serious, but enough to make you wonder. Actors suffered strange lapses of memory, fell backwards off high rostrums, injured themselves in fights. There were small technical troubles, light bulbs failing at crucial moments, sound equipment fusing during vital scene changes. There were administrative troubles. Paul Robeson announced that he would not after all be appearing as Othello and a replacement had to be found.

Everytime the play was quoted, Nicholas Hawtrey remembers, something bad happened.

Finally he was convinced and to everybody's relief the experiment was abandoned.

A similar experiment was tried by the actors in *Anthony and Cleopatra* at the Bankside Theatre in the summer of 1973. Several of them in a dressing-room started to shout out a speech from *Macbeth* just to see what would happen. The immediate result was a scene from a Hammer horror film. A storm blew up, a truly terrible storm which produced a savage deluge of rain. This beat down on the canvas roof which began to sag and fill up. In the meantime, the electricity from the storm caused a very dangerous short-circuiting with the result that the whole stage became an electric death-trap. The performance was thankfully stopped, the audience sent away, the roof collapsed and the theatre virtually fell to pieces. As a result of all this extensive repairs were required which involved cancelling the 1974 season.

The most appalling incident in this category was always known in the profession as 'The Oldham Tragedy'. Some of those involved have suffered such a deep shock that even after thirty years they will not talk about it. The facts, though, are simple and have been easy to ascertain from the files of the *Oldham Evening Chronicle*. Oldham Repertory Company one of the better known weekly reps, decided to celebrate its ninth anniversary with a production of *Macbeth*. The part was to be played by their leading man, Harold Norman who had been with the company for two years and was popular in the town and with the company. He was by all accounts a very talented actor and had recently played Iago, Ernest and Mr Rochester. A great future was prophesied for him; he was at this time 34. He was married to a young dancer called Audrey Thompson (his second wife) and they had a baby daughter. The company included Bernard Cribbins (Seyton), Weyman Mackay (Malcolm), Harry Lomax (Duncan), and Antony Oakley (Macduff). It was directed by Douglas Emery. Norman and Oakley were given directorial instructions to rehearse their fight, with sword and dagger, alone and in their own time which they did with enormous enthusiasm and professional expertise. Both daggers and swords were

179

blunted as is the theatrical custom. The play opened on Monday 27 January 1947. It went very well, Norman gave a fine performance and the company received good local notices. On the Wednesday night, 30 January, Douglas Emery was standing in the wings watching the fight between Macbeth and Macduff which ends the play. Both actors were stabbing and hacking with their usual energy but it did seem that the moves were slightly muddled and wasn't running as strictly as it should to the rehearsed routine. This night it was cut short for Norman fell to the ground, but instead of dying on stage as it had been rehearsed, he crawled slowly to the wings. 'Douglas, I've been stabbed, I can't take my curtain call' he whispered. Emery sent for an ambulance and Norman was taken off to the local hospital. In the meantime the play had finished and the audience was shouting for Norman who had given a magnificent performance. Douglas Emery then had to go in front of the curtain and explain what had happened to a hushed and shocked audience. The following afternoon the senior surgical officer at the hospital decided that there was evidence of bowel perforation and performed an operation. Norman made what appeared to be a good recovery; the *Oldham Chronicle* decided not to swamp a trivial incident with a lot of sensational publicity about the superstition and said very little about it. The part of Macbeth was played in his absence by the stage-manager Arthur Hall. But a few weeks later general peritonitis set in and exactly a month after the stabbing, Norman died. At the inquest, evidence was given by the stage-staff, the other actors, the medical authorities and the firm which hired out theatre daggers. Antony Oakley stated that he had never met Norman before they joined the company and that their professional relationship had always been very friendly. He was completely exonerated and the official verdict was death by misadventure. But a little later it was reported that the baby girl died of suffocation in the theatrical lodgings and the widow had suffered a nervous breakdown as a result of the double tragedy and had left the theatre. It was a quarter of a century after the tragedy that it was learned that a little time before the production, Norman had shared a dressing-room with an older actor and had started to quote *Macbeth*. He disdainfully ignored the tearful requests that he

180

should stop because it was bad luck and continued to quote. Six weeks later he was dead.

Two people who did believe in the Curse most religiously and who never scoffed at it were Sybil Thorndike and Lewis Casson. In 1926 they presented the play at the Prince's Theatre (now the Shaftesbury) with Henry Ainley as Macbeth, Sybil and Lewis as Lady Macbeth and Banquo, Basil Gill as Macduff and the youthful Jack Hawkins as Fleance. They invested a lot of their own money in it which has long been regarded as very bad luck. From the start it was one of those productions which goes wrong in every department. Lewis, who directed, was at his snappiest and angriest during rehearsals and he and Sybil bickered and quarrelled more violently than ever before. Bernard Shaw came to the rehearsals and tried to take over the production, making a fool of himself with his stupid comments and instructions (his directorial skills did not, it seemed, extend to other people's plays); at one point, as Jack Hawkins remembered at the end of his life, he had a blazing screaming match with John Laurie over the correct pronunication of the name Scone which Shaw insisted should be said *Skoon* to rhyme with moon. The first performance went well and the notices were good but a series of mysterious troubles hit the theatre like the plague: costumes caught fire, scenery fell down, equipment was stolen and to cap it all, Henry Ainley, suffering from nervous exhaustion and fighting his lifelong battle with alcoholism, had to leave the company. His place was taken by Hubert Carter, a huge, bull-necked, bull-voiced heavyweight actor who had so little control over his natural strength that he nearly killed Sybil on one occasion and nearly killed his Macduff on several successive nights. The company became very worried and tense and there were nights when Sybil was frightened to go onto the stage and had to force herself by a real effort of will. One evening, Lewis took her into their dressing-room; 'Sybil, the Devil *does* work in this play,' he said, 'there *is* horror behind it. The play is truly cursed.' Together they knelt down and prayed, reciting Psalm 91, 'surely he shall deliver us from this noisome pestilence'. Slowly the aura of evil and darkness lifted, they went on the stage without any further fears and the remainder of its regrettably short run passed without incident.

Quotation can be dangerous even outside a theatre if the context is nevertheless a theatrical one. Noel Johnson remembers a wartime ENSA tour of *Thunder Rock* in which the company travelled in a coach. One evening during the journey one of the younger actors started to quote *Macbeth* and stopped in mid-sentence as the others exploded with vituperation. It was then democratically decided that the mischief had been done and that they might just as well continue quoting. So, like naughty children working off years of repression doing what was forbidden, the entire company started to quote their favourite *Macbeth* passages. That night, the performance of *Thunder Rock* was one long accident. Nothing very serious happened, but a succession of irritating little troubles reduced the play to something resembling chaos: props were mislaid, scenery fell over, costumes were torn, entrances were missed, lines were forgotten, and Noel Johnson, fighting Humphrey Morton, fractionally mistimed a blow and knocked him momentarily unconscious. During the journey back, the company was wryly discussing the evening's troubles; suddenly somebody remembered the journey to the theatre that evening. 'My God!' he said, 'do you all remember which play we were quoting?'

† † †

The Curse has crossed the Atlantic and has been very active in America. Clayre Ribner, General Manager of the Shakespeare Festival at Stratford, Connecticut, remembers a truly terrible season in 1961. The company included Pat Hingle, Jessica Tandy, Kim Hunter and Will Geer. The first accident occurred during the dress rehearsal: one of the company riding a bicycle to the theatre was knocked over by a car and had to spend a week in hospital. During a preview performance, the stage lift taking up the three witches rose too high, one of the witches stepped forward onto the darkened stage, fell and injured herself badly. She also had to spend some days in the local hospital. Throughout the summer they were plagued with injuries and accidents and the local doctor was in constant attendance. Franklin Cover replaced Pat Hingle as Macbeth for the final month of the season and had to play the dagger scene at a command performance at the White House in front of

President Kennedy and General Ibrahin of the Sudan, the first time Shakespeare had ever been performed there. He had a very painful time with the play. One night he was chasing a witch in Act One and took a fall, landed on his back, missing a fog machine by inches. He lay painfully there for what seemed like hours until Banquo's solicitous 'My gracious Lord, may I help you?' brought down the house in mocking laughter. X-rays were taken and although nothing had been broken he was black and blue for days. Later he developed a cyst under his left arm. It was operated on locally and he played the remaining performances in great pain with blood soaking through the bandages. The complications developed when the dye of his costume worked its way inside, necessitating a further operation in New York. After all this, he firmly believes in the Curse but – as with so many actors – would dearly love to risk it all again. But the climactic disaster of the season took place during this final month. Douglas Sherman, a young actor from the company, was found stabbed and dying of knife wounds in the picnic grounds adjacent to the theatre. Police questioned everybody after the performance but the murderer was never discovered and it was thought that he might have committed hara-kiri. The following week, the little daughter belonging to actor Colgate Salsbury, fell to her death from the window of the apartment they occupied. But still the Curse was not satisfied. Jack Landau, the company manager, was later found murdered in his Boston apartment. His naked body was beaten, strangled and tied up in his bathroom. He had been stabbed nine times by an eight-inch carving knife. Three youths were charged with his murder but were subsequently released for lack of evidence.

In Minneapolis, a talented young actor, George Ostroska, playing his first *Macbeth*, collapsed and died of a heart attack whilst on the stage. By a strange irony, he was talking to the two murderers in the banquet scene, and had just come to the lines:

> There's blood on thy face/
> Thou art the best of cut-throats.

In 1940, Margaret Webster directed the play with Maurice Evans and Judith Anderson. The preliminaries of casting were unusually acrimonious and produced one ferocious row between her and Maurice Evans. The rehearsals were reasonably smooth but the physical production was immensely complicated. It involved light projections, which Margaret Webster had always disliked and distrusted, complex scene changes, recorded sound effects, a musical score in the pit, transparencies and all the usual Macbeth hazards including Banquo's ghost, the witches and all the apparitions. No expense or trouble was to be stinted.

During the New Haven rehearsals, the stage manager got stage manager's stage-fright, and became paralytic and helpless. The electrician caught the infection. The designer decided that his light projections were the most important aspect of the production and Margaret Webster decided that they were not. She finally had to tell him to leave the theatre and not come back till after the opening night.

The opening night in Boston was a real director's nightmare. None of the effects happened as they were intended and the performance was a mess. But this was nothing in comparison to the New York opening. All went well until the England scene in Act Four. When the lights came up, it proved to be Duncan's tent scene from Act One. The unhappy designer crept up to Margaret Webster in the darkness and whispered, 'Another surprise for me?' She nodded sympathetically. 'And for me too,' she said. It was only the rapid intervention of the stage manager who rushed up the iron ladder to the fly floor which stopped the over-eager flymen from visibly changing the set when they discovered their mistake.

Immediately after the New York opening, Margaret Webster went down with appendicitis. Then Pearl Harbour happened and the draft began to bear down on the company; the Thanes of Scotland and the Lords of England began to disappear almost weekly. At the end of the New York run a long road tour was planned, which involved some recasting including Judith Anderson's understudy. Margaret Webster went down with 'flu at this point and could do little about it. The tour was to open at Buffalo on a Monday night in February and on the Monday morning, Maurice Evans telephoned her to say that Judith Anderson had laryngitis and the new understudy did not yet know the lines. He suggested that she come up and play Lady Macbeth. She crawled out of bed and went to the airport. The flight was made very bumpy and dangerous by a blizzard which was in progress. Margaret Webster had played the part before and did know the lines but she was not at all sure about the directorial moves and business she had devised, and throughout the flight she was continually closing her eyes and trying hard to remember them. To add to her troubles, she felt weak and ill. At last, a man sitting across the aisle spoke to her sympathetically. 'I have some airsickness tablets if you would like one', he said. She shook her head. 'They're no good for what's troubling me', she said.

Happily she was able to get through the evening performance without disaster, and even with some credit; next day at her hotel was a huge and magnificent bouquet of flowers with a card saying, 'never again will I mistake a rehearsal of the sleepwalking scene for airsickness'. There was, however, a brief and bitter epilogue to all this. Her production of *Macbeth* was selected at the end of the tour to be tried out at Fort Mead to demonstrate whether the US Army would like, or more probably loathe, Shakespeare. As she was on her way to join the company, acute tonsilitis set in and she had to return quickly to New York.

The Curse can produce many different sorts of trouble quite apart from the more obvious physical and artistic disasters – it can, indeed, be as devious, patient and malevolent as a Victorian mother with six unmarried daughters. It had not quite finished with the Evans-Webster-Anderson production and chose a singularly unpleasant and long-delayed method to make its further presence felt – like a time bomb with a very long fuse, in this case twenty-six years, although the solitary victim was not anybody in or even remotely connected with the play. Amongst those who saw it in its initial New York run was William Redfield, a boy actor of thirteen who had scored a great success in Moss Hart's production of *Junior Miss* and was to make a small but ineradicable mark on theatrical history by being the only actor to get star-billing as Guildenstern which he played in the famous Burton *Hamlet*. After Redfield had seen the performance of *Macbeth*, he went backstage to visit a friend in the company who played Banquo. Sitting in Banquo's dressing-room they chatted and laughed, and Banquo told him a very funny and very well-known story about the English director, Basil Dean and a difference of opinion he had had with Sir Ralph Richardson over a play in which they had both been involved back in the early thirties. Sixteen years later, Redfield published a brilliantly witty and vivid account of the rehearsals and performances of the Burton *Hamlet*. It was called *Letters to an Actor* and it was plentifully garnished with amusing anecdotes. One of them was the Dean-Richardson story. It was published in England and Basil Dean, taking strong exception to the story, sued Cassells, the publisher. The vital point at issue was simple: could Redfield prove that the story was true? Clearly, he couldn't even though the story had been told and re-told on both sides of the Atlantic for many years and was part of contemporary theatrical folk-lore. The suit was surrendered and there were no damages other than court costs, but the book was embargoed within two weeks of its English publication and both Cassells and William Redfield ended up by being considerably out of pocket.

Another actor who will always remember *Macbeth* with alarm and embarrassment is Charlton Heston. He had played it a number of times, including a very successful performance on NBC television, before he played it under Burgess Meredith's direction in an open-air production at Fort St. Catherine, Bermuda in 1953. Trouble began at the rehearsals when Heston had a severe accident on his motor-bicycle; his legs were badly cut and he had to leave the company for a few days which upset him very much as never before in his life had he ever missed a single day's rehearsal. This was the point when other actors in the company began to talk about the Curse and to quote examples of it from recent theatre history, though there were some actors who had never heard of it. They did not have to wait long to see its effect for trouble started right at the first performance. Jack Fletcher, who played the Porter, was sitting in the wings, watching Macbeth's first scene with Banquo. Heston left the stage abruptly and rushed to Fletcher, pointing at his tights. 'Get them off me, get them off me', he whispered frantically. Fletcher and another actor grabbed him by the waist and pulled his tights off his body, while Heston groaned and writhed with the pain and sank gasping to the ground. It later transpired that while laundering the clothes, somebody had dipped Heston's tights in kerosene. Since it was an outdoor production both Macbeth and Banquo rode their horses bareback, and the sweat of the horses and the heat resulted in very nasty burns on his legs and groin. Enquiries were later made but nobody knew who or why this had been done or, more disturbingly, whether it had been an accident or an inexplicable piece of aggravation.

The Curse was relentless that night though it did exchange its physical malevolence for a more impish mood. The castle overlooked the sea and the ocean formed a very picturesque backdrop. It had been arranged that just before Lady Macbeth's death there should be a loud scream and then a dummy wearing the same dress she had worn for the sleepwalking scene should be tossed off the rampart. It would sail down, catching the lights as it went out of sight into the sea below. Very dramatic, very convincing, very realistic. But in order to use the same dummy for each performance, it was attached by ropes to the rampart. On the opening night is was very windy. The scream came, the dummy was tossed fluttering through the air and down out of sight. Then, without missing a beat, the wind picked it up and it fluttered right back up again landing with a loud plop at the feet of the actor who, as the messenger, was trying to say 'The Queen is dead, my Lord!' The audience naturally screamed with laughter.

Pain, and ridicule, and now confusion. The soldiers storming Macbeth's castle quite literally burned it down to the ground. Logs, faggots and various complex wooden structures had been placed round the set and soaked in kerosene. When the soldiers stormed on, they lit everything with their flaming torches. Once again, this was an effect which would have been exceedingly impressive if all had gone according to plan, but in that high wind the flames and smoke blew straight into the audience causing a stampede as people screamed in panic and distress. Order was eventually restored, but the burning of the castle did not take place again.

The Curse had one more trick up its sleeve. In spite of some impressive acting, the audience was finding it difficult to take the production seriously and were in that slightly hysterical mood when anything appears to be funny. Their final joy was at the end when Macduff brings Macbeth's severed head onto the stage on a long pole. Heston had just played the part on television and thoughtfully brought along with him the severed head which the TV property department had made. When it appeared it was seen that it was an exact and realistic replica of Heston's face covered with blood and looking very gory, but for some extraordinary reason the audience decided that this was the funniest thing since Charlie Chaplin and screamed with joy. As with the burning castle, the severed head was never seen again.

But at least there had been no fatalities: John Gielgud's wartime appearance in the play must surely hold the record in this respect. With rehearsals, provincial tour and West End run it occupied ten months and it was a very hectic and troublesome period for all concerned. Gielgud had played the part once before at his first season at the Old Vic in 1930 when he was twenty-six and just starting in Shakespeare. Everybody assumed that he was terribly miscast but he astonished everybody by being very good, public, critics and even fellow-actors. James Agate, the oldest, toughest and hardest-to-please of all the critics, was so impressed by the murder scene that he actually visited him backstage in his dressing-room to tell him how good he was and to prophesy that he would not be able to keep it up, a distinctly rash and unprofessional thing for a critic to do. It seemed that Gielgud proved him wrong, for he was deluged by splendid notices and the three week run passed without trouble or incident.

But recreating a successful performance twelve years later is very difficult and full of pitfalls. He had some distinguished names to support him, Gwen Frangcon-Davies and Leon Quartermaine, but the call-up and the difficulties of wartime casting had resulted in a rather makeshift company of frustrated old actors who couldn't get into the war, as Gielgud himself later described it. The music was by William Walton, the sets by John Minton, a brilliant young designer, and it was directed, rather unwisely, by Gielgud himself. Manchester in January 1942 was miserably cold and the company had to battle through the ice, snow and blizzards to reach the

188

gloomy and unheated Scala Theatre where the rehearsals were held. It was here that the first fatality occurred. Beatrice Fielden-Kaye, a splendid actress, who had been rehearsing the Third Witch had been forced to leave the company. She had been feeling very ill but she insisted on coming to the theatre every day to watch the rehearsals wrapped up in furs and being made much of by the company. On the final Friday night she died in her hotel from a heart attack. Tactfully, the company kept the news from Gielgud until after the opening five days later.

Older actors – and there were many of them – shook their heads gloomily and talked about the Curse and waited nervously for further trouble which was not long in coming. One by one the younger actors in the company dropped out, either for the army or from illness and in Edinburgh the actor who played Duncan, Marcus Barron, died of *angina pectoris*. The play opened in July 1942 at the Piccadilly Theatre to rather mixed notices. Gielgud was dissatisfied with his own performance, Gwen Frangcon-Davies, a small-sized actress from South Africa, was dwarfed by the impressively sombre settings and her obvious miscasting was now clear to everybody.

William Walton's music was greatly admired by Gielgud and the audiences, but rather less so by the Three Witches who had to dance round the cauldron rather more quickly than was comfortable to one of his more agitated musical frenzies, *presto agitato con fuoco*. Breathless, panting and sweating, it was a nightly ordeal. Annie Esmond, one of the witches, could not keep up with the relentless tempo, and one night she collapsed on the stage and died.

John Minton later committed suicide in his studio, surrounded by his beautiful and atmospheric pre-Raphaelite designs for his *Macbeth* sets and costumes. The flats used in the production were subsequently repainted for a light comedy which was sent out on a wartime tour. The star of this play was the charming and greatly loved Owen Nares, said to have been the first matinée idol. It was on this tour that he died.

† † †

The effectiveness of the Curse is naturally dependent on the number of performances the play receives. It is no coincidence that the Curse is most active in England and America where the play is seldom off the stage. On the Continent and in other foreign countries, *Macbeth* is not by any means the most popular Shakespeare play so performances are rare and there are very few – if any – examples of trouble. In Russia, a performance of *Macbeth* is a rarity – there have been only two since the War – and Russian theatre people are politely surprised that the play is considered unlucky. It is also possible that the Curse is less active where the play is in translation since these will not be the words Shakespeare wrote: however, there have been some notable examples of bad luck on the Continent so it would seem that translation carries no guarantee of immunity. The earliest production of the play outside England was in Amsterdam in 1672 when a Dutch actor, Jan de Hoffmeyr, played the part under his own management. He had become involved with one of the actresses in his company whose husband was playing Duncan. Relations between the two men became worse and shortly after the first performance, Jan de Hoffmeyr substituted a real dagger for the artifical one for Duncan's death scene which took place on the stage in full view of the audience. Duncan's death that night was horribly blood-stained and real. Jan de Hoffmeyr was arrested and served a life imprisonment. Nothing more was ever heard of him.

Two generations of Greek actors have suffered at the hands of the play. Dimitri Murat, who had his own theatrical company in Athens has recorded the disasters which he and his grandfather experienced.

After playing many heroic parts with his own theatre company, my grandfather decided to include *Macbeth* in his repertory, as he was very fond of this famous and excellent tragedy. Disaster! He was obliged to disband his company after years of lucrative touring and he realised that the bad luck was due to this ominous play. In the following year he formed a new company but as soon as he repeated *Macbeth* the bad luck returned. So, not willing to give up a play he loved so much, he assigned the part of Macbeth to a minor actor in his

190

troupe, thinking thus he could avoid misfortune. He was wrong for the bad luck persisted. Finally he was forced to give up the play. My grandmother used to say that if it had not been for *Macbeth* they would have been rich.

It seems that I did not learn from the unlucky experiences of my grandfather. In 1956 I decided to produce *Macbeth* in the Rex Theatre, Athens which I had been managing for seven years. From that day on there was trouble between myself and the owner of the theatre, so that I was ultimately compelled to resign. It took me two years to recover from the reverse and I can assure you that I will never again try to perform this marvellous but unlucky play.

Stanislavsky had always been fascinated by the play and spent many years preparing and rehearsing it with his Moscow Arts company. Russian indecisiveness and procrastination in addition to the usual accompanying troubles caused endless delays and postponements but in the early 1900s, the production was declared ready and a grand dress rehearsal was held. In the murder scene, Macbeth suffered an alarming lapse of memory and as was the custom in the turn-of-the-century Russian theatre, went down to the prompter's box for help. No prompt. He called out to the prompter. No reply. He stamped his foot angrily. Still nothing. Finally he investigated and found the old man slumped over the script – dead. With appropriate Russian fatalism, Stanlislavsky took the hint. He abandoned the production and never attempted it again.

A similar decision was made by the Portugese National Theatre in 1964 when Michael Benthall was invited to direct *Macbeth* in Lisbon as Portugal's contribution to the Shakespeare centenary in translation. It was a superb production, splendidly acted and received enthusiastic notices, but two days after the opening the theatre was burned down and it was six years before it was rebuilt. The production was abandoned and suggestions that it be revived in the new house have been coldly received.

But there was nothing cold about the reception given to a Japanese production in Japan some years ago. It was said that prisoners condemned to death were compelled to rehearse and play Macbeth with a company of professional actors and that Macbeth's death by decapitation and the subsequent exhibition of his bleeding head on a pole was not faked. The production played as many performances as there were condemned prisoners; they were widely attended and received with enormous enthusiasm, since the spectacle of combining punishment with popular entertainment appealed strongly to the oriental sense of justice. It is not, alas, known just how much truth there is in this exceedingly gruesome story, but anybody who suffered under Japanese hands in the wartime prison camps will have little difficulty in believing it.

† † †

In view of the number of cancellations, it is amazing that *Macbeth* has ever reached the screen at all. In fact it has been filmed more than any other Shakespeare play and the reference books list between them no less than nine, starting with an early silent version made in 1903 and starring Godfrey Tearle and Edmund Gwenn and finishing with Roman Polanski's version starring Jon Finch and Francesca Annis. The Curse is just as active in the film studios as it is in the theatre; none have been really successful and all have run into some sort of trouble. Godfrey Tearle, fighting on top of a building, was nearly killed in his death throes, and Edmund Gwenn sustained injuries which caused pain to him for the rest of his life. Sir Herbert Beerbohm Tree touring in America made his Hollywood début in a studio-shot version which was such a disaster that a ten-week season in New York was cut short after six days and his three-year contract was cancelled. The film has, unhappily, vanished without a trace and that is a great loss because on the evidence of what has survived of the film of his Svengali, Sir Herbert's highly melodramatic style did transfer rather effectively to the screen. When Orson Welles finished his 1946 version he discovered that the Scots accents which he had asked his actors to adopt were totally incomprehensible and the sound track had to be entirely, and expensively, re-made. A Russian version was to have been filmed in Georgia but nine members of the crew died of food poisoning whilst on location. A fire in the MGM studios in Hollywood in 1969 which destroyed millions of dollars worth of equipment was finally traced to a cigarette lying on a wooden desk in the producer's office. The desk contained a large pile of shooting scripts for a projected version of *Macbeth*. The Polanski film is certainly the best to date, but this ran into serious trouble. Polanski was sacked by the distributors because he was way behind schedule, but after a long and critical interregnum he was reinstated.

Only when the film has nothing to do with Shakespeare does it escape the Curse; to rehash the plot and transfer it to another place and another time in history is perfectly safe. This explains the artistic success and untroubled shooting of two well-known and very popular films, the Japanese version, *Throne of Blood* which has garnered well-deserved awards all over the world, and a modern Chicago-based gangster version made in 1955 called *Joe Macbeth* starring Paul Douglas and Bonar Colleano. This escape route has been followed by *Umbatha* in which the action is transferred to a Zulu village in South Africa, the plot intermittently follows its original with occasional patches of Zulu dialogue, and the chief attraction is a display of native dancing whose high spots are the play's dramatic climaxes. This profect was masterminded by Professor Elizabeth Sneddon of Durban University and was the most exciting offering of the 1971 World Theatre Season in London.

† † †

What about *Macbeth* in the other branches of the theatre, in opera and ballet? Unhappily, the Curse has crossed the orchestra pit and has operated with some success in the opera house. It inspired Verdi to write one of his dullest, most undistinguished operas, three hours of tedium broken by moments of the purest banality – the Banqueting Chorus might have come straight out of *The Student Prince*. It survives as a moderately popular item in the repertoire only because its dramatic content, since it follows the play closely, is considerable, though the extraordinarily difficult technical demands made on the principal singers are one reason why it isn't more frequently performed. Lady Macbeth ends her sleep-walking scene with a top D flat which one in twenty singers can reach in comfort. The knowledge of this hurdle can produce terrible tensions in sopranos who have failed to produce it; it comes at the end of a long and exhausting evening and the note has been known to emerge as a tired flattened squawk. More than one singer has refused to sing the part for this reason.

Operatic memoirs are full of disaster stories connected with the opera since its first performance in 1847. Spike Hughes has given a blow-by-blow account of the first English performance in 1938 which took place at Glyndebourne. Fritz Busch, the conductor, and Carl Ebert, the producer both loved the opera and were very anxious to present it. They also knew of the superstition and were fully prepared for trouble (typical of John Christie that he knew nothing of Macbeth's sinister reputation and, when it was pointed out, bluffly refused to believe 'all that nonsense'). Trouble was what they got, right from the start. There were some urgent casting problems: Lady Macbeth is a part which is almost unsingable, too high for a mezzo, too low for a soprano, and where do you find a singer with a sufficiently wide range who can reach the top and bottom, who can act and whose voice would not swamp the delicate acoustics of the Glyndebourne Opera House? Busch later admitted that nothing in all his years as an opera conductor had caused him so many headaches, so many sleepless nights. Finally, after many months of searching, he chose the American-born soprano, Franca Somigle, who studied the part for three months and finally asked to be released from her contract because the part was too difficult and was unsuited to her voice, though why it took her so long to come to that decision was not explained. The second choice was the much-recommended Iva Pacetti. She was signed up with Francesco Valentino, also American-born, who possessed what Busch described as the most beautiful voice he had heard for years.

Rehearsals started and it seemed that their troubles were over: advance bookings were good, pre-publicity very helpful, and Queen Elizabeth who had been born in Glamis Castle, promised to come to an early performance. It was, however, the calm before the storm, the Curse's now-familiar trick of lulling the intended victim into a state of false security. Ten days before the opening, Iva Pacetti was taken ill and was unable to sing. This meant that Rudolf Bing, the production assistant, had a number of sleepless

194

nights phoning round the world's opera houses to find a replacement. He eventually engaged the Yugoslav soprano, Vera Schwarz, who said she had never sung the part before but was willing to try. She took the next train and learned the part *en route*. By the first night she was very tired but she struggled bravely and her performance was highly praised for its dramatic effectiveness. As a special concession she was allowed not to sing that dreaded high D flat which was supplied offstage by Barbara Beaumont, a member of the Glyndebourne chorus, thus starting what has become a not-infrequent practice in the world's opera houses. All was being eagerly prepared for Royalty's first visit to Glyndebourne, a special gala souvenir programme was printed, and special food and wine laid on for a private supper in the Christie's house, but it was not to be. Queen Elizabeth's mother died and in the period of mourning which followed all her social engagements were cancelled.

However, Royalty of another sort did make its appearance a few days later. Christie had invited Toscanini to visit Glyndebourne as part of a long and devious campaign to persuade him to conduct there. Toscanini consented and turned up one evening to see *Macbeth* and it was an evening which surviving Glyndebourne administrative staff remember as one of confusion and tension. Furtwangler chose to turn up on that very same evening and everybody knew that the two men were at daggers drawn. Toscanini violently disapproved of the German conductor because of his Nazi sympathies and deeply resented his willingness to conduct in front of Hitler. If he saw him he might make a scene, might go up and abuse him, might even strike him. Toscanini's fiery temperament was notorious throughout the musical world, and the possibilities of diplomatic embarrassment were horrifying. The two men were seated in different parts of the theatre, and in the interval Furtwangler was taken into the Nether Wallop dining-room and Toscanini was escorted to the Christie's house for supper. Happily, the dreaded encounter did not take place but, unhappily, Toscanini never conducted at Glyndebourne. Twenty years later when he was at the Met, Rudolf Bing experienced a very similar sequence of troubles when reviving *Macbeth* there.

The Curse has also extended to the ballet but in a destructively negative way. *Macbeth* offers superb balletic possibilities – the witches, the ghosts, the dancing round the cauldron, the battles, the duels and fights, the banquet with its *divertissement*: what a superb and spectacular full-length ballet could be created out of Shakespeare, what a gift for an imaginative choreographer. Many have thought about it; John Cranko at Stuttgart had been contemplating the subject for some time, and how magnificently Marcia Haydée would dance Lady Macbeth, passionate, sexual, cruel, relentless. But Cranko's death by heart attack in the plane flying him back from New York in the summer of 1973 prevented him from realising this and many other projects. Fokine was interested; Balanchine is said to have thought about it. Sir Frederick Ashton went so far with the idea in the post-war years of the Royal Ballet as to make definite plans: designs and music (from William Walton) were commissioned, and some preliminary casting was done. Robert Helpmann and Margot Fonteyn as the Macbeths, Michael Somes as Macduff. But the ballet mysteriously refuses to come alive and why this should have been so is one of the great imponderables of the theatre. Ashton lost his enthusiasm. Three acts were reduced to two, then to one and it was finally cancelled leaving nothing behind except his synopsis, some design sketches and a few musical outlines.

The Ballet Theatre in London ran into far worse trouble with Robert North's projected ballet *Lady Macbeth*. Norman MacDowell, the dancer-director broke his arm, Belinda Wright rehearsing Lady Macbeth broke an ankle, her replacement tore a ligament and if all that wasn't enough, Norman MacDowell's house caught fire burning all his notes and sketches for the ballet. It was eventually abandoned.

Macbeth, as a full length spectacular, must be regarded as a Scottish white elephant, the ballet that never was. It briefly reached the stage in Russia and has been part of the Bolshoi repertory for the last two years but it has not been a success and it has recently been dropped. The only known *Macbeth* ballet which has survived is a short 30-minute piece for schools which was created by Edward Gailliard for his small ballet company, Ballet Minerva.

Even in the enclosed and boisterous world of music-hall, the Curse is not without influence. Billy Merson, who died in 1947 had a very distinguished career and his best-known song, of which he wrote words *and* music, dealt with the sufferings of an actor who is given a very hostile reception by his audience. It is very ironic and significant that the play in which the actor suffers his worst humiliations should be *Macbeth*.

> 'Twas through a Y.M.C.A. concert
>   I craved a desire for the stage.
> In Flanders one night I was asked to recite,
>   Gadzooks, I was quickly the rage.
> They claimed I was better than Irving,
>   They gave me some biscuits and tea.
> I knew it was not Union wages,
>   But that was their usual fee.
> Home I came, bought this dress,
> Played in the theatre and what success.
> I acted so tragic, the house rose like magic.
>   The audience cried 'you're sublime'.
> They made me a present of Mornington Crescent
>   They threw it a brick at a time.
> They jeered me, they queered me,
> They all tried to stone me to death.
> They threw nuts and bananas,
>   Fried eggs and sultanas,
>   The Night I Appeared as Macbeth

Another reason for the bad luck has been advanced by Michael Blakemore, and this is a strictly rational explanation dealing purely with the theatrical practicalities. *Macbeth* is virtually a one-part play. The imbalance is greater than in any other Shakespeare play for the central character carries the lion's share of the dramatic burden while the others are small parts standing round to feed him. Of these there are three good supporting parts – Lady Macbeth, Banquo and Macduff – while the rest are little better than walk-ons. Because they are so uninteresting it is very difficult to get good actors to play them which is one reason why it is rare to find productions which are well acted and well balanced throughout. On first glance, Macbeth appears to be a heavy villain on simple operatic lines, and the play can be taken to be a straightforward thriller à la Hitchcock (why did he never film it, one wonders?), with a few spectacular effects which the director eagerly looks forward to devising. The obvious and calculated theatricality of those fights, witches, black magic and ghosts enthrall the imagination and a series of beautiful and frightening effects are worked out. Both actor and director are thus deluded into underrating the play and its problems. Both are unpleasantly surprised. The director invariably runs into urgent technical difficulties and I've never heard of a production which didn't; he finds that this wonderful theatricality of the play is mysteriously slipping away between his fingers. The magnificent effects are not happening. *Macbeth* has evaded him, but why?

The actor finds that Macbeth is not a straightforward operatic villain; he is infinitely complex and full of disturbing inconsistencies – just *how* does an actor reconcile and make theatrical sense of a man who is simultaneously a successful soldier, a brutal murderer and a hen-pecked husband? The language in which all this is to be conveyed is full of the most subtle imagery, difficult to understand and difficult to put over. An actor needs to work very hard, to do a great deal of theatrical homework, and thoughtful preparation to make sense of it and yet not to lose the impulse and excitement which makes it interesting to watch. Romantic impulsiveness, instinct and a talent for inspired improvisation are no substitute.

What happens in the usual production of *Macbeth* is that the actor playing Macbeth gets progressively more worried and neurotic as he finds the part not as easy as he thought, while the rest of the company, standing around for hours with very little to do, gets increasingly bored and irritable. When action comes, it's rushing across the stage with bits of branches and leaves to represent Birnam Wood and then the dashing and staggering of the typical stage battle. Most actors find this rather embarrassing; depression and paranoia sets in, before long everybody is at each other's throats and that leads to trouble. The part is so physically and emotionally

198

exhausting that the actor playing Macbeth wears himself out because the part is a series of superb highspots with no valleys and resting-places in between. And when the end comes, the exhausted actor then has to fight four duels one after the other, up and down steps, rostrums and different levels, usually in the near dark. It's not in the least surprising that few productions take place without some broken arms, legs, gouged eyes, cuts, bruises and stabbings.

There are few actors who do not lust to play the part, whose great ambition is not to be able to shout out, 'Lay on, Macduff, and cursed be he who cries enough!' But it is a case of many being called and precious few being chosen. The artistic disasters can have a truly lethal effect on an actor's career. Lionel Barrymore satisfied a lifelong ambition in the early twenties and was torn to pieces by the critics with a viciousness which was unusual even for them. It killed his stage career for he left Broadway and went to Hollywood, and never set foot on the stage again for the rest of his life. His brother John had always wanted to play it and there were many offers, but, with the calamitous experiences of Lionel fresh in his memory, he always refused. The sad case of Basil Langton is a typical example of how the Curse can have an adverse effect on an actor's career. He had always wanted to play it and in 1950 he had his chance at the Downtown Theatre, off-Broadway. The director was Ray Boyle and his Lady was Gerry Jedd. From the start, he remembers, everything went wrong. There was trouble over the cast, over the contracts and over the production. As the opening night drew nearer, his wife advised him to get out of the production while he could. He refused. The first night was a disaster, and at the inevitable party afterwards some amiable fool (there's always one) put the finishing touches by saying, 'you know, you really did something for me, Basil. For the first time in my life I felt really sorry for Macbeth.' The critics treated him very badly; the notices were really crucifying, and the worst was from Walter Kerr who had previously been a great friend. This finished the friendship and it also finished his acting career. He did continue for a short time afterwards, but the impulse and ambition had gone; he then moved to writing and direction, both of which he now does very successfully.

Broadway, and particularly off-Broadway, has never been very hospitable to *Macbeth* which has seldom enjoyed commercial success there. The traditional situation in England, that whatever physical and artistic disasters are in attendance, the public always flocks to see it, doesn't seem to apply in New York where short runs are the rule. Gladys Cooper and her husband Phillip Merivale in all their dual glory, couldn't make it run for more than a week in 1934. Walter Hampden's revival of the same year survived only four performances and is remembered by Walter Kerr chiefly for the interminable gaps when the curtain was lowered after every scene to allow complicated changes behind it. Hampden had been unusually unlucky with the play which had always been a favourite: he presented it three times on Broadway, the first in 1918 survived only a single performance and the second in 1921 only six. In 1970, Rip Torn rehearsed what promised to be a very interesting experimental production which eliminated a number of small parts, cut the play down to a straight two hours and kept Macbeth on the stage throughout. Just before the opening, the off-Broadway Actors went on strike for more money and better conditions, the theatres were all closed and *Macbeth* was cancelled. In the following year there was a production at the Mercer O'Casey Theatre starring David Leary which surely breaks some sort of record for damage. Within three months there had been a fire which destroyed scenery, furniture and properties: there were no less than seven robberies in the course of which the hooligans tore out all the telephones from the walls, slashed the gauze scrims, made a bonfire of all the costumes and caused a financial loss of $80,000. And let it not be forgotten that it was during a performance of *Macbeth* that the historic Astor Place Riot in 1849 took place. Edwin Forrest, the leading American tragedian, was supposed to have organised it against Macready, his hated English rival, then on an extended American tour. Hundreds of patriotic Forrest supporters pelted the English actor with tomatoes and excreta thus forcing him off the stage. Outside, the military was ordered to fire above the rioting crowd reported to be 20,000 strong, but owing to the confusion of the moment, the soldiers fired *into* the crowd. Thirty-one people were killed. It must also be remembered that *Macbeth* was Abraham Lincoln's favourite play, and that the day before the assassination, he was reading aloud one of his favourite passages to a party of friends while sailing down the Potomac on the *Riverboat Queen.*

> Duncan's in his grave
> After life's fever he sleeps well.
> Treason has done its worst,
>   Not steel, not poison
> Malice domestic, foreign levy,
> Nothing can touch him further.

Macbeth is very popular with schools; they are always performing it and one wishes they wouldn't for it is a very unsuitable choice. Because the play is tough and virile it is thus naïvely assumed by so many theatre-minded, play-directing schoolmasters that it is right for adolescent boys. If the play defeats the combined talents of even the greatest professionals, it is unlikely to surrender to a group of inexperienced young amateurs. A muscular sixth-former may be king of the local rugger field or cricket pitch but he is likely to cut a very sorry, inadequate figure at Glamis Castle, even if he is supported by the headmaster's wife or the games-mistress of the nearby girls' school. There are few of us who have not at some time or other yawned and shifted irritably through a schoolboy *Macbeth* which we have been press-ganged into seeing merely because it is required reading for that year's examinations or because the English master has an obsession with the play and wants to try out some peculiar theory on his defenceless boys and their parents.

† † †

What do Harold Pinter, Prince Charles and Albert Finney's mother have in common? It is a question which may well one day grace *The Times* Christmas quiz. The answer, rather surprisingly, is that they all played Macbeth at school. Harold Pinter was well-spoken of by his East End school-friends. Gordonstoun, where both Prince Phillip and Prince Charles were educated, clearly thought *Macbeth* was a highly suitable play for Royalty as they both played in it in their time, Prince Phillip appeared briefly as Lennox before the war and Prince Charles as Macbeth in 1967. Penetrating the cloak of discretion which blankets all royal events is difficult, but it seems that these performances took place without incident or trouble, and that both royal actors were rather good. Albert Finney's mother wasn't so lucky. In a recent interview in *The Times*, her son has revealed that she once cherished theatrical ambitions and played Macbeth at the unusually tender age of thirteen. Unhappily she fell off the stage backwards during a performance, and although she herself wasn't hurt, it marked the end of her theatrical future.

The Curse is no respecter of amateurs and children. A production at St. John's College in Johannesburg in 1954 ran into an amazing sequence of trouble. A boy called Ivor Sander was selected to play Lady Macbeth but early in the rehearsals he was involved in a car accident and had to withdraw from the play. His replacement was a sensitive boy called Michael Shuter who rehearsed the part with great intensity and enthusiasm. Two weeks before the opening he fell from a high window in the middle of the night and broke an arm and a leg; he had apparently been sleepwalking and it was thought that the emotional strain of the part had had an adverse effect on him. Nevertheless he was able to play it with his leg in plaster and his arm in a sling. The third climax of trouble concerned the boy, Michael Moreny, who played Macbeth – his mother was killed in a car accident. The play was postponed for a fortnight and finally came to the stage with – happily – amazing success.

Schoolmasters who produce it and parents whose boys have appeared in it have many sad stories to tell. For Mrs Elsie Hawkesworth of London the play has always had deeply tragic associations. Her only child, a boy aged fifteen, played Seyton in his school production and shortly afterwards was killed by a lorry while on holiday. 'I wish that I hadn't known about the Curse,' she wrote, 'because if superstition is a fact it somehow destroys a certain faith in God for me.' In Florida, a large group of local children appeared in an amateur production at the Francis Wilson Theatre, Clearwater. Jesse Tilman aged eight, playing the Bloody Child, was killed by a car on his way to the theatre. It was only years later that those concerned realised that there was a connection between the tragedy and the play.

School children acting *Macbeth* are one thing but school children being forced to watch it in the professional theatre are quite another. There is nothing that we actors hate more that school matinées. We know that they are necessary evils but we can't pretend that – with precious few exceptions – they're anything but an exhausting nuisance and an aggravation. The children, unaccustomed to theatregoing, are noisy and restless either because they're rigid with boredom or because they're enjoying it too much. Children can reduce the finest performances to a shambles with their boisterous mockery and *Macbeth* suffers from this more than any other. Sensitive actors will always take this as a personal criticism but they are wrong: it is the Curse revealing a more cynical sense of humour. Wesley Addy playing the part at the Bucks County Playhouse in New Hope, Pennsylvania in 1969 found himself confronted by a very noisy audience of school children who interrupted his speeches and even pelted him with paper darts. 'This is the first time I have ever been subject to such conduct, you are the rudest audience I have ever played to,' he said to them, stopping the play. It takes a lot to provoke an actor to active protest but he clearly had no choice. He appealed to them and asked if he wished them to continue. This shamed them into good behaviour. They gave him a round of enthusiastic applause and the play finished without incident.

It's a great pity that school children all over the world have traditionally regarded *Macbeth* as the greatest comic masterpiece since *Charley's Aunt*. Sir Michael Redgrave had a very punishing experience with them one afternoon at the Aldwych in 1947. They had been tittering continuously throughout the play but when Lady Macbeth dies offstage, there is supposed to be a scream followed by cries and shrieks from her ladies also offstage. On this occasion the ladies forgot their cue and all that was heard was a sort of loud croak. Macbeth had no alternative but to ask, as per text, 'What is that noise?' and Seyton had no alternative but to reply, 'it is the cry of women, my lord.' This was too much and the school girls roared and screamed with laughter. Redgrave did the only

Michael Redgrave at the Aldwych Theatre, London. He had a short way with laughing schoolgirls. (Hegelmeyer)

thing an actor can do; he strode to the front, shouted 'Quiet!' reducing them to quivering silence and then proceeded with the play. At the end he received a considerable ovation from his youthful audience and was warmly commended by his colleagues for his action.

In America, 'out, out, damned spot' is thought to be excessively funny, and Judith Anderson playing the Lady with Maurice Evans during the war, found that the only way she could get past the point of danger was to cheat on the timing. 'Out! ... (long pause) Out, damned-spot (very quickly).'

John Irwin remembers a school matinée at the Abbey Theatre, Dublin: on the first night the company fought the first battle scene and then waited through a scene to fight the second. Unhappily somebody gave Malcolm the opening line of the *first* battle scene which was passed on and before the startled company knew what was happening the first battle was being repeated and nobody could stop it. The children in the audience were thrilled and noisy; 'Yiz have fought that battle wance before' ... 'Chazuz, they're givin' us an encore' ... 'six ter four I can tell yiz who wins, etc.' The play was reduced to chaos and the audience, he says, never laughed so much before or since.

The National Youth Theatre, directed by Michael Croft, presented *Macbeth* in 1969. The company consisted of senior schoolboys and school leavers and it had a very punishing time with the play. One of the boys received the news that his sister had fallen down a cliff to her death in the Hebrides; another boy fell backwards down a steep flight of stairs on the stage and sustained severe head injuries; a girl had £15 stolen from her dressing-room. But the most disastrous thing happened on the night that Jenny Lee came to see the play with a view to giving the company some Arts Council Aid. Gill Rutter who was in the company remembers that on that night the production, which had gone very smoothly and had in fact received excellent notices, just would not go right. The acting became sloppy, the production effects didn't work, a blanket of gloom and tension hung over the whole evening which was definitely not one of their best and which resulted in the grant not being given. The following night, she remembers, the play was as good as ever, but it was too late. Shortly after the production finished, Michael Croft had a heart attack.

A recent rep production in the North of England ran into bad technical trouble before its audience of schoolboy critics; one of them, Stephen Tate, remembers the details:

... it had the audience in stitches. The company was experimenting with some moving scenery which consisted of two large boards suspended by wires and they were raised or lowered as was appropriate. At first this was very effective in providing a contrast for the different scenes and acts. However, disaster struck as Macbeth was delivering one of his soliloquies. One of the wires attached to the scenery broke loose and the board began to swing uncontrollably to the front of the stage and struck an astonished Macbeth on the back of the head. He was obviously stunned but he decided to continue while weaving in and out of the swinging scenery providing a pantomime atmosphere for the youthful audience who were on their toes waiting for further mishaps. They were soon to be rewarded for their patience, for at the end of the play when, with a crudely-made sword, Macduff plunged into Macbeth. At this point, to the hysterical delight of the audience, Macduff's sword bent double. His complexion turned a deep purple and it was quite clear that he wanted to sink down the nearest hole.

† † †

The Curse can turn friends against each other and ruin scholastic careers. Keith Hancock, the Public Relations Executive, remembers a production at St. Paul's School, Darjeeling, India when he played the Bleeding Sergeant at the age of eighteen. The boys involved who made up one of the senior forms, had hitherto been well-behaved, well-disciplined, hard-working; they were respected by their masters and great things were expected. In their final term, they planned to present a single performance of *Macbeth* as part of the speech day, prize-giving festivities. Rehearsals started and suddenly everything changed. The boys suffered a mysterious change of personality; they became quarrelsome, aggressive, spiteful and insubordinate. It seemed that a devil was possessing them. There were fights, absenteeism and other breaches of discipline. A group of them suddenly turned against one of their number and bullied him so mercilessly that he was driven to protect himself. One day he threw a glass decanter against his arch-tormenter and a sliver of glass went into his eye. The surgeon was unable to save it and the persecuted boy was expelled and thus prevented from taking up a

Cambridge scholarship on which he and his parents had set their hearts. Keith Hancock was mysteriously attacked by a strange illness and he too was unable to go to university. The performance went without trouble or incident and was much admired, but the boys had behaved so badly that it was decided they must be punished. Accordingly, ten senior boys were ordered to the headmaster's study, and forced to bend over and take six strokes of the cane administered by their very tough, squash-playing headmaster; ten strapping, muscular, rugby-playing, eighteen-year-old boys who had never been in trouble before. It was all very mysterious and disturbing.

Of all the literary virtues, discriminating selection is the most important and the most difficult. In an investigation like this, so many fascinating stories are contributed, dramatic, tragic and horrifying, one is confronted by such an *embarras de richesses*, that there is an irresistible temptation to tell all. How can I omit the story of the production at the Flora Robson Playhouse, Newcastle in 1965 which because of technical difficulties had to be cancelled at 4.00pm on the opening day to the disappointment of the critics who had travelled up from London ... of the stage-hand who committed suicide during the rehearsals of the Chichester production of 1966 ... of the charming and talented Nicholas Meredith who died in New York during a *Macbeth* season with the Old Vic ... of John Lindsay who fell off a high rostrum, was replaced by Bernard Kay who learned the part overnight, and returned after a week with his leg in an iron ... of Duncan Macrae who broke his leg while rehearsing the play at the Glasgow Citizens and bravely struggled through a number of performances until he collapsed and was then replaced by John Casson ... of Donald Wolfit who was nearly killed by a cannonball which fell from the thundertrack and dropped onto the stage a few inches from where he was standing ... of the stage-hand who trod on a stage brace at the Winter Garden before the war when Robert Atkins was presenting the play, fell onto his back and was paralysed for life ... of John Woodvine who played the part at the Mermaid Theatre and received such appalling notices that he claims it set his career back by five years ... of the Theatre Royal, Newcastle being gutted by fire during the run of

207

John Woodvine at the Mermaid Theatre.

Macbeth in 1898 ... of the Lady Macbeth who suddenly married and eloped with her Porter whilst on a bus-and-truck tour of America and thus caused panic stations, drastic re-casting and confusion in an already despondent company ... of the actress who fell through a trapdoor at Greenwich and suffered injuries which kept her in hospital for a whole year (happily now recovered and working full blast) ... of Alfred Lunt and Lynne Fontanne who yearned to play the Macbeths and planned it for years but every time they were all ready to go into production something happened to stop and delay it, and this went on for years until they finally decided to give it up, and that was a real tragedy for the American Theatre for they would both have been superb ... of the German director, Hermann Herrey who directed *Macbeth* in Berlin's Kurfurstendam Theatre just after the war and who was torn to pieces so savagely by the press that he lost his job, lost the friendship of his most embittered critic, lost his health and finally emigrated to America where he found a new career as an architect ... of Mike Gambon who rehearsed the play for a month without incident only to receive a telegram an hour before the first performance telling that his father had died ... of the young actor, Stefan Langfelder who scrawled the final soliloquy, 'tomorrow and tomorrow and tomorrow, creeps on this pretty pace of day' on a blackboard in his old school in Long Island and then killed himself by gas poisoning ... of Julia Neilson who played in the 1937 Stratford production and crashed her car into the window of a Cotswold antique shop one sightseeing afternoon and insisted on returning to the theatre to play in *Macbeth* that same evening although she was covered in bruises and bandages ... of Richard Dennis playing the Porter at Billingham in 1970 who fell through the trapdoor, jabbed his foot on a rusty nail and whose agonised shriek of pain, 'Oh! F-U-C-K!' echoed round the crowded theatre eliciting a laugh his author never anticipated ... of the repertory manager whose production of *Macbeth* was so horrendously bad in every department that he was covered with confusion and embarrassment when he saw the queues at the box-office, and would go to his patrons and gently beg them not to come and see the play?

Happily, not all these stories are so tragic; some of them are very funny, for even the most chilling subject has its light-hearted side. Actors are fond of quoting Edith Evans' reaction when invited to play Lady Macbeth and who refused for a number of very sensible reasons. '1. she doesn't develop as a character, 2. she sits at that Banquet scene and doesn't do a thing and gets played right off the stage, 3. she doesn't have a death scene and 4. I could *never* impersonate a woman who had such bizarre notions of hospitality.' Margaret Webster remembers having to deputise for one of the witches at ten minutes' notice on one of her alarming bus 'n' truck tours during the war. The witch was sleeping blissfully at her hotel having totally forgotten that there was matinée. Just before the curtain went up, Margaret Webster rushed to the prompt corner to ask anxiously, 'Stop, *which* witch am I supposed to be?'

† † †

I myself played and presented *Macbeth* under my own management on the Edinburgh Festival Fringe. I ran into deep trouble from the start. A railway strike prevented the costumes and props from arriving in time and I had to obtain emergency replacements at short, and horribly expensive, notice. I was knocked off my bicycle in Princes Street and suffered from concussion, recovering just in time for the evening performance. My father died during the brief run and later a much-loved aunt. I lost every penny I put into it for there were two other rival *Macbeths* playing at the same Festival, and as if all that wasn't enough I had the worst notices of my life and didn't work for six months afterwards. Nevertheless, I don't regret it at all: the part is a unique challenge and however miscast or bad the actor may be, and I was undoubtably both, he cannot fail to learn something from the experience.

Old actors are also fond of re-telling the stories of Sir Ralph Richardson who played Macbeth at Stratford in the 1952 season. He was not ideal casting at the best of times and these times were not of the best, for he was tired and in bad health. He was deeply unhappy about his performance and throughout the season would indulge in long orgies of lacerating masochism. One day, he went to a group of actors in the greenroom. 'I'm the worst Macbeth I've ever seen. If I was the public, I'd ask for me money back.' Suiting the action to the word, he went to the box-office and said to the startled girl inside, 'It's the *worst* performance I've ever seen, it's a disgrace the public should be forced to pay to see it. I want me money back.' The girl didn't, in fact, recognise him, being new to the job, but she knew enough to give Sir Ralph a firm but polite refusal. Later that evening, during the performance, he approached his Macduff, Raymond Westwell.

'Give me five pounds,' he said.

'I *beg* your pardon, Sir Ralph?' asked Westwell, startled.

'Give me five pounds.'

'But why, Sir Ralph?'

'Because if you don't, I'll tell everybody that you played Macduff to my Macbeth!'

A treasured gem in the *Macbeth* apocrypha has an American couple watching Sir John Clements from the front row of the stalls at Chichester. It was a Thursday night and Sir John had just started to deliver the final soliloquy. 'Tomorrow and tomorrow and to-morrow ...' The American husband turned eagerly to his wife; 'did you get that, Honey?' he said, 'That means Sunday.'

But certainly the funniest of the *Macbeth* stories, and one which makes a fitting conclusion to this investigation deals with an am-bitious but not overtalented young actor who was employed in Sir Donald Wolfit's travelling Shakespeare Company. His contribu-tion to *Macbeth* was as the final messenger who has to run on stage and stammer out, 'My Lord, the Queen is dead,' and then run away. For many seasons he did just this, and then he became bored and asked Sir Donald if he could play a larger part. Wolfit refused. The young actor continued to ask and Wolfit continued to refuse. The young actor became increasingly depressed and the matter developed into an obsession. Thoughts of revenge filled his waking hours and one evening he decided to sabotage the play. That night he ran onto the stage. 'My Lord,' he shouted, 'the Queen is *much better and is even now at dinner.*' He then ran off, leaving the aston-ished actor-manager to deal with the situation as best he could.

† † †

What conclusions can be drawn from this enquiry? To be valid, an investigation must show both sides of the question. The evidence that *Macbeth* is cursed is formidable and, one would have thought, beyond reasonable dispute, but could a determined sceptic, a liter-ary devil's advocate, make out a case that it isn't? Possibly, but it is unlikely to be much of a case. It must be admitted in all honesty that there have been productions of *Macbeth* – not many, but some – which have taken place without trouble: where nobody dies, or breaks an arm or loses an eye or suffers a bereavement whether

"Get on a camel—a few lines from 'Lawrence of Arabia' and this could run for ever!"

Even the most tragic subject
has its lighter side …

212

I'd take the part, myself - if I wasn't so busy...

MACBETH
Resians

The English will blame anyone for their problems..

CALMAN

MACBETH
CRITICISED

THE OLD VIC
PETER
O'TOOLE
IN
MACBETH

'No I assure you sir, the understudy is on tonight'

'Which would be more amusing, the new Ayckbourn or Macbeth?'

birkett

"How would you like a small part in 'Macbeth', this guy said."

'So it's a Royal Command
Performance, but I still think it's a hell
of a way to play Lady Macbeth.'

human or canine; where the company remains united and friendly, when the notices are good and careers, if not actually advanced, are certainly not impaired. Two such productions spring instantly to mind and they were both black: Peter Coe's at the Roundhouse in 1971 and Orson Welles' *Voodoo Macbeth* at Harlem's Lafayette Theatre in 1935. Do black actors, one wonders despairingly, have a specially strong magic to protect them from the forces of evil? And for some actors *Macbeth* has been lucky, as with Barry Foster who received from David Lean his best film offer to date in *Ryan's Daughter* while playing Macbeth at the Mermaid Theatre; as with the late Michael Goodliffe whose eldest son was born while he played Banquo at the Aldwych in 1948 (he is the only one I know who didn't like the play and twice refused offers to play Macbeth); as with Julia Jones who has stage managed no less than nine productions between 1946 and 1962 without mishap; as with Edgar Wreford who has been in six productions and loves the play very dearly. This is a purely arbitrary selection from those letters I have received. There are doubtless many others.

It must also be admitted that troubles have occurred in other plays: the Globe Theatre was burned down during a performance of *Henry VIII*, Molière died of a heart attack during a performance of *La Malade Imaginaire*; actors have been stabbed and cut to pieces during the fights of *Romeo and Juliet, Richard III* and *Julius Cæsar*. But obviously the amount of disaster in these plays is trivial in comparison to that which has been found in *Macbeth*.

Any actor into whose hands this book should chance to fall must decide for himself if *Macbeth* has a curse on it or not. If he decides that it has, the inescapable question follows – what can be done about it? Regrettably, the only answer is – *absolutely nothing*. The only possible solution would be to ban the play, but in view of its relentless popularity this will be impossible while the theatre survives. Every actor and actress, every director and designer will want to get their hands on it. They are all incorrigible optimists and will console themselves by saying '*it won't happen to me!*'

> *I hope they are right.*
> *I wish them luck.*
> *They will need it.*

Epilogue

Macbeth has neither sub-plot nor epilogue. *The Curse of Macbeth* has both. The story behind the story is as interesting as, and forms a valuable supplement to, the story itself.

It was in May 1970 that my firstborn, *The Truth about Pygmalion* was published: this is not a fanciful analogy, for writing a book is supposed to be very much like having a baby according to those who have achieved both. Heinemanns generously gave me a publication party which was held in the Dress Circle Bar at Her Majesty's Theatre (where else?) and of the hundred guests invited seventy-five turned up. A pyramid of the book had been erected on a table by Heinemann's ever-resourceful Head of Publicity, Nigel Hollis, (now it's Publishing Director) and about thirty were sold which in itself was a rare occurrence, for friends of any new author always expect to be given a copy and get very resentful if they are expected to pay for it. That my friends did buy, and cheerfully, is an indication of how well they had been trained.

It was a very joyful and noisy party: my heart was filled with a delicious glowing happiness as I surveyed the guests. It seemed incredible that I should have as many as seventy-five friends at one and the same time, but there they were, mostly theatre people but not all. There were policemen, lawyers, security men, hospital nurses, secretary birds, advertising tycoons, unpublished authors and a motley collection of Soho eccentrics; all that and Fenella Fielding too.

'What are you going to write for us next?' It was Rachel Montgomery, my editor at Heinemanns, asking the one question which every first author secretly dreads. It was a question which was going to occupy my mind during my waking hours rather consistently during the following months, and there would be no easy answers. *The Truth about Pygmalion* had been a huge success with rave notices, over sixty of them, which Heinemanns said was unheard of for a young author's first book; there had been a sheet deal with Random House in New York for an October publication to coincide with a tour of the American Universities I was due to make with *The First Night of Pygmalion*, the two-handed play from which the book had been adapted, and there had been enquiries after the film and musical rights. I knew very well how difficult it is to follow a success and the book had certainly been that. The obvious solution was to describe the dramas and comicalities of another famous first night, but I had no desire to be trapped by what might well turn out to be an empty formula, nor did I wish to be known simply as a First Night historian. And even if I did, was there another first night which offered the same abundance of superb material as that of *Pygmalion* where I had a good plot, three colourful characters, and a wealth of witty dialogue to start off with, and all I had to do with the splendid story was simply to tell it? I looked despairingly at four hundred years of theatrical history and realised that the answer was an un-qualified 'NO'.

So I continued to think and to solicit advice from my friends both in and out of publishing. In the meantime, I was rehearsing a rather responsible part in an American musical called *1776*, (in which I was required to sing, dance *and* act) due to open at the beginning of June at what was then the New Theatre and is now the Albery. In fact the *Pygmalion* publication party had taken place in the middle of rehearsals and I had to obtain special leave of absence to attend it. The opening was a triumph for Anglo-American relations, the notices were those about which publicity directors dream, and the company settled down happily for what turned out to be a six-month run. Eight performances a week in a heatwave in a theatre without air-conditioning and with the added trouble of wearing periwigs and heavy eighteenth-century costumes was a great strain on the company and the wear on our nerves and tempers was noticeable. It was this which triggered a small but significant incident one day. I was drinking a cup of tea in the wardrobe with a group of others in the company in the interval, as was our custom, and one of them, the late Ted Gilbert, was telling a funny story about a production of *Macbeth* in which he'd once appeared. He was saying, 'now when I was playing Lennox in the Scottish Play ...' and this provoked a question from a young drama student who was working for a few weeks as a dresser. Being new to the profession, he knew nothing about its mystique and superstitions and he asked, in all innocence, 'Oh! What Scottish play is that?' I remember a slightly amused, condescending look pass between the company and I explained gently that this was the Shakespeare play set in Scotland about a homicidal Thane who becomes King, and that on no account was the name to be mentioned within the four walls of a theatre. 'Oh! You mean *Macbeth,*' he said, again in all innocence. There was a scream of anger from Ted and he shouted, 'Get *out* of this dressing-room you horrible little boy!' In the embarrassed silence which followed, I led the bewildered young student out of the room, explained the situation and made him perform the traditional routine of turning round three times and asking to be re-admitted. As an added precaution we made him recite, 'Angels and Ministers of Grace, defend us,' which is supposed to have cleansing properties. After that, the tea-party was resumed.

It was this little incident which reminded me very sharply of my own painful initiation into the world of superstition and fear. My first job in the theatre had been in 1950 after I had been demobbed from my two years service in the army in Greece. I was engaged to be an unpaid assistant stage manager, for in those halcyon days Equity permitted an aspiring and untrained young actor to work an eighty-hour week for nothing if he could find a theatre which would let him. As there was no Tannoy system, my duties included visiting all the dressing-rooms in turn to call the half-hour, the quarter, the five minutes and the beginners: to hurtle up and down six flights of stairs four times in thirty minutes was excellent exer-

218

cise if nothing else and I doubt if I had ever been in better physical condition. The senior actor in the company was an old man in his seventies called Harold J. Wilkinson, 'Wilkie' to his intimates and he has already been mentioned in Chapter One. I remember how timidly I knocked on his door. 'Come in!' he shouted and I entered for the first time in my life that holy-of-holies, the Star Dressing-Room. 'Half-an-hour, Mr Wilkinson,' I said. He was making-up for his performance as the Headmaster in *The Happiest Days of Your Life,* and he looked at me with petulant curiosity. 'Who the devil are you?' he enquired. 'I'm the new A.S.M.' I replied, and told him my name. 'The last one was no bloody good,' he grumbled and went back to his make-up which was kept in a scruffy old cigar box.

I was suddenly seized by a desire to impress him with my theatrical knowledge. I wasn't exactly conceited but I did want to let him see that this verdict would never apply to me. On the dressing-room table was a curved dagger left over from the Christmas production of *Aladdin* and a quotation from *Macbeth* seemed to be in order. 'Is that a dagger I see before me?' I said in what I hoped was a dramatic Macbethy tone of voice, and to my alarm he turned, gazed at me in horror, stood up pointing a shaking finger at me and shouted *'Get Out!'* 'But Mr Wilkinson, what have I ...?' I stammered, but I got no further for he picked up his make-up box and threw it at me. It hurtled through the air, grazed my forehead thus causing a bleeding scratch and crashed at my feet scattering make-up sticks and little bottles everywhere. *'Get out you bloody little fool!'* he screamed and the commotion brought my immediate superior, the Stage Manager herself, running to the scene. 'What's the matter, Wilkie?' she asked. 'He quoted, he bloody quoted!' shouted Wilkie. She turned to me. 'You quoted?' she moaned in an incredulous voice, 'You *quoted?* How could you, and on a first night. Well ... *really.*' 'But what have I done? What's it all about? I just don't understand,' I stammered being very close to tears myself. My obvious distress did have the effect of calming them down. Wilkie gently explained the old superstition, which was of course news to me, and then told me what to do. I must go out of the room, turn round three times, fart, knock on the door and ask very humbly to be forgiven and re-admitted. I did all this but when it came to the fart I tried but couldn't. 'Mr Wilkinson,' I shouted through the door, 'I can't fart.' 'Then bloody well try,' he shouted impatiently. 'I have tried and I still can't.' There was a pause while he privately debated the matter. 'Then make the noise, anything, as long as it sounds like a fart.' This was easy. I did so and the door opened. He was smiling. 'Come on in, you bloody fool,' he said cheerfully, shaking me by the hand, 'and *never* quote that play again. Never while in the theatre. In fact, it would be safer if you never quoted from it anywhere even outside the theatre. And if anybody asks you to be in it, say no. It's very dangerous.'

All this came back to me forcibly as I was drinking my interval tea in the New Theatre and I realised that this was the answer to my problem. A superstition in which people passionately believed, even to the point of actual violence, was clearly one of absorbing interest, not only to theatre people but to the world outside. To gather up all the horror stories connected with the play and to try and find out the reason for the bad luck would make up a book which not only had never been written before but which theatrical literature urgently needed. I did not waste any time. I wrote out a synopsis of five thousand words, had it beautifully and expensively typed and bound, and sent it to Heinemanns.

They rejected it. Oh, they thought it was a fascinating idea but didn't think there would be anything like enough material to fill a book. Would it not be better, Rachel enquired, to write it as a series of articles and sell it to the Sunday colour magazines? At this point my agent, Joyce Weiner, retired and like an unwanted heirloom I was passed over to Debbie Owen, wife of David Owen, later the Labour Government Foreign Secretary. I went down to meet her in her beautiful house overlooking the river in darkest Limehouse. She liked to idea of a book to be called *The Curse of Macbeth* (already that title had forced acceptance, irrevocably and unarguably), but suggested that ten thousand words or even twenty thousand would give a future publisher a clearer idea of the riches which the book offered. I agreed and seeing that it would probably end up with my having to write the book in advance and purely on spec, I decided to start the investigation.

I began by consulting my fellow-actors in *1776*. These chats

220

usually took place in the stagedoor lobby where there was a long wooden bench and a hot drinks machine and enough space (just) to lounge and stand around. The superstition forbids you to mention the name of *Macbeth* while actually standing inside the four walls of the theatre, and it was intriguing to see just how literally this was taken by my colleagues. Some of them bluntly refused to discuss the matter until we had stepped out of the stagedoor into the alleyway (a public byway) which separates the New from the Wyndhams Theatre. Strictly speaking this put them outside the theatre so the Fates were not being flouted and Augery was not being defied. The fact that they were all in full make-up and costume and thus exposed to the public which thronged the alley in the height of that 1970 summer did not deter them, though this is, strictly speaking, forbidden by one of those unwritten theatrical laws. I often think that those American tourists who passed the stagedoor during that summer must have had their most treasured preconceptions of English life delightedly confirmed when they saw a group of eighteenth century gentlemen, gorgeously costumed and periwigged, standing in solemn conclave in a dingy twentieth century alleyway. Other actors would have to be dragged out onto the fire escape or even the roof before they would discuss their *Macbeth* experiences. Some would refuse to discuss it anywhere in or outside the theatre and would have to be coaxed to a nearby pub or to my Soho flat in 25B Lisle Street before they felt safe. And one actor wouldn't discuss it at all anywhere, under any circumstances, and to this day has firmly refused. All of which goes far to show the terrible power which this grim superstitition has over the minds of some people.

I wrote hundreds of letters to other actors in London and suggested meetings. Sometimes they were eager to tell, sometimes not. Typical of this group was a postcard from Sharon Duce who had been involved in a production of the play in York. Writing from the comparative safety of her Hampstead flat, she said:

> I was all set to tell you all about the things which happened to us over the Scottish Play, but alas, I'm too scared to do even that for fear of bad luck.

I compiled a list of all the principal *Macbeth* productions of the last fifty years. I haunted the British Museum and the London Library reading obscure books of theatrical history. I roamed around the picture libraries of the national newspapers looking at old tattered production photographs. I began to get interested in witchcraft and started to correspond with its authorities and practitioners. I put in an appeal for information in the correspondence columns of a hundred magazines and newspapers all over the world. When I started on the book I did not regard myself as a superstitious man but as the evidence to support the superstition piled up and letters from actors all over the world flooded in, and as I saw the extra-ordinary effect it has on people, I did start to believe in it myself. I became obsessed with the subject and devoted every waking moment to the book. I started by taking letters, books and papers connected with it into the theatre so that I could work on it in the interval and when I was not on the stage. Some of the actors found out and objected strongly; their alarm infected me and I found myself believing that this alone would bring bad luck to the play so I stopped bringing them. Normally, I would have taken them on train and car journeys but being reluctant to tempt the Fates I stopped even that. This caution extended to my cycling round the London streets: I began to be very cautious and never carried *Macbeth* memorabilia in my saddle-bag. Soon the horrible idea crossed my mind that the mere fact of writing the book might be unlucky. But that, I sensibly decided, was a chance I just had to take.

By the end of 1971 I had completed twenty thousand words and had changed my agent twice, ending up with a charming ex-Indian Army officer called Paul Moncrieff. He sported brocade waist-coats, a monacle and scented Balkan Sobranie cigarettes: he knew little about the theatre but he liked my synopsis and was confident that he could sell it. He had a friendly arrangement with a New York agent, an old gentleman who looked rather like Mark Twain and was called Joshua Sanders. He was reputedly the oldest agent in the business and had a list of famous clients which looked like the Pulitzer Prizewinners for the last fifty years. He liked the idea and the synopsis and started to send it round. But the American publishers were even less interested in it than their English counter-parts. Eighteen months of writing and hustling and nothing to show for it. I began to get very neurotic about it all. And then something quite amazing happened which changed the whole picture.

One day in October 1972 I was in the Occult Bookshop in Cecil Court making a rather special enquiry. I had heard from a number of sources, including Sir Alec Guinness, of a theory that the Witches' cauldron scene contained an authentic black magic spell and was thus the cause of the Curse. It was an intriguing idea and I had been told that a book of mediæval spells called *Grimoires* might contain something like it. If I could find it written down, this would go a long way to confirming the theory. The assistant wasn't able to help me, and I was about to leave when a woman, who had clearly overheard my brief conversation, turned round.

'You won't find it,' she said, 'It exists but its never been written down. Never.'

'You appear to be an authority on the subject?' I said.

'I should be,' she said with a smile, 'I'm in the Profession.'

'"Profession" you mean that you're an actress?' for it is only in the theatre that people refer to themselves in this manner.

'No, luv,' she said with a strange little smile, 'I'm a witch.'

I gazed at her in astonishment. I had never before met a witch and I had no idea what one would look like but I never thought it would be like this. She was a plump cheerful woman in her middle thirties: she had brown hair, smooth skin, she wore a brown over-coat and sensible shoes. There was nothing remotely occult about her, though perhaps there was just a touch of Madame Arcati in the large leather handbag she carried. We started to chat and with a stab of excitement I realised that this was a heaven-sent oppor-tunity to find out some of the things I urgently wanted to know, and from an authoritative source. I suggested a cup of tea. She agreed, and we went to the Wimpy Bar on the other side of the Court.

I ordered tea and Danish pastries and watched her while she tucked in with Bessie Bunter gusto. 'Are you a white witch or a black one?' I asked facetiously, and she giggled. 'White, luv, white as snow. Don't have anything to do with the black stuff. Not my line at all.' The accent was suburban Cockney, the humour was briskly cheerful: she was like a nanny or a school matron or a very cosy wardrobe mistress and I wasn't entirely surprised to discover that her name was Millie. She told me a little about her life. She lived in Watford quite near the theatre (coincidence!) in a semi-detached house with a little garden and she had two husbands – a legal husband and a witch husband who was her partner in her occult practises. It seemed to be a very unusual domestic situation but apparently the three of them lived together in peace and harmony. She ran a small but thriving herbal cure business and wrote the occasional article on witchcraft for the trade papers. She spoke contemptuously about the popular conception of witchcraft as shown in the popular press. 'All that running about naked round the camp fire, lot of nonsense. We in the profession think it's ever so funny. If people want to do it then let them get on with it, but what's it got to do with witchcraft?' She rattled on cheerfully for a few more moments and then she became brisk and businesslike. 'Now what do you want to ask me, luv?' I launched into my story. I told her about the book, my trouble in getting it accepted, the terrible boredom and apathy amongst the publishing houses who clearly didn't know a good thing when it was on a silver plate before their noses, and this latest theory that the Curse was due to the authentic black magic in the Witches' scenes. She listened intently.

'Yes, you're quite right, luv. *Macbeth* is all you've said. It *is* unlucky, it *does* have a curse on it and we in the profession have always known about it. Whenever I go to see if I feel funny. Evil is a strange thing, love, you can see it, smell it just like you can a cold wind or a nasty smell and evil is both those things and a lot more besides. Whenever I see *Macbeth* I can feel the evil all round me and to keep it off I keep turning round this little ring on my finger.' And she showed me a gold ring with a Celtic cross on it. 'And when the play is over and the audience have gone I can still feel the evil lingering in the empty theatre. Now about the cauldron scene, "eye of newt and toe of frog", yes you're quite right, it *is* black magic but you won't find it in the *Grimoires*. In fact it's not written down anywhere. No real spell is ever written down, it's far too dangerous and anything which is written is not a real spell. It's usually a lot of nonsense.'

'But the *Grimoires* ...'

She giggled happily. 'All rubbish, luv. You might just as well get a cookery book. There's more magic in *Mrs Beeton* or the *Penguin Food Guide* than in those silly old *Grimoires*. Yes, that speech is real magic but don't you go getting a newt's eye or a frog's toe or the liver of a blaspheming Jew, always assuming you could find one, and thinking you can make a potion which will let you see into the future because you can't. You see, love, all those things mentioned are code words for something else which we in the profession know about but don't ask me what they are because I'm not going to tell you. This information is potentially far too dangerous to be given to outsiders however well-intentioned or innocent their interest. And you won't find it in a book anywhere so don't waste your time looking. That's why there's a curse on the play and on everything and everybody connected with it. Actors, scenery, furniture, even the audience. Yes, the bad luck can extend even to the audience.'

'And would it extend to my book about it?'

'Yes, luv, of course it would,' she said cheerfully.

I then explained that it had already done so. I hadn't had any personal bad luck in the last two years while I had been doing my preliminary research, and my acting career had flourished mightily, but the book had already had no less than twenty rejections and what could I do about it?

'Easy. As there's a curse on the book, what you have to do is to get it taken off. And you do that by appealing to a higher authority. Dedicate the book to the White Goddess, every religion has a mother-figure who is all powerful. Catholics call her the Virgin Mary. What you've got to do is this: when you get home write out a dedication sheet to the White Goddess, attach it to the book and if you do that I promise you, love, that the next publisher you send it to will take it.'

'Are you sure?' I asked eagerly.

'Yes.'

'But how do you know?'

She gave a strange, sly, secretive smile. 'Don't worry, luv,' she said quietly. 'I just *do* know. That's all. I *do*' There was a long pause while I contemplated the full significance of what she had just told me. Then she looked at her watch stubbed out her cigarette and gathered up her shopping bag. The conversation was over. 'Must go now, luv. Nice to have met you and thanks ever so much for the tea and all them lovely pastries. Good luck with the book!' The brisk cheerfulness was back again. She shook hands with me and off she went out into the crowded, darkening Charing Cross Road.

I never saw or heard from her again.

All this was later confirmed by another Witch who is a theatrical secretary in the West End and clearly knows whereof she speaks. She is Vi Marriott who works for Frank Dunlop at the Young Vic and is even warmer, cosier and more motherly than Millie. 'Yes, dear, it's all absolutely true, and I can tell you that the only way to get rid of the Curse is to cut out the witches' cauldron scene: but you can't do that because it's the best thing in the play, it's the core and centre of the play, everybody knows it and loves it, so you're stuck with it'.

I lost no time in carrying out Millie's advice. I went home, typed out the dedication sheet which is in the front of this book, and sent it to Mr Sanders in New York with instructions that it must be pasted onto the title page of my twenty thousand word synopsis. He did so and the White Goddess lost no time in making Millie's prediction come true, for within a fortnight there was good news. Mr Sanders had sent it to a small publishing house in New York owned by an expatriate Englishman called Rushton-Blake. Cyril Rushton-Blake was young, only 28, he was deeply interested in the theatre and the occult, and the book seemed to be made for his list. It was. He apparently was so enthralled that he read the twenty thousand words overnight and telephoned Joshua Sanders immediately saying that he liked it and wanted to commission it. He did, however, have one very good, sensible suggestion to make. Would it not be a rather good idea to extend the enquiry into all superstitions, rather than confine it only to *Macbeth*? And not only superstitions in the theatre but also in opera and ballet of which he already had a fair knowledge. And what about a special chapter on theatrical ghosts of which there were many on both sides of the Atlantic? And let it not be confined to England and America but let the investigation take in the whole world, so the result would be as complete a survey of its subject as was possible.

All this exciting news was quickly passed on to me via Paul Moncrieff who added that the advance was to be five thousand dollars, evidence that Rushton-Blake had great faith in the book and its commercial success and was contemplating a large print order. I agreed that his suggestions were good and that a better book would certainly result. Back came the news that the contract was being drafted and would be in Moncrieff's hands within the week.

It wasn't. By the end of the month, there was still no sign of it and Moncrieff telephoned the New York office to find out what had happened. The news was not good. Cyril Rushton-Blake had been knocked down by a car and was lying in the Intensive Care Unit in the local hospital. An icy dread filled my heart. Was the White Goddess going to take away with the other hand what she had already given to me with the first? A week later came the news I had been fearing: Cyril Rushton-Blake had died without regaining consciousness. The Curse of *Macbeth* had claimed yet another real-life victim.

It was a terrible blow, a shocking tragedy. He was in the prime of life, and by all accounts a charming and delightful man. I had really been looking forward to meeting him and spending a weekend on his farm in Connecticut as he had promised, and now I never should. But my other feelings were of sympathy for his widow, an elderly woman from Baltimore who had been his business partner for the last year. I learned from Paul that the future of the firm was undecided. Nobody knew whether Mamie Rushton-Blake was going to continue the firm or not. I wrote her a letter of condolence and sat back to await further events.

Five weeks of tension followed. Was I back to Square One? But no, for although the White Goddess had been temporarily stunned, she had now recovered and was prepared for further battle on my behalf against the Forces of Evil. The good news arrived that Mamie Rushton-Blake had decided to continue the firm and proposed to honour all her late husband's previous commitments. She wished to go ahead with the book and the contract was on its way. Once again we were in business and it was Round Three to the White Goddess. From this moment the book existed as a fact rather than a project and I now started serious work on it with the secure knowledge that it was all going to happen and that I was not wasting my time. The first thing to do was to advertise the book and its forthcoming publisher and request further information from the public. The second thing was to fly out to New York to meet Mrs Rushton-Blake and Joshua Sanders, to discuss the book, settle a number of ideas, to carry out extensive research in the New York museums and to speak to as many of the New York actors as was possible.

However, the Forces of Evil hadn't quite finished with me. They had sufficient energy to adminster two small kicks. They contrived to delay the arrival of the contract for two months and the arrival of the cheque for the first third of the advance by a further two months so that when it finally arrived in the August of 1973 a devaluation had taken place and I lost fifty pounds on the transaction.

The other kick was much more serious and could at that late stage have destroyed the book completely. Some years earlier a slim volume of mine had been published by a gentleman who I will call Clive Murdstone: this is not his real name but 'twill serve and he has now retired from publishing where he can do no more harm. Our relationship had been very friendly: ignoring all the heartfelt warnings from those who had suffered at his hands, I found him charming, good humoured, very efficient and well-organised, generous in his hospitality and entirely honest. My surprise can be measured when he suddenly re-appeared in my life breathing fire and brimstone. He had seen my appeal for *Macbeth* material. He had noted that it was commissioned by an American firm. He then proceeded to write a letter to Mrs Rushton-Blake in the most unpleasant and aggressive terms informing her that he had an option on my next book and that I had absolutely no right to enter into any contract with her over *The Curse of Macbeth*.

He was, of course, talking nonsense. No less than three further

228

manuscripts had been submitted to him after the publication of the first and all had been rejected. Unhappily, the first two rejections had been verbal so there was no proof of it. But for the third there was a letter and I had it. Therefore he had no further claim on anything else I wrote. Paul Moncrieff wrote a very courteous letter pointing all this out and received almost by return a very angry letter denying that any further manuscripts had been submitted. He also threatened legal action. This letter arrived on the morning I was due to fly to New York. I called at Paul's office and we discussed the matter. Clearly, Murdstone didn't have a real case but if it came to court – and Paul thought that it might – there could be some complications. The letter of rejection seemed to me to be pretty conclusive but Paul was an old hand at the ancient game of Agent versus Publisher and said that on closer inspection it was worded in a rather ambiguous way. It said *'we've gone cold on the idea'* which Murdstone might conceivably claim was not a rejection at all. He was a very litigious man and Paul pointed out that it was those who are dishonest, and indulge in sharp practice, if not outright criminality, who are the first and the quickest to seek the Law's protection against imaginary evils. The nuisance and aggravation could be damaging and it would be much better not to let it get as far as a court case. There could be a freeze on the Rushton-Blake contract and another lengthy postponement and this was something neither of us wanted.

So what was to be done? Paul decided that the best solution was to re-submit one of the earlier slim volumes and if it was rejected again, as it surely must be, then he would make sure that the covering letter would be clear and unambiguous. This plan was slightly complicated by the fact that another publisher had already bought and paid for this slim volume, but they generously agreed to waive the contract until the matter had been settled one way or another. Of course, I could always quickly turn out another book, working day and night to produce some terrible thriller, known in the publishing world as an *option breaker*, but this would have to be specially written, whereas the slim volume was ready. It was sent off and after a long delay Mr Clive Murdstone sent it back. He didn't want it. My option clause was now officially broken and as he had no further claim on anything I wrote, my contract with Mamie Rushton-Blake over *The Curse of Macbeth* could continue as planned.

The subsequent war between the Virgin Goddess and the Powers of Evil can best be likened to a heavyweight boxing contest between Sonny Liston and Muhammad Ali, a long drawn-out struggle for supremacy with an endless succession of victories and defeats, achievements and setbacks, despair alternating with triumph. The Virgin was smiling as I flew into New York and I was able to relax comfortably in her pleasure. New York was bright and sunny during that late October 1973 and it was wearing its prettiest autumn clothes. Honorary membership of the Lambs Club just off Times Square had been arranged and I stayed there for only thirty dollars a week. On my second day I walked up Fifth Avenue to Central Park to meet my new publisher. The premises were in the Penthouse at the top of the Sherry-Netherlands Hotel. Mamie Rushton-Blake had a beautiful office on the top floor overlooking the Park. It was filled with golden autumnal sunlight, Chinese bells tinkled merrily in the gentle breeze, the Chopin waltzes sparkled in the background and over a bottle of nicely-chilled Veuve Cliquot served in exquisite crystal glasses, I was able to relax in the depths of a very comfortable green velvet sofa. Cyril Rushton-Blake had clearly been a man with very good taste and a talent for gracious living and I felt the poignancy and sadness of his death even more keenly. A large framed photo of him showed him to have been a very good-looking young man.

But the charms of his office did not, alas, extend to his widow. Mrs Mamie Rushton-Blake, poor soul, was desperately unattractive. She was short and fat and like all short fat women in history compounded the felony by wearing a tight short black skirt. She had a round featureless face and pebble spectacles: her voice was a flat, nasal Brooklyn whine. It was a great disappointment. But she was, I admit, very friendly and enthusiastic and spoke glowingly of the book which she invariably referred to as The Project.

'You've gotta meet your editor,' she said suddenly. 'I've got you the best, no question, the best.'

'Who is it? Anybody I know?'

'Harry Hoover. Harry is a freelance, but really good.' She waddled over to the door. 'Harry ... *Harry* ...' she shouted.

I was delighted to learn that I was going to be in the hands of such a good editor and very curious to meet him. The reader will understand that with a name like Harry Hoover I fully expected him to be a tough, muscular, laconic Humphrey Bogart sort of man. I could see him slouching in with a cigarette at the corner of his mouth, extending a hairy paw with a 'Hi! Kid.' and perhaps a 'Glad to meetcha, okay?' He would then invite me to have a coupla highballs in a little, dimly-lit bar filled with sporting photos and managed by an overweight, musclebound, ex-boxing heavyweight whom he would call Bugsy, and before the evening was out it would be Harry and Richie. He would introduce me to his baseball and boxing friends as *my Limey pal.*

That's what I imagined so the reader can understand my surprise and amusement when what clattered into the office was a very tall, thin old lady with dyed blonde curls lots of jangling costume jewellery and a roguish smile. 'I'm deeelaaarted to meet you,' she shrilled in a high-pitched voice. 'Aaaah just luuurv the English, you have such a cute accent and I luuurv all that white hair.' It was more Beatrice Lillie being outrageous rather than Humphrey Bogart being tough-guy, but with so much goodwill coming from these two inestimable ladies, how could anything go wrong? We chatted for an hour about the book and the opportunities for research which New York offered. Mamie promised to send me a parcel of books on witchcraft and the occult which the firm had already published, and she invited me to join her and Harry for dinner there and then. She took me to the Sherry-Netherlands Restaurant de Paris where she had an account. It was very grand, very lavish and very expensive. There was a band, and anxious to live up to the image they obviously had of me as the irresistably attractive, TV Personality-Of-The-Year Englishman (early 1930s Ronald Colman style) I asked them to dance. It was a bizarre experience. One was very old and thin, the other was very old and very fat so it was rather like pushing round first a bundle of twigs and second a pumpkin. But I clenched my teeth and thought of Equity, muttering Henry VIII's famous pre-coital prayer, *'the*

231

things I do for England.' The evening ended with a taxi back to the Club and many expressions of mutual esteem and unquenchable optimism.

I didn't see much of them thereafter for I was busy researching into the history of *Macbeth* in America. I spent most of my days talking to the old actors at the Lambs and the Players, most of whom did not know that *Macbeth* was unlucky but I managed to put the fear of God into them and I doubt if any of them will ever dare quote from it again. I spent many happy and fruitful hours in the Lincoln Drama Library where Dr Carl Meyer, the curator looked after me and supplied my wants with enormous efficiency and enthusiasm. During the three weeks, I checked into Mamie's office to tell her how well everything was going and to discuss the book. I said goodbye affectionately to both ladies and took them out to dinner at the Players. I had, it seems, become rather fond of them.

During the next five months I buckled down and wrote it, working through the day and usually well into the night for that is when the concentration is at its keenest with nothing else you can do and no interruptions. I had a really magnificent collection of stories, anecdotes and miscellaneous material and the writing came easily. I completed seventy thousand words, sent it to Paul who sent it off to Mamie. I sat back, exhausted but happy, to await the second instalment of the advance.

And this is where the trouble began again, for the Powers of Evil, having been inactive for several months, suddenly shuddered back into horrible life. It caused a number of editorial disputes which not only held up the book but spoiled the friendly relationships between myself and the Rushton-Blake team. Harry would scrawl her comments and corrections on the Xerox copies of my original manuscript sheets and Mamie would send me long letters outlining her ideas for the book. The post was kept very busy and the number of words I was thus forced to write to them probably exceeded that of the original book. The main points of contention were as follows:

1. The Title. Mamie didn't like *The Curse of Macbeth* because she thought that *Curse* was an unlucky word and the presence of a

Shakespeare title on the dust-jacket would brand the book as academic and ... horror on horror ... *educational*, than which nothing, but *nothing*, could be more destructive. She favoured *The History of Dramatic Superstition* which I and everybody whom I consulted, thought was dull, drab, dismal, dreary and depressing. I pointed out the dramatic and sensational appeal of my title and told her that on that alone some Hollywood film company which specialised in horror films would snap it up. But she was sold on her title, and no power in heaven or earth was going to change her. Both Joshua Sanders and Paul Moncreiff pleaded with her but she was adamant.

2. American spelling. This became a major issue. She said that English spelling would bewilder, confuse and alienate her public and the book would thus die a quick death. I countered this by pointing out that my *Truth about Pygmalion* had been published in America with its original English spelling, and that far from dying a quick death it had sold out its first print of five thousand within three months; I continued to argue on this point, informing her that many theatre books had been published with English spelling and that her probable reading public was, surely, sufficiently well-educated not to be bothered by *theatre* instead of *theater*, *colour* instead of *color*, *dress circle* instead of *mezzanine* and *programme* instead of *program*. She refused to be drawn into an argument but merely repeated her original assertion, that English spelling would be bad for the book. I replied, with as loud a shriek of anger as my Olympia typewriter made possible, that if her reading public consisted of semi-literate shopgirls, overworked traffic cops, drugged out hippies, and the mentally-retarded flotsam and jetsam of New York life ... which was obviously what she *did* think ... then we were all wasting our time because these people wouldn't buy the book in any case. For Christ's sake, I screamed, if we're publishing a minority book, don't patronise your public but treat it like adults. She made no reply.

3. House style. This is the bleeding ulcer, the gangrenous, rotting sore in the flesh of many authors in their blitzkrieg with their publishers. In the case of Rushton-Blake, the house style consisted of words of one syllable, short sentences of one or perhaps two

233

lines, short paragraphs of perhaps three or four sentences. So all my beautifully phrased, carefully constructed, elegantly flowing long sentences were cut down to one or two lines each producing a text which was like a series of captions in *The New York Daily* (a horrible tabloid). Writing with a Punch! Harry (which was, incidentally, short for Harriet) was reluctant to concede the existence of any punctuation outside the comma and full stop, a typical piece of feminine wilfulness which aroused me to further transports of fury. I tried hard to explain to her the purpose and value of the semi-colon and colon, but she wouldn't listen. So the bulk of my colons were changed to full stops and most of the commas too. Her ignorance of the theatre ... admitted in conversation but all-too-evident in her editing ... led her to ask for guidance on every page. Technical terms like tabs, floats, wings, flies, corpsing, tagline, all had to be explained before she could get to work. She seemed to be the sort of editor ... regrettably common in American publishing... who regards herself as not doing her job unless she has made at least thirty corrections on every page whether they were needed or not. 'Look Busy' was the attitude which leaps to mind here, so we had the ridiculous situation of work being artificially made without cause or reason. *A Regency novel* was thus changed to *a novel set in Regency times* and I had to write to her to tell her that the two were not the same. 'Why are they not the same?' she wrote immediately. So I had to write and explain just why they were not the same. A reference to Eric Porter caused some confusion. Did I mean Eric Portman? No, I did not. Eric Porter was who I meant and surely she had heard of him. No, she hadn't. He was the star of *The Forsyth Saga* I explained and surely even *she* had seen that. Oh yes, she replied, she was a great fan but she didn't know that he was the star. Well, he is, he is very famous and my reference to him must remain unchanged.

The Power of Evil was having a tremendous time with all this. But there was worse to come. Both ladies thought that there was far too much about *Macbeth* which should be merely another chapter in the investigation rather than the climax and centre-piece of the book, so a great many cuts were made reducing it to little more than half its original size. They refused to have an Index stating that the book was only a light-hearted piece of gossip and that nobody would want one. A modern Dante writing his *Inferno* would reserve a special circle of his Hell for publishers who put out works of non-fiction without an index, and I have met a great many scholars who have complained bitterly about its absence in my book. If this correspondence is ever published it will make an interesting companion work, illustrating the unbridgeable gulf between English and American publishing, and the folly of putting your book into the hands of one who has had little experience of her trade and no knowledge of the book's subject.

I could see exactly what was happening. Mamie was so intoxicated by the power she was wielding as the director of the whole firm, and so determined to show everybody who was boss, so determined to show the world that even though she was only a woman she was as good, as tough, as powerful as any man, that she would not concede an inch, imagining, in her ignorance and naïvety, that a display of foolish, wilful obstinacy would be mistaken for real strength. My book was to be yet another chapter in the turbulent history of Woman's Lib. Clearly, it was to this, and not to her author, that she owed her first allegiance. I pleaded, coaxed, roared, begged and shouted, but she would not budge an inch. And there was nothing I could do about it.

'If you really feel that Rushton-Blake are destroying your book,' said Paul Moncrieff smiling reassuringly through a cloud of scented cigarette smoke, 'then you must demand the manuscript back and return the advance. Then we'll find somebody else. But it won't be easy. And do you have the money left?' The answer, as we both knew, was *no*. Also, I was so bored and irritated by the six months' correspondence that I couldn't face the prospect of starting all over again. Half a book is still better than none. So I decided to let them go ahead with it as they wanted.

The writing of the book took a full year and there wasn't a moment in that year when I didn't wonder nervously if the Curse on the play was going to attach itself to me. And it did, though some months were to pass before I realised just what was the precise method with which the Powers of Evil chose to make their disapproval felt. They knew where my Achilles Heel lay ... in my acting career which was, is and always will be the most important part of my life. They saw to it that I ran into one of those bleak periods which all actors mysteriously get. My last job had been in July 1973 just a month before I started to write the book and *I didn't work for a whole year.* Auditions failed, letters were unanswered, phone-calls were not returned, interviews and meetings led nowhere. The combined efforts of myself, my friends, my agents and various well-wishers in the profession produced nothing. All doors, even those which had once been open, were tightly shut. I had suffered bad patches, (who hasn't?) but never as bad as this. I became increasingly worried and neurotic.

The book was finished in March 1974 and was followed by the four months of editorial harrassment already described. The letter which contained the final and formal acceptance of the manuscript arrived at the end of July and my work was done. This was the cue for the absentee White Goddess to return and make it up to me for all that I had suffered, for with a superb sense of timing, the Curse was lifted the following day with an offer to act in *Pygmalion*, a play which has always been a source of good luck. My relief and happinesss at finding myself out of the tunnel was in no way diminished by the fact that the production was to be in Belfast which, at the height of its troubles, was arguably the most dangerous place in the world. And with a further sense of dramatic timing, the Goddess arranged for the cheque for the second part of the advance, admittedly rather reduced by two agents' commissions but still leaving over three hundred pounds, to arrive on the day of the opening which makes it the most generous first night present I have ever received. The White Goddess continued to look after me throughout my two months in Belfast, protecting me from death and mutilation, and arranging for the production to be a huge, stampeding success, to break all records at the Lyric Theatre and to bring a great deal of much needed laughter into the lives of the residents of that unhappy city.

But the Powers of Evil were not to be subdued for long for shortly after I returned to London in October 1974, they provoked me into a stupid act of defiance. I received a late-night phone call from a friend, who was a Sergeant in the CID. Eddie was interested in antiques and it was his custom to drive up to Inverness every couple of months to buy silver in an antique auction and re-sell back in London where prices were higher. He invited me to join him. He would pay all expenses for the three-day trip and it wouldn't cost me a penny. I would get a free holiday and he would get the company. I accepted and decided to try a small experiment. I would take a copy of *The Curse of Macbeth* typescript and do some more polishing. I would also take a notebook and write this epilogue telling the story to date. I would work on both during the long hours in the car and in the hotel and see what happened. It was exceedingly foolish to tempt providence I fully admit, and I should have taken warning from the alarming evidence I had uncovered while researching the book but I was consumed by an intense curiosity to see what happened: if I have a streak of devil-may-care irresponsibility it must be my Irish blood.

The trip was a total disaster and I am lucky to be alive to tell the tale. Owing to a slight domestic crisis (Eddie's wife wasn't at all keen on the trip and tried to stop it), we were several hours late in starting so, far from reaching Inverness by eight o'clock in the evening, it was midnight before we even got to Edinburgh. The City was full of commercial visitors for a trade fair and it was all of three hours before we found a hotel. The Frankensteinian porter was anything but pleased to see us and firmly refused to give us any sort of refreshment, not even tea and biscuits, and we were thus forced to go hungry to bed.

The car had been giving a lot of trouble and a number of small technical faults had made our progress up the motorway a distinct hazard so Eddie decided to change it at the local Avis rental for another. Within fifteen minutes of leaving some more serious technical faults made themselves known ... defective brakes, a petrol gauge which didn't work, and a bonnet which opened and shut itself all the time making it necessary for Eddie to drive very very slowly. A man from the Avis rental drove out from Edinburgh to mend the car and apparently did so, but ten minutes after he had left, the same faults reasserted themselves reducing Eddie to impotent cursing and thumping.

I noticed a couple of passably attractive girls hitch-hiking and I suggested that we give them a lift hoping that their presence would lighten the gathering tension of the journey and restore the harmony and humour with which it had started. Unhappily, it turned out that they were both French and spoke no English so as Eddie and I spoke no French we sat in a bored and sullen silence for the next six hours. We left them in Aberdeen and then drove to the local airport for yet another change of car. And that was the moment when we discovered the loss of six hundred pounds which Eddie had drawn from the Edinburgh branch of his bank to cover the costs of the trip. The money in ten pound notes was in a thick brown envelope. We searched every inch of the car but it was nowhere to be found. Suspicion naturally fell on the two girls: the money might have fallen from Eddie's pocket and the girls might have picked it up and kept it. I did remember leaving them alone in the car at one point while we both went to have a pee. Eddie telephoned the local police. They picked up the two girls who were staying in a Youth Hostel. They were naturally very upset at the mere suggestion that they might have stolen six hundred pounds and very angry when the police insisted on searching their luggage in the hostel dormitory. Anger gave way to something approaching screaming hysteria when the police insisted on a body search just in the hope that a thick envelope of ten pound notes might, just *might* be concealed about their persons. It wasn't. I doubt if Anglo-French relations have ever been worse. The money was never recovered which made it a very expensive holiday.

We journeyed to our hotel, too late for a meal but the manager sulkily produced some tired and tasteless ham sandwiches. We repaired to the bar. I took my manuscript and a glass of wine and sat alone by a roaring log fire and worked while Eddie made himself very agreeable to a group of locals round the bar. Everything seemed to be calm and peaceful until one of the locals, a heavily-built man with very black eyebrows, wanted to know what I was writing. 'A book,' I said. 'What book?' he asked. I told him. A chill hovered in the air and he lumbered over to me and looked at it. 'I dinna think it's guid manners tae write in a bar when the folk's enjoyin' themselves. Are these Sassenach manners?' he asked aggressively, and he snatched the file of papers from my hand and threw it on the floor. I gathered it up and walked out of the bar. I was in no mood for a fight and it seemed to be tactful to leave the scene of the dispute rather than add to it.

The following morning there was a terrible atmosphere in the hotel. Over breakfast, the manager came to me and suggested that we both leave the hotel without delay. It seemed that after I had gone to bed Eddie had got very drunk and insulted everybody in sight. He had broken a lot of glasses, he had nearly started a fire and had damaged some fire extinguishers. He then started to fight the barman and had to be dragged off by the manager and the hall porter, subdued and finally put to bed. Eddie finally came down to breakfast looking very guilty. He apologised profusely, gave them a large cheque to cover the breakages and harrassment and said he didn't know what had come over him. I didn't realise it at the time but this was the first symptom of what later turned out to be a complete nervous breakdown resulting in a long spell in and out of the London Hospital and a medical discharge from the Police. However, my first and urgent desire was to get away from Eddie and back home as quickly as possible. God knows what trouble he would cause for us both during the remainder of his trip, but whatever it was, I wanted no part of it.

I arrived home unhurt with my precious manuscript undamaged. I had got the message and never again would I tempt providence so foolishly. However, I was not to be let off the hook so easily. The following week, I had a burglary and the manuscript was stolen. Who it was and why they stole it I do not know for the manuscript was never recovered and the police declared themselves baffled that a burglar should have stolen something which officially had no commercial value. 'We seem to be getting a very good class of burglar these days, Sir,' said the CID Inspector rather ponderously. Could it have been a publisher? Or an agent? Or a rival author? Or the man from the Inverness Hotel who had taken such an unreasonable exception to my working on it in the crowded bar? Happily, there was no great harm done for I had my carbon copy.

Six months later the book was published, *A Dramatic History of Superstition* with a plain black and white jacket, and a lot of very unsuitable and badly-reproduced photographs. I decided to go over and help out with the publicity and promotion. It was typical of Mamie's ineptitude that she engaged for this difficult and demanding job a young man who had never done it before. However, I had to admit that he worked hard and managed to get some quite useful radio and TV interviews though none which really counted. One of the chat-show interviewers was a tall, intimidating man whom I shall call Lou Blitzkrieg. We met in the studio just five minutes before we were due on the air. Innocently, I asked him what he thought of the book.

'Don't know. Haven't read it,' he replied curtly.

'You haven't *read* it?' I echoed in astonishment, at which point he proceeded to lose his temper.

'No, I have *not*,' he yelled for all the building to hear, 'My job is to *ask questions*, okay, and not to *read fucking books,* okay. I haven't got time to read, I'm a busy man, okay ... and you ask me fucking stupid questions like that?' He eventually calmed down and then asked me to give him ten leading intelligent questions he could ask me. I did, and the interview proceeded smoothly.

† † †

A Dramatic History of Superstition sold a thousand copies but very slowly and received a few tepid notices: for a time it occupied a prominent table in the All Night Bookshop in Times Square and became a popular choice for first night presents among the Broadway fraternity (and sorority). But apart from this, it was a disaster and Mamie Rushton-Blake never even got her advance back. Her obstinacy had been her undoing: on every point of issue she had been proved horribly in the wrong. It gave me no pleasure to say 'I told you so,' but say it I did at a very chilly lunchtime meeting in London when she was over here trying to sell her other wares to the English publishers. It was chilly because I was seething with a profound inner fury and though I made a valiant attempt to conceal it, I wasn't entirely successful.

Fortunately, the contract allowed me to retain the English and world rights and for the next five years I sent it round and round the London publishing houses. It was my original typescript they saw and not the mutilated abortion which the Rushton-Blake firm had spawned. Once again, the Powers of Evil were triumphant and they continued to be so until 1980. The London publishing fraternity were infinitely polite and charming in their letters of rejection: they found *The Curse of Macbeth* fascinating, full of enthralling arcane information, elegantly and stylishly written, a book which they themselves greatly enjoyed reading and one which filled a long-regretted gap in the theatrical bookshelf ... *but* in these hard days they didn't think that they could sell it, they didn't think that anybody but a few theatrical fanatics would buy it, that they were compelled by the financial recession to be very selective and to play safe. Therefore they were exceedingly sorry, but ...

I received forty-seven such letters over the years which must surely be a record worthy of that Guiness Book. Then the White Goddess having been on an extensive holiday returned to do battle. Peter O'Toole returned to the stage to play Macbeth, received the worst notices since Alec Guinness at the Royal Court, and with a holocaust of appalling publicity made *Macbeth* at the Old Vic the most talked about theatrical event in the world. I had written a programme note on the Curse and as a result I found myself looked on as an authority on the subject. I was interviewed extensively by press and radio and managed to let it be known that the book had been rejected by forty-seven publishers and that if any one of them had shown a bit of initiative they would have made a real financial killing during the early weeks of the play's run.

The White Goddess saw to it that David Picton-Phillips was listening to his radio while driving to his home in Somerset. He wrote to me and asked for a meeting which took place at a Bookfair in the basement of Quaglino's Restaurant. He looked at the American edition and his reaction was immediate. 'Terrible title, have to change that. Dreadful dust-jacket, my design department can do much better. We must have an index, and of course English spelling. And a lot of very relevant photographs. And then we'll have a success on our hands.'

A week later we met and he talked to me over a delicious lunch at

Peter O'Toole at the Old Vic, 1980. A classic case history of the Curse.
(Frank Herrmann/*The Sunday Times*)

Bacco 70 a restaurant in Old Compton Street much favoured by the literary fraternity: it was the first of a series of splendid publisher's lunches. His wife, his production manager and his salesman had all read it and they loved it. 'I just can't imagine why those forty-seven publishers turned it down. They must be mad. But we'll show 'em. Don't worry: *we'll show 'em.*

We were in business, and once again the White Goddess had called the tune.

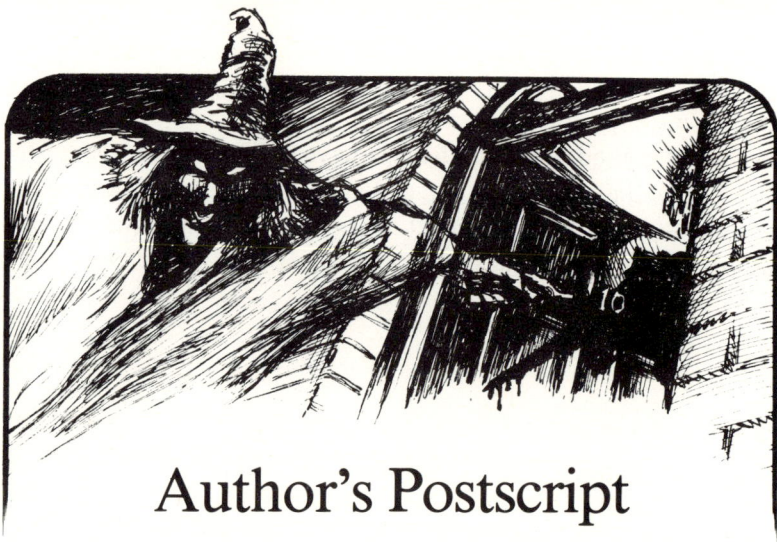

Author's Postscript

I have been living with this book for a long time now.

I have lived with *Macbeth*, slept and dreamed with *Macbeth*, eaten and drunk with *Macbeth*, bored my friends with him, kept the Post Office busy with him, persecuted librarians and booksellers with him. *Macbeth* has been dominating my life, as all obsessions must, and now I find that he has invaded my subconscious mind. One night I dreamt about *Macbeth*. Normally I never tell my dreams, they are the most boring things in the world for others, and in addition one usually forgets them. But not this one and since it is very relevant to this book, I shall describe it.

I dreamt that I had been invited to dinner at No.10 Downing Street. The dream is clearly a flashback in time for the prime minister on this occasion was Harold Wilson. I find myself sitting at the end of a long table covered with magnificent silver and floral decorations. The faces of the other guests are dim and misty as is the way in dreams. At one end of the table was Mr Wilson, puffing silently and ominously on his famous pipe; sitting next to him, laughing and smiling nervously, is Mr Edward Heath, the next prime minister. At my end and next to me, is Mrs Mary Wilson and I am finding it very difficult to make conversation with her for in this dream she is very silent and withdrawn. I search around for something to say to her but her attention is continually distracted by her husband. She casts baleful eyes at him as if to rebuke him for not being a good host. Suddenly, I have an inspiration. 'Mrs Wilson,' I say, 'have you ever played Lady Macbeth?' She looks at me with heavy, sinister eyes and her voice is the echo of a charnel-house. 'Yes I have,' she says, '*and I'm playing it right now!*'

Thanks

To all who have helped I say thank you very much:

Franklin Cover, New York
Walter Kerr, New York
Clive Barnes, New York
Trader Faulkner, London
John Nettleton, London
Brigid Skemp, London
Jay Fox and Bonnie Walker Fox,
    New York
Renée Rose, New York
Don Bonnell, New York
John Graham, London
Magdalen Egerton, London
Nicholas Hawtrey, London
Hugh Goldie, London
Jim Dale, London
John Bennett, London
Jill Bennett, London
Dr Levi Fox, Stratford-upon-Avon
Ian Richardson, London
Michael Denison, London
Dulcie Gray, London
Thora Hird, London
Joe Melia, London
Hersey Piggot, London
Anthony Tuckey, Liverpool

Peter Hall, London
Joseph Fox, London
Ken Wynne, London
Professor A. N. Kincaid, Oxford
Robert Gillespie, London
Peter Porteous, London
Michael Gambon, London
Geoffrey Bayldon, London
Donald Laye-Smith, London
Mrs Barbara Richards, South Africa
Christine Hole, Oxford
Hugh Cross, London
Paul Hardwick, London
Michael Warwick, London
Frank Seton, London
James D. P. Smith, Bushey
William Abney, London
Max Miradin, London
Angela B. Hill, Shadwell
Barry Foster, London
Stan Turney, London
Martin Jarvis, London
Fitzroy Davis, New York
Melinda May, London
John Maas, Philadelphia

Jane and Francis Carr, London
Nigel Hawthorne, London
George Baker, London
Roger Lancelyn-Green, Wirral
Michael Goodliffe, London
Fred Lawrence Guiles, New York
Bridget Boland, London
Marianne and Barrie Hesketh,
   Isle of Mull
E. Hardman, Widnes
Abraham Sofaer, New York
J. M. G. Blakiston, Oxford
George Hagan, London
John Haylock, Brighton
Tony Britton, London
Harry Tuthill, Cape Town
Eva Bornemann, Germany
Herb Moulton, Vienna
Franz Schrafranek, Vienna
Robert Rushmore, Massachusetts
Michael Harnick, Bronx
Jutta Grunthal, Haifa
Olive Peel, Durban
Ruby Betts, Utica
Oleg Kerensky, London
Sir Alec Guinness, London
Spike Hughes, Ringmer
David Shipman, London
Jean McConnell, Tonbridge
Vera Lindsey, London
Richard Schenkman, Yonkers
Anne Harlan, New Haven
Kathie Warren, High Barnet
A. J. Beale, Walton-on-Thames
Hugh Beeson, Jr, New York
Brendan Gill, New York
Vi Marriott, London
Jack Lyne, London
Walter Horsburgh, London
Bernard Archard, London
Jack Lemmon, California
Henry Marshall, London
Richard Attenborough,
   Richmond Green
Sheila Campbell, New York

Ellen Pollock, London
Patricia Hayes, London
Clive Revill, London
Laurence Irving, Tenterden
Dudley Moore, London
Paul Myers, New York
Bob Thomas, California
Zena Dare, London
John Mills, London
Sir Robert Helpmann, London
Robert Potterton, Dublin
Denis Shaw, Windsor
Wilfrid Granville, London
Renée Bourne Webb, London
Tenniel Evans, Bucks
David Williams, Liverpool
Michael Codron, London
John Savident, London
T. Robertson, Stalybridge
Emlyn Williams, London
Donald Sinden, London
Ronald Harwood, West Liss
Robert Selbie, Chichester
Jean Kent, London
Enid St. John Parry, Somerton
Patrick MacClellan, Isle of Man
Derek Fowldes, London
Sir Laurence Olivier, Brighton
Peter Saunders, London
Eric Paice, West Wratting
Leslie Phillips, London
Paul Huson, New York
Amanda Reiss, London
Peter Barkworth, London
John Shrapnel, London
Clayre Ribner, New York
Gerald Blake, New York
Julia Jones, London
Charles Lewson, London
Barry Morse, London
Anthony Quayle, London
Elizabeth Armstrong, Harrogate
Armand Georges, Rickmansworth
Michael Hordern, London
Dennis Wheatley, London

Graham Beynon, Loughborough
Frank Thornton, London
J. K. Hunt, Warwick
Maureen Norman, Great Yarmouth
Peter Bull, London
Charles Bowden, London
Kenneth Tynan, London
Otto G. Stoll, New Jersey
Ted Gilling, London
Jack Doughty, Oldham
A. L. Rowse, Oxford
Sandy Dunbar, London
Geoffrey Toone, London
John Drummond, Isle of Man
B. M. Hancock, Birmingham
Margaret Rawlings, Wendover
Viscount Furness, London
S. W. Milverton, Oldham
Edgar Wreford, London
Sharon Duce, London
T. R. Goulding, Blackpool
Margaret Webster, U.S.A.
Tony Robinson, Port Elizabeth
Sir John Gielgud, London,
Andrew Cruikshank, London
David Rustidge, Oldham
Stephen Tate, York
Robert Perfitt, St. Neots
Miss H. Crompton, Oldham
J. Clegg, Liverpool
Robert Morley, Wargrave
C. Birchenough, Maulsfield
Patrick Garland, London
Meryl Wold, Denver
Eric Porter, Stratford-upon-Avon
Nicholas Grimshaw, Richmond
Judy McKeown, London
A. V. Dalby, London
Brigit Ferguson, Lamberhurst
William Redfield, New York
Jack Fletcher, New York
Frederick Teahan, New York
Dimitri Murat, Athens
A. R. James, Ovingdean
Arnold Gates, New York

Theodore Hoffman, Brooklyn
Kay Ward, Columbus
Phillip Weller, Washington, D.C.
George Nestor, Lambs Club,
    New York
William Shust, Players Club,
    New York
Sandy Marshall, Lambs Club,
    New York
Frank Alford, Lambs Club,
    New York
Bill Buckley, Lambs Club, New York
Alan Hewitt, New York
Emerson Beauchamp,
    Washington, D.C.
Louis Marder, Chicago
Catherine Hughes, New York
David Leonard, Ballet Bookshop,
    London
John O'Brien, Ballet Bookshop,
    London
Michael Sinclair, New York
Bob Pearce, Kuala Lumpur
Margaretta Scott, London
John Harrison, High Wycombe
Arne Meier, London
P. Murray-Hoodless, London
P. W. Janes, Farningham
Paul Rogers, London
Ian Holm, London
Raymond Adamson, Beckenham
John Woodvine, London
Derek Salberg, Salisbury
J. G. Trewin, London
John Moffatt, London
Fred Marshall, Colchester
Gill Rutter, Egham
John Irwin, London
Timothy Schultz, Williamstown
Leda Sulta, New York
H. Clarke, Eastbourne
Lyell Rodieck, New York
Mrs Elsie Hawksworth, London
J. Almieda Flor, Lisbon
R. A. Cable, Dover

Robin Hood, London
Mary Lynn, London
Meg Ritchie, London
George Manuel, Cape Town
Clara Hackett, New York
Victor Lownes, London
Douglas Emory, Beckenham
Mrs D. Beckett, Eastbourne
Noel Johnson, London
Cardew Robinson, London
Richard Dennis, London
Ann Rogers, London
John Bryans, London
Michael Ridgeway, London
Gerry Small, London
John Moore, London

Margaret Ware, Huddersfield
Brenda Cleather, London
June Grey, London
Herb Felsenfield, Milwaukee
Bob Hoskins, London
Stephen Mead, London
William Lewis, New York
Dennis Handby, London
Basil Langton, New York
Marjorie Beddow, New York
Jeanne Belkin, Brooklyn
Bill Lemessina, New York
Barbara Rubinstein, New York
David Cattanach, New York
Joe Wiebkin, Fulham.

I would also like to thank Adrian Hillier, designer and Mike Wicks who have worked so hard on the layout; Alan Cameron for the chapter headings and Neville Fox the printer: between them they have made this book a thing of beauty.

Richard Huggett.

Index

Included are names, theatres, organisations and the titles of plays, films, TV serials, books, and theatre newspapers. These last are printed in italics.

252

254

258

TIMOTHY WEST

Is this a clanger I see before me?
Timothy West attacks O'Toole and disowns Old Vic production

DAGGERS OUT FOR MACBETH

by Michael Owen

ACTOR Peter O'Toole stayed silent today at the centre of an extraordinary row as Old Vic theatre director Timothy West disowned the Macbeth production that opened last night to giggles in the audience and derisive reviews from the critics.

O'Toole's much-awaited return to the London stage went down like a lead balloon and the Irish actor missed the first-night party he was expected to attend at the theatre.

Mr West said today: "I am afraid I do have to disown it. Peter contractually had total artistic control and though I tried to talk to him about how he was playing it he would not listen.

"I had enormous reservations but by the time I was able to see it in rehearsal it was too late to try to get him to see reason.

"I talked to him quite a lot in rehearsals but he just replied: 'No, that's how it is going to be.' I'm afraid he took a very unbalanced and uninformed view.

"There was nothing I could do unless I decided to stop the production and refund the money to people. That was not on.

"I do feel responsible in a way but a lot of people have booked their tickets because they want to see Peter as Macbeth.

"It's not too late to change it if Peter will listen to reason. It could be re-staged in a couple of days."

O'Toole was unavailable at his Hampstead home today. A spokesman said: "Peter has nothing to say until he gets on stage and starts his performance tonight in the usual way.

"He has been told that the notices were not good and I believe he just laughed. I don't think he was expecting Lord's Prayer reviews.

The star stayed in his dressing room for an hour after the performance last night but was in good spirits. He greeted friends saying: "It's such a big role I'm still punchy from it. I don't know what to think yet."

Bryan Forbes, who directed the production, and was equally savaged by the critics said last night: "It is one of the most difficult plays to do, as difficult as King Lear. I thought some of the company did quite well tonight."

Today he stood by his cast and the production. He said: "I believe in old fashioned things like loyalty. I have not read the notices, but just because seven or eight gentlemen—some of whom I know and who can't put pen to paper—don't like it, well, it's not the end of the world.

"I always think life is a challenge. One takes on new

Continued Page 2. Col 6

An ultimatum over Macbeth

Continued from Page One
critic Felix Barker said of the play that if film director Bryan Forbes had been working for the cinema, "90 per cent. of the scenes would have been consigned to the cutting floor."

Other critics were no kinder. The Daily Mail's Jack Tinker said: "The performance (of O'Toole) is not so much downright bad as heroically ludicrous."

Michael Billington of the Guardian described the production as "old fashioned fit-up Shakespeare in which everyone stands up to let the star do his number".

And the Times says it "gruesomely evokes the kind of thing one used to get from weeks on a bad night."

Mr. West said there were many quite simple changes which could improve the production.

He added: "We were hop-

ing for a miracle — hoping that Peter would pull something out of the bag.

"I feel responsible because in the end it is m y theatre. I am sad about it and for the enormous number of people who have booked so heavily to see Macbeth."

Bryan Forbes said today: "Any play can do with changes. It depends on how much you can afford with sets and various things. One can always be bright with hindsight."

He made no criticism of any of the cast, however.

"I would have thought what he said was strangely at variance with the fact that when I last went to the box office before the performance it resembled something like a Harrods sale. Tickets worth £182,000 have been sold in advance.

TIMOTHY WEST . . . holding talks today.